LIFE IN THE PAST LANE
VOLUME THREE

A LOOK INTO MEDIA HISTORY THROUGH
THE EYES OF THOSE WHO MADE IT!

BY JASON HILL

LIFE IN THE PAST LANE—VOLUME THREE
©2016 JASON HILL

ALL RIGHTS RESERVED.

No part of this book may be reproduced in any form or by any means, electronic, mechanical, digital, photocopying, or recording, except for in the inclusion of a review, without permission in writing from the publisher.

Published in the USA by:

BEARMANOR MEDIA
P.O. BOX 71426
ALBANY, GEORGIA 31708
www.BearManorMedia.com

ISBN-10: 1-59393-936-1 (alk. paper)
ISBN-13: 978-1-59393-936-6 (alk. paper)

DESIGN AND LAYOUT: VALERIE THOMPSON

TABLE OF CONTENTS

ACKNOWLEDGMENTS 1

FOREWORD/PROGRAM NOTES 3

INTRODUCTION/OVERTURE 5

    THE CHILDREN'S HOURS

ACT I: MORE FOR THE KIDS 9

    Interview with Tony Parish—NBC staff announcer for Chicago radio

ACT II: PROFESSIONAL TALKERS 31

    SCENE ONE: MR. HIT PARADE 33

    Interview with André Baruch—Newsman, Talk Show Host, Disc Jockey and Sportscaster

    SCENE TWO: KEEPER OF THE SECRET WORD 49

    Conversation with George Fenneman and his years with Groucho

ACT III: UTILITY MEN 65

    SCENE ONE: OSGOOD CONKLIN 67

    Discussion with Gale Gordon—Much more than Miss Brooks

    SCENE TWO: MAN OF MANY INTERESTS 79

    Chat with Sheldon Leonard—From Benny to *I Spy*

SCENE THREE: WILL YOU EVER GET A REAL JOB? **95**

Talking with Jim and Henny Backus—Alan Young, James Dean and Mr. Magoo

SCENE FOUR: THE CUTUP **119**

Interview with Jerry Hausner—Bit player's bit player

ACT IV: MORE MUSIC MEN **133**

SCENE ONE: PHILLY AND ALICE **135**

Phil Harris on his band days and beyond

SCENE TWO: WAYFARING STRANGER **157**

The words of Burl Ives—Balladeer to Oscar winner

SCENE THREE: SOUTH RAMPART STREET PARADE **173**

Discussion with Steve Allen about his music and much more

PHOTO GALLERY **193**

ACT V: THE SERIALS **235**

SCENE ONE: *VIC AND SADE* **237**

Interview with Bill Idelson about his years as Rush

SCENE TWO: SOAP QUEEN **257**

Betty Lou Gerson tells about her work on day time serials and more

SCENE THREE: WRITER AND PUBLISHER **273**

Conversation with Carlton E. Morse—He did not do soaps, but some of his work followed that type of format

ACT VI: COMEDIENNES **291**

SCENE ONE: FROM BLONDIE TO JANE JETSON 293

Interview with Penny Singleton—Domestic tranquility

SCENE TWO: SERIOUSLY FUNNY 307

Discussion with Eve Arden-Stage, Movies and Radio/TV

SCENE THREE: MCGEE'S NEIGHBOR 321

Shirley Mitchell speaks of her radio days

ACT VII: TECS 339

SCENE ONE: PHILO VANCE 341

Chat with Jackson Beck—from radio to cartoons

SCENE TWO: SAM SPADE 355

Interview with Howard Duff about Sam and his movies

SCENE THREE: THE SAINT 375

The words of Vincent Price and his many faceted career

AFTERWORD/EPILOGUE 391

A few extra words concerning radio detectives

BIBLIOGRAPHY 395

INDEX 397

DEDICATION

For Janet Waldo—My very best California Friend.

ACKNOWLEDGMENTS

Once again I must thank all of the usual suspects who make my part in this endeavor so much easier.

First and foremost there is Michaela Nelson, my final editor and good friend. She is the one who catches every small error in my copy and prevents me from looking like an uninformed fool. Next I have to give praise to Valerie Thompson for her wonderful work in setting up the final layout of it all.

Then there is, once more, my Massachusetts connection, Paula Slade who continues to help me through the mysterious world of publishing.

And of course I must thank Ben Ohmart, my publisher, for his ongoing faith in our abilities.

Finally, I would be remiss not to thank the many people whose words on my radio show made this all possible.

J. H.

Foreword/
Program Notes

Once more we enter into the Past Lane of media history. It has been fun for me to revisit the old interviewees from the 1980s, but the journey is not yet finished.

In this volume you will meet some folks you know well and some others you may not know at all. We will visit the worlds of juvenile shows and radio detectives. We will say hello to three often very funny ladies. We will look in on the staples of old day-time radio, the soaps. To top it all off, we will hear from a couple of people who were so necessary in tying productions together. I am referring to the announcers who made it all seem so logical. We will also delve once again into the genre of music and musicians.

As you know, if you read the first or second volume of this series, the people included were all in-depth guests on my old radio shows that aired in the middle and late 80s called *Life in the Past Lane*. That series and another short form venue called *Antique Audio Digest* were on many stations, some under syndication.

I have mentioned it in the first two books, but I feel that I must say again that the main motivating force behind getting this material down on paper was Norman Corwin. He got to be a good friend and mentor during the twenty-five years between my first contact with him and his passing not long ago at the age of 101. He repeatedly told me to put it in print so others might learn more about the field he held so dear. I finally concurred, not wanting to have those wonderful people forgotten when I too am gone.

It has been a labor of love to listen again to those old air-checks and to transcribe them for you to enjoy as well. I must comment that while much of the old work on radio and in the movies was not always so good, I tried to concentrate on some of the brighter spots. All I ask is that you read on and listen once more to those mostly golden years of the past.

Introduction/Overture: The Children's Hours

Do you remember when kids used to play outside no matter what season and regardless of the weather? If you are anywhere near my age you will recall how we used to invent all sorts of games and become champions at them along with the more normal sports and games. Our parents could never get us to come back inside before dark and sometimes not even then.

There was one thing that could get us inside early though. It was the steady late afternoon stream of radio shows aimed directly at us. So many of those shows were on daily and on the weekends that I cannot begin to list them all, but I would like to bring up a few of them. They fall into several categories so let me see if I can sort some of them out.

First, let me bring up the daring pilots who flew into our homes on late afternoons. We could hear the exploits of *Hop Harrigan* and his sidekick, mechanic Tank Tinker, who incidentally was played by Jackson Beck, who will be featured later in this book. Hop was "America's Ace of the Airwaves" and during WWII, which covered most of the run, he fought in many of the battles of that time. Next, there was *Captain Midnight*, leader of "The Secret Squadron." It was a show that also appeared on television at a later date. Another intrepid aviator who came to us was "America's Favorite Flying Cowboy," *Sky King*, or Schuyler King who dropped in on us day after day in his airplane, Songbird.

Speaking of cowboys, there were many of them, but most of them were on in prime time or on the weekends. One of them that was an afternoon feature was *Tom Mix and the Ralston Straight Shooters*. He was based loosely on a real life cowboy and, as was the case on many of these shows, the title came in part from the sponsor, Ralston

Purina. A very young cowboy was *Bobby Benson and the B-Bar-B Riders*, which was at one time an afternoon broadcast before moving to Saturdays. Also on Saturdays we could find *Hopalong Cassidy* known as "The Knight of the Range." He was always a gentleman and he never, never kissed the heroines. In the evenings we could hear from the likes of *The Lone Ranger* and *The Cisco Kid*. *The Lone Ranger* came to us originally from Detroit and became a favorite through the years on both radio and TV. Interestingly, his "Faithful Indian Companion," Tonto, was not a part of the earliest shows, but the producers soon realized that it did not seem right for the Ranger to be speaking to himself out on the range, so Tonto was invented to fill the void. He could talk to Silver, but that did not quite cut it. *The Cisco Kid*, who was called "O'Henry's Bad Man," was always on the run at the end of each broadcast with his sidekick, Pancho. For a while Pancho was played by Mel Blanc.

That brings us to an intriguing connection to one of the characters in the super-hero category. That would be Britt Reid, *The Green Hornet*, "The Masked Crime Fighter." Britt was the great-nephew of John Reid, *The Lone Ranger*. Something very peculiar happened during the run of that show. At the start, Kato, Britt's houseboy, was Japanese. After Pearl Harbor he instantly became Filipino. No one seemed to notice the change at the time. The other super-hero I must mention is "The Man of Steel," *Superman*, who was the last survivor after the destruction of his home planet, Krypton. As the "Mild-Mannered Reporter" at the Daily Planet, Clark Kent kept his true identity a secret during his never ending battle for justice and the American way. His secret was not so secret because all of us knew who he really was.

Superman was a product of comic books and comic strips. There were many other examples of that genre on radio. One of those was *Popeye, the Sailor*. Here again we heard Jackson Beck as Bluto, Popeye's continual adversary. In print our hero always got his monumental strength by devouring a can of spinach. On the air it was Wheatena, the sponsor's product. We could also hear episodes from yet another airman. He would be Terry from *Terry & the Pirates* and his adventures in the Far East. Another comic strip character brought to life was *Little Orphan Annie* with her benefactor, Daddy Warbucks and of course, her ever present dog, Sandy.

Other adventurers to be found on the dial came to us from settings both North and South of the Canadian border. There was a juvenile football hero from Hudson High School who traveled the globe to solve problems aided by his Uncle Jim and his two teenage cohorts, Billy and Betty Fairfield. That show ran forever, but another one that had a relatively short run was *The Adventures of Frank Merriwell,* straight out the old dime novels that were once so popular. From North of the border came several members of the Royal Canadian Mounted Police. One such was *Renfrew of the Mounted,* a no nonsense law man who always got the perpetrator. The most popular Mountie was Sergeant Preston on *Challenge of the Yukon.* His trusty lead dog, Yukon King, almost always got credit for solving the enigmas they had to deal with on each and every episode.

Not to be overlooked were the futuristic, space based programs. *Flash Gordon* took us to the planet Mongo to fight Emperor Ming in the 25th century. Flash and Dr. Hans Zarkov and Flash's girlfriend, Dale Arden could handle every threat Ming and his entourage could throw their way. Gale Gordon was one of the actors who played Flash. He will also be featured later in this book. The other space-based series I want to mention was *Space Patrol* featuring Commander Buzz Corey and his gang bringing law and order to the interplanetary realm.

One category we have not yet approached here is a very important one because it gave a start in the business to many very young actors who made media history at a later date. What I am referring to are the story tellers who got into many diverse areas of historic work. There was the Sunday morning *Horn and Hardart Children's Hour,* which told a variety of children's stories using an entirely juvenile cast. We had *The Singing Story Lady* performed by Ireene Wicker. She did some fairy tales, but she also did a series of programs based on the youthful days of many famous people from the past. A couple of those people were Michelangelo and Ludwig von Beethoven. It was a whole new concept. Then there was a Saturday morning show called *Let's Pretend,* written by Nila Mack who said there was no better way to tell kid's stories than with very young performers.

It was a lot of fun for us kids in those days. Simply by turning on the radio we could travel the globe and beyond with stories written just for us. If that was not enough, many of those shows offered precious premiums we could send in for. We could get all sorts of secret de-coders and even a shake-up mug. The possibilities were endless.

As I said at the beginning of this piece, I have only brought up a few of the many broadcasts. If you read on into Act I you will learn more about some of the ones I mentioned here.

Act I:
More for the Kids

When considering the many facets of radio's Golden Years there are many people who must be included whose names would not be at all familiar to most listeners because they never received on-air credit for their work. At the same time, these people were just as important as the many stars who did get credited. I am referring to the many unsung heroes of the airwaves called staff announcers. They not only did opens and closes, they also filled in with many bit parts in the bodies of those shows we do remember. Some of them went on to be known for bigger things, people like Henry Morgan and Mike Wallace. Others just continued on doing their jobs until radio passed away.

One of those folks was Tony Parish, who did his thing for quite a few years without ever getting proper recognition. On September 11, 1986 we had a lengthy on-air live discussion, mostly about the world of what was talked about in the Overture. He was involved in many of the better known kid's shows as well as many other venues.

****

JASON: Here we have one of those people who did so much, but never got proper credit. I know this may be a loaded question, Tony, but how are you today?

TONY: I've never been better and I've never had more. That's an old fill.

JASON: I'm not sure I know what that means.

TONY: Never felt better, never had less.

JASON: I'm confused. I'll just let that one pass for now.

TONY: (Singing) Never felt better, never had less, not even happiness.

JASON: I didn't know I had a singer on the line.

TONY: I'm singin' an old one for you, dad.

JASON: How about if you just sing through the whole show. Then you won't have to do any talking.

TONY: But that would upset the whole format. I didn't mean to start out that way.

JASON: Okay, let's move on to what we were going to talk about.

TONY: What were we going to talk about, Jason?

JASON: First of all, tell me a little about yourself and your background in radio.

TONY: Oh golly, that goes back a piece, about 46 years. I marvel at the fact that I can talk about it in an offhand manner because, 46 years ago, if I had to project 46 years into the future, there wouldn't have been any future. It happened that way, not by career choice. I was tending bar for a guy named Pat O'Leary, a place called The Parkside Bar on East Main Street here in Madison, which later turned out to be The Dangle Lounge, which you may know a little about. I got tabbed by someone to do a stage show in town run by the Catholic Theatre Guild. It was called *Black Friars*. I don't know if they are still in existence. They were casting a play called *Brother Orchid*, which turned out to be *Brother Rat* on film. George Raft played the lead character in that one. I wound up in the show with no prior experience. The woman who produced the show happened to be the secretary to Ralph O'Conner, who was the manager of WIBU with offices on the 4th floor of the Commercial State Bank building. One thing led to another. She kept saying, "You have a beautiful voice. You should be on radio." So I went and Ralph O'Conner listened. He made a wire recording because tape was unknown in those days, and he played it back to me. I ran out of the place screaming because I'd never heard such a horrible thing in my life. Two days later I was back there working as an announcer. I didn't realize they were that hard up. In a nut shell, that was the beginning. It went from there in all kinds of different ways. After a year and a half I thought. Since I was 4-F in the draft during the war, that New York was waiting for me so I went there. I found out they weren't.

JASON: You ended up in Washington, DC, didn't you?

TONY: No, I wound up in Norfolk, Virginia.

JASON: Close to Washington.

TONY: I was in the NBC studios in those days and I can't remember the chief announcer's name, I think it was Pat Harrington, not the comedian. I would be there every day and one day two of the people from WTR in Norfolk came in looking for bodies. I auditioned for them. They offered me a job at 65 bucks a week. Bear in mind, it was 1942. I took the job because I didn't have a job and that was it.

JASON: What brought you to Chicago?

TONY: Well, a circuitous route. I was up all night in Norfolk. I'd monitor CBS out of DC. I heard, one night, a name I knew. I said to myself, "This is Segunner Bach." I said, "This guy used to be a customer at my father's speak-easy." My father had a speak-easy years ago here in Madison. By the way, the family name is Perritori and that's where the speak-easy comes in. I thought that he had to be the same guy. I got on the horn. I called him and I said, "Hey, are you Gunner Bach?" He said he was. I said, "I'm Tony Perritori." He said, "From Madison?" I said, "Yeah." He said, "What's the problem?" I said, "I'm buried alive in Norfolk, Virginia. What can you do for me?" He said, "Look, the next time you can catch a MATS plane come up and audition." I was doing a lot of freebies for the army at the time so I didn't mind leaning on them for military transport to go up there for free. So I went up and auditioned, came back and a couple of months later I got a call. They offered me a new job and I went up in '44 to WTOP in Washington. I spent a year, almost a year and a half there. I do believe it was the most exciting time of my life because that was the end of the Franklin Delano Roosevelt era. It was the end of the war in Europe. I covered the Breton Woods Conference in New Hampshire. I had the most emotional experience of my life being in the line of march during the funeral for FDR when his body was brought up from Warm Springs, Georgia. While I was doing my job I think, emotionally I peaked that year. Then one thing led to another and I came home to visit my folks, stopped in Chicago to visit some people I knew. They said, "They're looking for an all night jock at WIND. Are you interested?" I said, "Not really, but if it's available I'll go over and take a look." So I auditioned, came here to Madison to visit my family and then went back to DC. One day they said, "You've got a call from Chicago. Do you want it?" Well, I took it because it was closer to home, closer to the busy radio world and in my old neighborhood again. That had a tremendous draw for me.

JASON: Was that around '45?

TONY: Yeah, I got there in '45, the fall of '45. I did the all night record show in '45 and '46 and then struck out to work staff at WBBM.

JASON: Where you were exposed to a lot of kid's shows.

TONY: I was exposed to them as a kid.

JASON: I was too, but you became a part of those shows. I'll play some segments from a few of them to jog your memory. They may be before your time, but I'm sure you know some of the people on them.

TONY: I'm all ears!

JASON: Let's begin with *Tom Mix*.

****

ANNCR: The Tom Mix Ralston Straight Shooters are on the air and here comes Tom Mix, America's favorite cowboy with another thrill packed western adventure.

TOM: (*Singing*) Shredded Ralston for your breakfast, start the day off shining bright. If you like that cowboy energy with a flavor that's just right. Its delicious and nutritious, bite size and ready to eat. Take a tip from Tom. Go and tell your mom, Shredded Ralston can't be beat.

ANNCR:	The Tom Mix Ralston Straight Shooters bring you action, mystery and thrills in radio's biggest western and detective program. Tonight you're about to hear Tom involved in a baffling mystery called "Secret Mission." (Music sting) Tom has agreed to undertake a dangerous secret mission from which he may never return. Right now, Tom and Sherriff Mike Shaw find themselves in a strange city after the plane in which they took off in from Twin Rivers Airport near Doby was grounded because of bad weather. With them is a man who calls himself Mr. Moonlight. A moment ago another car driven by a beautiful young woman ran into the car in which Tom, Sheriff Mike and Mr. Moonlight were riding from the airport into town. The young lady's car was so badly wrecked that they agreed to take her home in their car. In a moment, strange and baffling things are going to happen.

****

JASON:	Tom Mix was a silent movie star and made a small fortune doing them. He was also a real life cowboy.
TONY:	Curley Bradley, who played on the show was as real life cowboy as you'll ever get.
JASON:	I remember him better from some later shows that he did. Curly Bradley, *the Singing Marshall* in 1950 was one.
TONY:	No, no, come on Jason, we're getting far apart here. No, really, because I was still in Chicago in the 50s and I don't recall Curley being called The Singing Marshall. He sang the signature for Ralston Purina, but he was an out and out cowboy. He and Mary Afflick, who was the producer of the show, got married in about 1948. It was called AB Productions,

	Afflick-Bradley Productions. I don't know what happened after '52 when I came back to Madison. I kept in touch with Don Gordon, my good buddy, who was the announcer on the show.
JASON:	Don was on so many of those shows.
TONY:	Don was a hell of a commercial announcer, fine announcer. Forrest Lewis played the part of Wash. There were three contract roles, Curley, Forrest and Sheriff Mike. All the rest of us came in and out as bad guys, heavies, you know how that routine goes.
JASON:	There is somebody else on my list for that show, someone who played a character named Jimmy at one time—George Gobel. Does that ring any bells at all?
TONY:	My earliest recollection of George Gobel is doing his early evening network TV show with Dagmar. You know, Jason, I don't know how old you are. We're talking stuff back and forth. You know a lot of things that I know, but I don't know, but I'm older than you are.
JASON:	A little bit, yes.
TONY:	Where are you from originally?
JASON:	I grew up in Chicago, during the great Chicago radio market days. Who's interviewing who here? Okay, go ahead.
TONY:	What were you doing between '45 and '52 when I was in Chicago?
JASON:	Listening to Jack Armstrong and Captain Midnight.

TONY: The All-American Boy. (*Singing*) Wave the Flag for Hudson High. Boys. Show them how we stand.

JASON: We'll get to that one in a little while. First I want to switch over to another show that I don't have any cuts from unfortunately. The show was Sky King. There was an announcer on that...

TONY: And he's still a very good friend.

JASON: The announcer I'm thinking of was Mike Wallace.

TONY: The announcer was indeed Mike Wallace.

JASON: I remember Mike also from a late night show called *The Chez Show* from the Chez Paree night club on Chicago's near north side.

TONY: Sure, with Buff Cobb. Mike was married to Cathy. My wife Roma remembers her well because she preceded me in Chicago radio. Her first husband cut quite a swath in Chicago circles. That's an odd story.

JASON: It's an interesting one.

TONY: All right, so Mike Wallace has a wife by the name of Cathy. Now Mike is in New York with CBS, 60 Minutes, etc. and his ex-wife Cathy is now married to Bill Paley, Mike's boss.

JASON: The boss of everybody at CBS.

TONY: If there's a God he comes around sooner or later.

JASON: There was another show he was the announcer on that surprises me a little because if came from Detroit. That one was *The Green Hornet*.

ACT I: MORE FOR THE KIDS | 17

TONY: I didn't know that because I didn't know Mike did the Detroit scene at all. All I know of Mike is Chicago and New York. You're in a better position to know, but I don't remember that he ever came out of Detroit.

JASON: Well, sometimes research isn't perfect because people do write mistakes. Sometimes it's a matter of trusting your sources. Shall we move on to The All-American Boy?

TONY: Why don't we do that?

****

OPENING: (*loud*) Jack Armstrong—Jack Armstrong—Jack Armstrong—The All-American Boy. (*singing*) Wave the flag for Hudson High Boys. Show them how we stand. Every scholar can be champion, known throughout the land.

ANNCR: Wheaties! The breakfast of champions, bring you the thrilling adventures of Jack Armstrong, the All-American boy. Say, just because the regular 1940 football season is drawing to a close, do you think that a lot of the game's best players will want to stop eating a champion training breakfast in the morning? Do you think they're going to pass up their regular bowl full of those champion whole wheat flakes, Wheaties and change to just an ordinary kind of breakfast? Well, not so you'd notice it. Plenty of All-Star athletes have been eating Wheaties all season long and they keep right on eating them straight through the year. Why? Take Tuffy Leemans for example, that great half-back from George Washington University, now with the New York Giants football team. Tuffy Leemans tells you, "With plenty of Wheaties to back me up, I know I'm, getting off to a swell start morning. Make mine Wheaties in training season and all year long." Did you get that fellows and girls? Tuffy Leemans goes for Wheaties all year long and right here I'm going to let you in on one of the most exciting discoveries I know about. Listen, do you know that a big bowl of those toasted Wheaties flakes with a champion flavor is every bit as good for you in the fall and winter as it is in the spring and summer? It's a fact. Food authorities, who help decide the kind of breakfast champion athletes and everybody else need in this weather, tell us that Wheaties are rich in heat energy units, the special fuel it takes to help keep us warm on chilly mornings. You don't need to eat a hot cooked breakfast, not if you'd rather have Wheaties because the heat of cooking doesn't count for a thing. It's those very important heat energy units in a food like Wheaties that help keep you warm. Why, your regular bowl of Wheaties will give you the same number of heat energy units as you'd get from an equal amount of whole wheat served steaming hot from the kitchen stove. And I'll tell you another reason Wheaties give you every bit of the well-known essential nourishment of the whole wheat grain. Of course you know that a square deal in nourishment is what every athlete wants from a good training breakfast. Now, I'm not going to say a word about how good and satisfying Wheaties taste when you eat it with lots of milk or cream and a glass of fruit juice. No, I want you to enjoy that breakfast of champions yourself tomorrow morning. Be sure to get some Wheaties right away.

And now, Jack Armstrong, the All-American Boy.

Uncle Jim's car has stalled. It won't start. Jack, Billy, Betty and Uncle Jim are on their way to the head hunting country in the mountains of the Philippines to locate a constabulary sergeant who has some knowledge of the missing professor Loring. With them, they have a chart and a luminous ring which will help them locate some valuable uranium which Uncle Jim needs to complete his experiment in atomic power. Their automobile has just been pulled across an un-fordable stream by a caribou, a water buffalo in the Philippines, but their engine is now wet and won't start. Just at this moment the unscrupulous adventurer, Dr. Shipetto, who is trying to steal the chart and ring from Uncle Jim has arrived in his car on the other side of the stream. With him are Black Beard and Lazarro and others of his crew and there's no doubt what they'd do if they can get across the stream before Uncle Jim and Jack can get the car started. Listen.

****

JASON: That was the longest running of the children's serials, all the way from 1939 until '51. Tony, is there anyone on there that you recognize? I know it may have been before your time.

TONY: I recognize a couple of the people. Charlie Flynn was playing Jack Armstrong. I'm trying to remember the guys who played Uncle Jim. You're flooding me with memories of 40, 45 years ago. I used to remember, but I don't now. I seem to recall that both Jim and Don Ameche were on it at one time, on the first Jack Armstrong.

JASON: Don played Captain Hughes for a while.

TONY: I did a summer replacement with Jim on ABC in the late 40s. We did a series of half-hour network radio dramatic shows. I got to know Jim well.

JASON: Jim was big on radio.

TONY: I used to see him at Ricardo's, which was my stomping ground, on the corner of Rush and Hubbard.

JASON: Which is still there.

TONY: Yep, still there, run by a Greek family now. I was working staff at WBBM then. I would come out of the basement level and be right there at Rush and Hubbard. Right at the Chicago River. I spent eight years in Chicago and I think I spent eight years at Ricardo's, which is probably an unsurpassed record. I did go to other places at times, but that was my home base. It was so much fun. I was part of the act. I sang with the waiters. I cleaned up in the morning with Carlo Bianchi when the clean-up man didn't show up. I lived on the third floor at one time. It was like home. I spent eight wonderful years on Rush Street. I don't know if I ever inspired to anything on radio, it must have been an unconscious thing, but I know that I always was and still am an invenerate radio listener. I have the radio on all the time. I used to drive my wife nuts. I slept with the radio on all night long. Now that I don't see any more, I'm right back to square one enjoying radio as much as I ever did because it allows my mind to be free. I am not transfixed by what is on TV.

JASON: There's so much of television that could be done without the pictures. You can sit and listen to the sound with your eyes shut and not miss much.

TONY: That's what I'm doing now. I find that I cannot follow most shows because the dialogue is not attuned to the blind. It's geared to people who see.

I say they are the unfortunate ones because their mind does not operate. I'm privileged that my mind can run rampant. I'm not bothered by what I see on the screen. I'm listening and I'm back to the old radio days where you could be a hero, a coward or you could be ten feet tall. You could be a pygmy, you could be male or female, I don't care what. You could be whatever you wanted to be by the sound that came out of the radio.

JASON: Let's go back to another one of those radio heroes, since you mentioned heroes. Here's one that I'm sure you remember well.

****

SFX: [*oriental cacophony*] Terry and the Pirates (*more noise*) Quaker Puffed Wheat brings you Terry and the Pirates. (*gong*)

ANNCR: I wish I could give you a fuller picture of what has happened to Terry and his friends in Calcutta, India, but things are confused by intrigue, undercover activities, spy paths that criss-cross and many unseen enemies, but this much we do know. Somewhere hidden in Calcutta is a master spy, a Nazi enemy agent. That German operator is an evil genius who is helping the Japs to adapt and improve their deadly robot bombs. They made the enemy pay by working with the British secret agents in Calcutta. But all has not gone well, nor will it, as you'll see in just a moment. So stand by. (*Cymbal clash*)

JINGLE: Oh, here comes Quaker with a bang, bang. Quaker Puffed Wheat Sparkies, the wheat that's shot from guns—the families favorite breakfast, the wheat that's shot from guns. Quaker Puffed Wheat Sparkies have the vitamins, do tell. The guns help with that extra puff and boy, do they taste swell. Here comes Quaker with a bang, bang, rat-a-tat-tat bang, bang.

ANNCR: Hello gang. Say, who has no questions, but requires many answers? A door bell, of course, but I don't rush to answer the door bell when I'm eating the cereal shot from guns. No siree, no interfering with my breakfast pleasure. Try that swell meal tomorrow. Take your choice of Quaker Puffed Wheat Sparkies or Quaker Puffed Rice Sparkies. They're both shot from guns. The rice is nice. The wheat is sweet. They're magnified eight times bigger and brim full of glorious sunlight flavors and as crisp as you want. Yes, they chirp while you crunch them. They're filled with vitamin B1 and niacin and nutritious. Quaker Puffed Wheat Sparkies and Quaker Puffed Rice Sparkies, full of hearty nourishment.

Well, gang, Pat Ryan has stepped into a mess of bad luck. He and Terry tried to invade a spy hide-out and Pat got shot in the leg for his pains plus a bawling out by General Leander, the chief British agent. Pat has now been put into the hospital and Terry has been ordered to remain in his hotel room. Flip Corcoran is the only cheerful one. As Pat entered the hospital Flip went out to join Terry at the hotel.

****

JASON: That show we just heard a small portion of was *Terry and the Pirates.* There were a lot of recognizable voices on that one. Jackie Kelk from The Aldrich Family was one.

TONY: By the way, do you know who Florio is?

JASON: Certainly, but I wonder if our listeners do? Or should we let that one go?

TONY: I just thought I'd drop that in as an add-on and let it go and let you take it.

JASON: But he was not on *Terry and the Pirates*. Florio is Florio Benedetti who works with me here at this station. He does the Big Band Show as Ben Benedetti.

TONY: And he is a beautiful man with a beautiful voice. Okay, I got that out of my system. *Terry and the Pirates*—I did a thing with that. I played a guy by the name of Akin, the cobra, a typical Russian. I was an accent guy. I played heavies. On the *Tom Mix Show* I was Caesar Chino, an Italian gangster—type casting, I guess. On *Captain Midnight* I was—but Boris Aplon was the resident heavy, Ivan Sharp. Sherman Marks was one of the contract players.

JASON: He played Ichy, the mechanic, Ichabod Mudd.

TONY: On the *Sky King Show*, Mike Wallace was the announcer. Penny was played by Beryl Vaughn. Beryl was Ken Nordine's wife.

JASON: Ken is still going strong.

TONY: Yep, and you told me Paul Barnes has passed away.

JASON: About two years ago. Paul was a good friend. He was also one of the people who played the lead role on *Captain Midnight*.

TONY: The only Chicago people I would still be conversant with would be Jack Brickhouse and Fahey Flynn.

JASON: There was another guy you should remember from *Sky King*—Earl Nightingale.

TONY: Oh, Earl Nightingale. I was working staff at WBBM. I wish I could recall exactly, but I think I know the scenario. His father had a piece of an advertising agency and Earl knew exactly what he wanted to do. He came into BBM as an announcer, a staff announcer. I don't know what kind of a background he had, but he had his whole thing laid out. He was going to replace the original guy who played *Sky King*. And then he just stepped in and took over. Now you're going to have to help me, Jason because I have forgotten. It was a syndicated show all over the country, but there was a guy on BBM who did an hour or hour and a half every afternoon and went through about four wives. They did a confidential live show where it was all intimate conversation and they sold all sorts of junk. Have I struck a responsive chord?

JASON: Not at all. I do recall that in his later days Earl did a bunch of motivational programs on cassettes. I remember that because I had a recording studio at the time and we did a lot of duplication for him. What a racket that was!

TONY: No, no, come on. He also replaced this guy. I saw it laid out in advance and saw it perpetrate itself the way he said it was actually going to happen. He came to work staff at WBBM and I was there along with Will Shirley, Fahey Flynn and John Cannon. John went to New York and did a big shtick there. This Earl Nightingale was like a piranha. He came in and tore people apart and did it on purpose. I don't know if that explains anything.

| JASON: | I think it does. I met the man a few times in later years and he still seemed like that. Everything had to be done yesterday for him. |

| TONY: | I never met any other guy that deliberately set out to take someone else's job away from him, but that's exactly what he did. I guess he had a perfect license to do it. It's just that when you're that brazen about it, that leant a different aura to it. Anyway, that's neither here nor there. We're talking about kid's shows and these guys were no longer kids. It's just that I can't recollect old time radio without these kind of things or without going back to the late 20s when Ralph Ginsberg and his powerhouse ensemble would come on the air every day, Monday through Friday at noon on WGN. Those were golden days. Those were the days of Eddie and Fannie Cavanaugh. |

| JASON: | I remember them. |

| TONY: | Do you really? |

| JASON: | Not first hand, but I do have some information on them. |

| TONY: | You used to send in a line and if they could make a song out of it you would get—Oh, what would you get? |

| JASON: | Some sort of prize? |

| TONY: | Oh yeah, I remember. You would get Broadcast Corned Beef Hash. |

| JASON: | They also did what was probably the first talk show. |

TONY:	How about the three doctors, Rudolph, Sherman and Pratt?
JASON:	Now you're going back a little too far for me.
TONY:	You see, you've got me on a kick and I keep going back and going back. But, I'll tell you what, my brother Vito and my sisters, who may be listening in—I have four of them—they are gurgling I'm sure because I'm talking about stuff that they remember too because the Perritori family grew up with a radio. We watched it the way people watch TV. We watched the thing to hear what came out of it.
JASON:	Watched the green eye?
TONY:	And on Sunday—*The Eddie Cantor Show.*
JASON:	Among others—Eddie finally went to a quiz show type of format. Jack Benny was on, on Sunday night as well as Edgar Bergen.
TONY:	Do you remember Cantor's closing theme? I cry whenever I think of it. (Singing) I like to spend each Sunday with you. As friend to friend, I'm sorry it's through.
JASON:	Let's get in one more kid's show before we have to sign off. We already talked a little about this one.

****

SFX:	Captain Midnight (*Diving airplane*)
ANNCR:	Yes, Captain Midnight! Brought to you every day, Monday through Friday, by the makers of Ovaltine, America's favorite food drink. Now, have you heard the news? The news about that marvelous new

two-piece, bright colored shake-up mug Captain Midnight has for you? That big, handsome 2 in 1 shaker-upper you use to make ice cold chocolate shake-ups to drink every day? Well sir, Captain Midnight has one for you, almost as a gift, and listen, it's something you'll want to send in for tonight for sure. Will your eyes pop when you see it, probably different from anything you've ever seen. So listen carefully while I tell you how swell it is. It's big, even bigger than a regular drinking glass and its bright colored, bright orange bottom part and a brilliant blue shaker top. And its decorated with the official Secret Squadron insignia. There's a handsome embossed medallion, a full one and three-quarters inches across on the side of your mug showing Captain Midnight's head, like the Lincoln head on a penny. Then, on the blue top there's the Secret Squadron pledge in raised letters. And to make sure you know just what it's like, let me explain. It's a 2 in 1 shake-up mug. There are two separate parts to it. When the top and bottom are put together it's a shaker and when you take the top off, why the bottom's your own special drinking mug. Remember, you can use your shake-up mug for years because it isn't made from ordinary glass or breakable china, but of a special sturdy, durable, hard to break plastic. You can have one for just 15 cents in coins and the label from your jar of Ovaltine. Now, to get your shake-up mug and enjoy those wonderful, ice cold, creamy shake-ups, here's all you do. Just tear the label, the whole label, from your jar of Ovaltine. Print your name, address, city and state on the back of the label. Put the label in an envelope with 15 cents in coin and mail it to Captain Midnight, Chicago, Illinois. Supplies of these swell shake-up mugs are limited, and I know you want to start to enjoy those big, ice cold, chocolaty shake-ups right away. So be sure to send in that Ovaltine label and 15 cents to Captain Midnight, Chicago, Illinois this very night.

****

JASON: On *Captain Midnight* there were some familiar voices.

TONY: Oh gosh yes. On that bit Tom Moore was the announcer and Ed Prentiss would have been Jim 'Red' Albright, which was Captain Midnight's real name. Tom Moore was Tom McNutt. He was a preacher's son out of WNUP in Peoria. And again, Ivan Shark was the resident bad guy. Sherman Marks played Captain Midnight's sidekick. These came out of WGN. Both *Tom Mix* and *Captain Midnight* originated at WGN. I worked across the street at the Wrigley Building at the time. I was a staff announcer. Neither one of those locations for broadcasting are there anymore. They're still there, but the studios have moved. WMAQ and WENR were at the Merchandise Mart. I got there late in the heyday of the radio game, but I heard those guys when I got there. The prestige guys would have a speed boat on the Chicago River. They'd do a show at BBM, at the Wrigley Building, then duck down to the boat on the river to the Merchandise Mart and hit the express elevator that they had only for radio people, and get up to the 19th floor because they had another radio show to do. They would take their cues and timing over the phone. They would have a stand-in to run through rehearsals. Those were heady days.

JASON: People were all allowed to do cross-overs in those days. They weren't tied to any one outlet. They could work all over on the same day.

TONY: Sure, sure—Virginia Payne—Virginia Payne…

JASON: Soap Opera Heaven.

TONY: I have a mental block. I remember Virginia, but I cannot remember—Oh, yeah, *Ma Perkins*. That was the only show that was on rival networks at the same time, on CBS in the morning and NBC in the afternoon. Virginia Payne, at the time, which was '47, was making $75,000 a year. And, Jason, in '47…

JASON: That was a whole lot of money.

TONY: A fortune. Another thing, General Mills had a full hour of soaps on NBC called the General Mills Hour, from one to two in the afternoon with Ed Prentiss as your host. They had four different soaps. I did a thing on one of those called *Today's Children*. I played a hero, the first and only time in my career. I did a second romantic lead by the name of Carlos Fernandez.

****

As you must have noticed during the course of the previous discussion, Tony Parish lost his sight after his radio days were over. You should also have noticed that he did not lose any of his spirit because of that fact. Since that time he has left our world and is entertaining somewhere else. As he stated, he was able to appreciate the audio work of others even more after going blind. That is, after all is said and done, what entertainment radio was all about. We did it all with our minds, not our eyes. I'm flattered to know that he was a regular listener to my own show.

ACT II: PROFESSIONAL TALKERS

What I'm speaking of when I use the terms Professional Talkers or Professional Mouths are the people who provided the glue that held many productions together. While some simply did intros and outros along with commercials there were also many who became integral parts of the shows they were featured on. One such person was Harlow Wilcox, sometimes called Waxy, who could weave in Johnson's Wax commercials in a never ending series of sneaky ways on *Fibber McGee and Molly*. Jack Benny had Don Wilson and Ken Carpenter at different times. They could do a lot of the same things as Harlow. They both became active characters on Jack's shows. George and Gracie had many of these people, each in a different time frame, one of whom was Bill Goodwin, the perennial playboy. Bill later had his own program.

The people in question are, of course, the announcers. In Act II we will hear from two of those gentlemen, each of which became known for a particular series even though their bodies of work went far beyond that. They were both talented and versatile people who could fit easily into any format offered to them. They were definitely Professional Talkers of the first water.

ACT II:
SCENE ONE
MR. HIT PARADE

It is a difficult thing for me to be able to say much in the way of introduction for this man. Difficult, because during the course of the interview, his answers to my questions were so complete that there would be little more to add. That is not to say that his career was just a short story that could be covered quickly. Oh no, not at all. He was many things during his long and fruitful life that went way beyond announcing. One of those things was his more than average ability on the piano. He could have made a good living going that route had he pursued it.

The man I am referring to is André Baruch. On July 23, 1987 we had this long enjoyable conversation.

****

JASON: A member of the National Broadcasters Hall of Fame since 1979 is André Baruch. At one time his dignified voice leant itself to being a character by the name of Two Gun Andy on the Bobby Benson Show.

ANDRÉ: I think it was called *Bobby Benson and the H-bar O Ranch.*

JASON: *Bobby Benson and the B-bar-B Riders*

ANDRÉ: Your memory is better than mine because that goes back so many years that I can hardly remember it.

But I do remember that Bobby Benson was played by Billy Hallop, who eventually became one of the *Dead End Kids* and he had a sister who was a radio and television actress. She was on *Night Court*. She passed away while she was doing that show. She was the bailiff.

JASON: Florence Hallop was also on *Duffy's Tavern* and *Coast to Coast on a Bus* and some other later shows. Let's talk about how you got from Paris, where you were born, to the media in this country.

ANDRÉ: I came here from Paris, France when I was thirteen. My parents came over then. I went to High School and got through it very quickly because in France the educational system is a little swifter than it is here. At least it was then. I was in college at a very early age. We lived in Brooklyn and inadvertently one day a friend and I were wandering along the Boardwalk at Coney Island, which, if you don't know Brooklyn, is a sort of resort area. We came to a place called Have Motor Hotel, at the base of which were a series of stores. We saw a store window with the call letters WGCU. I asked my friend what he thought that was. He said, "I think it's a radio station." At which point somebody came running out and said, "Can anybody here do anything?" My friend pointed to me and said, "He plays piano." The man grabbed me by the back of my neck and pushed me into a studio which was velvet draped and sat me down at a piano, went to what was a carbon mike, punched it on and said, "Ladies and gentlemen, we now present that distinguished concert pianist Mr. Paul Hart." He then whispered to me, "What are you going to play?" I said, "I'm going to play 'Dizzy Fingers' and 'Nola' and—" He said, "No, no, you have to play classical music." I said, "Oh, then I'll play a Chopin Etude, a Minute Waltz, a Beethoven Sonata and a Bach Fugue." "Mr. Hart opens his program today with . . ." And he went on with the introduction. I went on to play about fifteen or twenty minutes. When I finished he said, "Very good. Do you want a job?" I said, "Doing what?" He said, "Playing the piano, of course." I said, "Well, I can't. I'm going to college at the present time." He said, "What time do you finish your studies?" I said, "Somewhere around one o'clock I'm finished. Then I have homework to do." He said, "Why don't you come here. We don't open until three or so. Between what you're doing, playing piano or whatever, you can do your homework." I said, "Fine, how much does it pay?" He said, "$25 a week." Well, $25 a week in those days is like two hundred today. I was delighted. I worked there as a pianist. I did newscasts by reading the newspaper and in general, had a good time and learned a great deal at that little radio station. As it turned out, I worked in a lot of little radio stations in Brooklyn until I applied for a job as studio pianist at CBS in New York. When I got the appointment and got to the 21st floor at 45 Madison Avenue, which was the home of the Columbia Broadcasting System, there were two lines. One was for announcers and one was auditioning studio pianists. I looked at both lines. One was much shorter than the other. I didn't know what it was for, but I got in the shorter of the two lines. When it came my turn they handed me a piece of paper with a lot of foreign compositions, composers and conductors and, since I spoke several languages it didn't pose any problem for me. I just thought it was an intelligence test. Most of it had to do with music so I just read it off. When I was finished the production man said, "Well, if we need you we'll call you." The following week I did get a call. They said, "Come on down to the station." I did and I walked in. They said, "Mr. Baruch, you have the job." I said, "Wonderful, what does it pay?" "$45 a week." "Great, do I bring my own music or do you have a library here?" That stunned him for a moment and he said, "Look, you are hired to be an announcer and that's what you're to stick to. We have a lot of concert musicians around here. We don't need you for that." That was the first time I found out I was an announcer.

JASON: In other words you're saying a lot of accidental things happened to get you started.

ANDRÉ: A great many accidental things happened. I don't think this is true of a great many people. Good accidents happen, bad ones sometimes, but during my career a great many good ones happened.

JASON: You did a lot of announcing for a lot of shows and there was something else that you did that many people don't know about. You did play-by-play for the Brooklyn Dodgers games for a while.

ANDRÉ: Red Barber moved from the Dodgers to the Yankees and left an open spot with Vin Scully and since I was doing commercials at the time for the American Tobacco Company and Lucky Strike—they sponsored the Dodgers—Walter O'Malley called me in and he said, "Do you know anything about Baseball?" I said, "Yes, I've been a fan of Baseball since I first came to this country. I used to come to Ebbets Field as a kid." By kid I meant thirteen, fourteen, fifteen years old and I had studied the game. I started calling out the names of Baseball players. He asked me what positions they played and did I know them? I said, "Of course" and I called them all out. He said, "Would you like to work for the Dodgers?" I said that I would love it. This was a big thrill. So I started in 1955 with the Brooklyn Dodgers along side of Vin Scully. It was a real thrill. I'll never forget it. My only mistake was not coming out to the coast with them, but I had so many shows at that time that I could not move.

JASON: You had a lot of shows going for a long time before that.

ANDRÉ: I had the *United States Steel Hour, The Hit Parade, The Kate Smith Show, American Album of Familiar Music*, a couple of soap operas and the salary from the Dodgers was rather low, which I didn't mind. I'd've done it for nothing, but when it meant moving to the coast it would mean a whole new start, in spite of the fact that O'Malley was much wiser than I was. He told me that I would be making a lot of money. I said, "I'm sorry, Mr. O'Malley, but I can't do it." To this day I regret it. However, I'm still a Dodger fan.

JASON: You mentioned *American Album of Familiar Music*. That was one of the earlier shows you worked on. It was one of the many shows put together by Frank and Ann Hummert, who did so many soaps.

ANDRÉ: That's right. There's a very interesting story about them. They were sponsored by Bayer Aspirin and Mr. Hummert was a very astute advertising man. I recall one day I read the copy during rehearsal and after the rehearsal I came in to him and I said, "Mr. Hummert, I read this copy and there is one complete paragraph, a rather large one; there are no verbs in there and it makes no sense whatsoever." He said, "Let me see it." He put on his *pince-nez*, looked at it through his glasses and then said, "By

Jove, you're right." I said, "Shall I change it?" He said, "No, no. The attorneys have looked at this. We cannot change it." I said, "But it makes no sense." He said, "Just read it clearly and distinctly. No one ever said to me that copy has to make sense."

JASON: There were a lot of things like that, that happened through the years that people just didn't catch.

ANDRÉ: Oh sure. I read scripts with "Ladies and gentlemen of the audio radiance", things of that type. I made a lot of fluffs in my time. There was one that was attributed to somebody, which was unfortunately mine. When I was doing a show with Frank Hacop and Junior Sanderson; I said at the end of a commercial, "Friends, get the breast in bed, use Braun's bed,"—instead of use Braun's Bread.

JASON: I have that somewhere. I know I've heard it. Some other things you did with the Hummerts were *Just Plain Bill* and a couple of other soaps.

ANDRÉ: *Second Husband, Little French Princess*—

JASON: *Marie, the Little French Princess?*

ANDRÉ: Right

JASON: A lot of people went through that show who were memorable, but not too many people remember them now.

ANDRÉ: You do.

JASON: You said that Frank Hummert was an ad man. The advertising agencies WERE radio in those days. They had almost complete control over it and Frank's group, Docket, Santo and Hummert was buying something like 18% of all available day time radio at one point.

ANDRÉ: Yes, agencies at that time had complete control over the creative people as far as most programs were concerned. Today it's entirely different, both radio and TV. The reason for that is because of the deracinated presentation of commercials. A program no longer is sponsored by one product or service except in rare instances on television when you have one big sponsor doing an entire special. Generally the sponsor buys one or two spots in a half hour program or in an hour show they might buy three. The prices are so prohibitive that they usually don't buy a whole program.

JASON: These days it costs as much or more to buy one 30 second spot as it would have cost to produce a whole season series years ago.

ANDRÉ: That's true.

JASON: It's gotten to a point of overkill. You have to wonder how much worse it can get.

ANDRÉ: As a matter of fact, if you take *Your Hit Parade* for an example. It was one of the most popular programs which ran from 1935 until about 1959, first on radio, then on both radio and TV and eventually on TV only. That program was sponsored by the American Tobacco Company only, nobody else.

JASON: When you talk about *Your Hit Parade* you're talking about something close to home. You're married to Bea Wain. Is that where you met her?

ANDRÉ: No, I didn't meet her originally there. I saw her for the first time when she was with a group called V-8 and was signed with the Fred Waring Chorus. V-8 was a marvelous swing octet. The nearest thing to it today would be Manhattan Transfer, that kind of group, very creative, very innovating in their singing. To this day that music still sounds great. Fred came in to me and said, "I want you to listen to a group." I listened to the V-8 and said, "They're wonderful!" He hired them, but I didn't speak to Bea. The following season Bea was singing with the Kate Smith Choir under the direction of Ted Straeter and I was announcing the *Kate Smith Show*. That's where I first met her and asked her for a date. Eventually we went out and got married on May 1, 1938.

JASON: So you're looking at a golden anniversary next year.

ANDRÉ: Indeed we are. She still looks super and is singing well. We have an act which is doing very nicely and her voice seems to have mellowed. She doesn't have the usual big vibrato that is synonymous with singers who age a bit. She has a clear, young voice and she sounds great.

JASON: You worked with Kate Smith and of course, Ted Collins, on radio and also on television.

ANDRÉ: On some television, but mostly radio. By the time it got to television Ted Collins was announcing the show himself. He decided he was as good as anybody and that was that.

JASON: Ted was really the driving factor of that show and of Kate's life as well.

ANDRÉ: He directed everything about her. He took her off the Broadway stage and made her a star.

ACT II: SCENE ONE: MR. HIT PARADE | 41

JASON: A lot of people that we know well got their start on *The Kate Smith Show*. I'm thinking of possibly Abbott & Costello or Ezra Stone from *The Aldrich Family* or even Henny Youngman.

ANDRÉ: I watched them come on. A lot of them got their starts on her show. No question about it.

JASON: You worked for some time too on *The Shadow*.

ANDRÉ: I did *The Shadow* with a fellow named Brett Morrison, who was Lamont Cranston. It was after the time of Orson Welles in the role.

JASON: You did a lot of music shows. You worked with Guy Lombardo. Mark Warno had his own radio show for a while and of course there was *Your Hit Parade*.

ANDRÉ: You must understand that we were staff announcers at CBS and there was a brilliant cast of announcers, twenty-one of the best in the business. I'm referring to people like Norman Brookshire, Ted Huesing, Ralph Edwards, Ken Roberts, Frank Gallup—*ad-infinitum*—David Ross, Harry von Zell, all brilliant announcers, knowledgeable, good voices and intelligent people. We each did a minimum of, let's say, five or six shows a day, sometimes more if necessary. We did everything. We did sports. We did news. We did commercials. We did music and remotes. Remotes meant that we'd go out and introduce the new bands. People like Benny Goodman, Harry James and Artie Shaw were side men originally in the CBS house orchestra. So when they became band leaders we didn't think much about it. We had been on friendly terms with them as just side men. We knew them that well. To this day, the few that are still left are good friends, and there aren't too many of them. Les Brown is still with us. Woody Herman is not doing that well, not feeling well, but he's one of the few that's left. Harry James is gone. Benny's gone. Artie is still around, but he's not into the music scene anymore.

JASON: Actually, Artie just won an Oscar for a movie that was made about him. He didn't, but the documentary did.

ANDRÉ: Yes, I think it's called *All You've Got is Time.* It's a wonderful documentary on Artie Shaw. If you're interested in music it's a must see.

JASON: I'm a little curious as to where one can see a lot of those documentaries and shorts. They don't really show them in the normal movie houses.

ANDRÉ: I think that one is being shown in theatres quite a bit. I'm a member of Motion Picture Academy of Arts and Sciences so that's where I see them.

JASON: Since we're speaking of movie shorts, there was something else that you did for many years. You were the narrator for Pathé News.

ANDRÉ: I was usually the voice of gloom and doom for Pathé News. There were other narrators there. There were Dwight Weist and Dan Donaldson and Red Barber did sports. The race track announcer was Clem McCarthy. He was a gravely voiced announcer and he used to start off every race with, "Racing fans, they're off!" You could hear the sand going through his throat. He was a wonderfully colorful character.

JASON: I remember him well, not a voice you could easily forget.

André: He did the races. Red did sports and as I said, I did death and destruction. Each of us was assigned a category. You became type-cast. The funny thing was, I used to do sports for RKO. The only thing they'd let me do was short subjects on sports. Universal only let me do comedy and at Warner Brothers I did something else. Each one said, "You can't do that. This is what you're slotted to do." Yet, I was doing something different for each company. I was free-lance so I didn't care what they said, but I was with Pathé News for a good number of years, from 1935 until they went out of business, a period of about twenty years.

Jason: What do you suppose happened to that sort of thing in theatres? Is it mostly because of television news?

André: Television news is immediate. Film news—Pathé News and Fox Movietone and Paramount News only came on twice a week, Monday and Thursday, I believe. They weren't immediate. They were on film. Although the people were wonderful, the camera men and the editors were great, it was always a rush job. Originally the sound track was right on the film. Sometimes I'd finish working at 9:00pm, doing my chores, voice-overs for Pathé News and then at 2:00am I'd get a call. They'd say, "André, you have to come back in." I'd say, "What's the matter?" "Well, the laboratory ruined the film." Later, when audio tape came in, we'd do it on tape and they would do it separately on film, the voice track. So I never had to go back in again nor did any of us, but it was intriguing. When television came in you got the news practically on the hour, almost as soon as it happened. Today there are so many people in the field that they can cover almost anything and they do, so gradually the news reels went out of business. They were no longer profitable. We had to just read from a piece of paper. A man would stand in back of us with a hand on our shoulder. When it came time to talk he would use a tap on our shoulder. We just hoped he didn't tap too hard. The copy looked like a road map. They were in such a rush to get this out that you really had to be quite astute at looking at the film and back at the paper to find out what was going on and to time everything perfectly. Today, with the advent of tape, you can do it over and over again until you get it right. But even on live television they can read from a Teleprompter. We never had Teleprompters.

JASON: It was a little like doing animation. You had to watch the film and read.

ANDRÉ: That's right. There's a difference between the announcers of the 30s, 40s or 50s and the announcers today. Today, those you find at stations are Disc Jockeys or they do sports or the do news—period. They're locked into whatever and the fees that are being paid to some of the news people on television are so outrageous that I say to myself, "What makes a sportscaster, one who's reading off a Teleprompter, worth $800,000 a year?" That's incredible to me, or a newscaster, even though he may be head of his division, head of the desk, editor-in-chief, may make $2,000,000 a year. It seems incredible. The announcers of the 30s, 40s and 50s, and I use that word announcers a little unadvisedly because most of them were very well educated. Many of us had to go out on remotes to do sports or conventions or whatever was necessary without a piece of paper in front of us and without any notes and just off the top of our heads report what was happening, whether it be a fire or a prize fight or a political convention. The reason we could do it was because we had to do it. We had to do everything, whether it was announcing a band or doing a commercial or doing a drama or whatever. Most of us could act and we did.

JASON: I think something else that most of the announcers did, at least the better ones, was to write their own continuity for advertising and so on.

ANDRÉ: Sure, I wrote a lot of stuff. Even today, on the recreation of *Your Hit Parade*, which is syndicated throughout the country, I wrote all of the material and did all the research—wrote the show. No problem. A lot of us can write. I write columns on golf and on radio for various publications.

JASON: What else keeps you busy today?

ANDRÉ: I do commercials here in California such as J. W. Robinson's, which is a very exclusive and very elegant chain of stores, department stores. I do commercials for Belgian Waffles, Van De Camp Foods and, I don't know, I do a lot of commercials. I also do industrial voice-overs and narration for films. I do some acting. What else? I don't know. I'm always busy.

JASON: So you're nowhere near retirement?

ANDRÉ: There's no such thing as retirement in our business because you'd turn blue. As I mentioned earlier, my wife, Bea Wain and I have an act. Not long ago we did a tour of ten cities with Bea singing and me doing a lot of humor to work with her. It was very successful. We played in large theatres and large convention halls with a minimum of 3,000 to 10,000 seats. It was a wonderful experience for us so we retained the act and we still do it. Bea is singing better than ever. They'll never hold a benefit for us because throughout the many years we've both been in the business we've been constantly active in various phases. Bea and I did a show called *Mr. And Mrs. Music*, which was a disc jockey show. For eight or nine years we did a 'Mr. and Mrs.' talk show over WPBR in Palm Beach, Florida. We did talk shows on the ABC and the NBC networks. I did news commentary at CBS for a while on radio. So we have a lot to go back on. When I think you have the experience to do these things there's never a problem of having to look for work. Someone's always calling and saying, "Can you do so and so? Do you want to do so and so?" We keep just as busy as we want to. Sometimes it gets a little too busy. It's a joy to be in a business that you enjoy and we both do. I can't remember ever being under any real stress except when I was doing auditions for big shows and not making it. I never made the audition for *Your Hit Parade*. I came in 73rd. But the man who won it was so nervous that George Washington Hill, who was a tycoon and chairman of the board at American Tobacco Company, at the rehearsal said, "Get that son of a so and so out of here!" They called the announcers room and I was the only one available. That's how I got *Your Hit Parade*. I stayed on it for many years.

JASON: That was another one of those lucky accidents. Many have had them, but once you got in you had to have the talent to sustain it.

ANDRÉ: That may be so and we hope that we have had a modicum of talent to sustain us throughout our career. I think we do. I think Bea, especially, because of her ability to sing well and phrase beautifully and you understand every lyric. I think that is what has extended her career. As far as I'm concerned, I don't know, I guess it's because I can do most anything that has to do with radio or television. It's been great fun.

****

So many people have jobs that make them wonder when they wake up in the morning why they have to go in for another dreaded day at work. Obviously, André Baruch was not one of those people. He approached every task with zest and energy and apparently made the most of every day. If you enjoy what you are doing your work is just another part of a pleasant day. George Burns often said that if you don't enjoy your business you are in the wrong business.

André was honored many times with awards for his chosen field of endeavor. He could have made it in many kinds of careers, but he chose show business and never regretted it for a minute. I opted for the title of this segment, Mr. Hit Parade, because he was with that show for so many years, but as you have read, that was just the tip of the iceberg.

One thing that we did not discuss was his involvement with the origination of Armed Forces Radio during the 40s. He was instrumental in setting up several of the stations that served our troops so well during the days of World War II.

André lived to celebrate his 53rd wedding anniversary with his wife, Bea, after which he was taken from her and from us.

Act II:
Scene Two
Keeper of the Secret Word

Here we have another example of someone who was born well beyond our national borders. Beijing, China was his place of birth, but he was not there for very long. He was only nine months old when his parents brought him to San Francisco. They were in the import-export business and just happened to be living in China when my guest was born, so he really had no Chinese ancestry. This is just a point of interest and has absolutely no bearing on the career of the man in question.

This is another of those versatile professional talkers who did a great deal more than merely announcing program content. I'll go into that versatility a bit more at the end of this segment, but for now let me introduce to you George Fenneman, foil of one of the best of the media pranksters. We talked on July 6, 1987.

****

JASON: George, before we go back to the old days I want to talk a little about the present. I understand you've recently done some things now that you're very proud of, that have won for you some local Emmys out there in California recently.

GEORGE: Yes, it's been very good for us. I'm a semi-retired person. For the last eleven years I've been the spokesman for Savings of America or Home Savings as it's known here. We had fifty branches. We now have 350. I did a couple of shows. One was called *On Campus*. I did that for ten years and it seemed to win an Emmy almost every year, local Emmys. It was a show that dealt with the independent colleges of Southern California. I also did one about photography called *Talk About Pictures*. My co-host on that was a professional photographer named Lee Wiener. We won an Emmy Award for that show too. We did 125 of those during the last six years. I've been into photography for many years. It was a pleasure to meet Ansel Adams and David Douglas Duncan and all the great photographers. It was kind of a labor of love.

JASON: That explains why you did a show a while back, probably in 1957, called *Funny, Funny Films*, where people submitted their home movies.

GEORGE: We were ahead of our time, you know that? It was an interesting show. We laughed for thirteen weeks. We were on prime time on ABC on Sunday nights. We had a problem getting enough film because we went on the air before we had all the film we needed. Today, I suppose you'd be inundated as everybody has home movies or a video camera. It was kind of cute. We had some funny stuff.

JASON: These days there are quite a few of those blooper shows. They usually end up using home movies on those.

GEORGE: We did quite a bit of that too. We had some wonderful films of families teaching their kids to roller skate and ride bicycles. They literally destroyed themselves on 8mm film. We had some 9 & 1/2mm film that I'd never heard of with the sprocket holes right down the center of the film, French amateur film. We had some interesting bits of film.

| JASON: | Let's go back to the beginning. Maybe you can tell us how you got your start in radio? The first reference I have is *You Bet Your Life*, in 1947, which we must discuss later, but I know you must have done more before that. |

| GEORGE: | Actually, I started when I was in High School. I got a part on a series called *Golden Days*. I played the role of Joaquin Mariatta, a California bandit in the early gold rush days. I did it with a very, very bad Spanish accent. I was a real young person then, about eighteen or nineteen. That was my first really paying job—I think I got five bucks for that one. Then the unions came in and I got a job as a staff announcer at KSFO in San Francisco. That paid $35 a week. That was about 1942. Six months later I auditioned for the Blue network, which later became the American Broadcasting Company, at a big raise in pay. I wound up with $55 a week. Then I got my first commercial—*Sunday Evening Serutan News*. That paid 35 bucks and I was on my way. |

| JASON: | You did three shows with Jack Webb. The one that I liked best is not the one that he is best remembered for. It was *Pat Novak, for Hire*, cleverly written by Richard Breen. |

| GEORGE: | That started in San Francisco on KGO, the Blue network. The interesting thing about Jack Webb and myself, when he came up to San Francisco originally he came to do what they call vacation relief announcing. In other words, when announcers took their vacations they hired someone to fill in for them. I must say that the San Francisco announcers had been entrenched in radio for many years. It was hard to break into radio in those days. I think they felt that this man was an interloper in his Val |

McCan hound's tooth checked overcoat and he was from Hollywood. What I'm getting at is that I kind of befriended him knowing how difficult it was to be new in that situation. I showed him the various things you had to know when you were working for the network. He never forgot that. From then on, whenever he could he'd put me on his shows. I wound up on *Dragnet* and *Pete Kelly's Blues* and of course the one you're referring to *Pat Novak, for Hire* was really the beginning of the Jack Webb style. And Breen was certainly a talented, talented writer. The show was really ahead of its time.

JASON: The dialogue moved so fast. You had to catch it quickly because the next line was usually even better that the first.

GEORGE: Breen had those marvelous analogies. That's the word for it, you know, "as cold as" or "as hot as." Almost all of the dialogue consisted of those. Then when Jack came back to Hollywood I was already here. He remembered. The friendship remained. He put me on a lot of his shows. I'm the voice you hear on *Dragnet* that says, "The story you are about to hear is true. The names have been changed to protect the innocent." I did the commercials for radio and television.

JASON: You mentioned San Francisco radio. That was major market in those days, more so than Los Angeles.

GEORGE: At that time it was starting to move to Southern California because of the star system, I think, but at that time it was Chicago, New York and San Francisco as the hubs. It was very tough to break into radio there, very difficult to audition. I can remember auditioning time and time again at NBC, a horrendous experience. They would hand you three pages of musical references and foreign languages and you had to ad-lib. It was quite a fight. I had to audition a lot before I finally won one.

JASON: In 1950 you did a show with Dick Haymes called *I Fly Anything*. You were an actor rather than an announcer. You played Buzz, the side-kick of Dockery Crane.

GEORGE: Somewhat of an experience. I'll tell you, Dick Haymes, perhaps one of the great singers of all time, one of the great God-given voices of all time, was one of the neatest guys to work with. He was just a charming son of a gun. I was the announcer on the show at the beginning and then the producer-writer, Dwight Hauser thought maybe I could play the side-kick. Well, I did and on the first few readings we did, because of Dick's musical background and his perfect pitch and ear, whenever I would end a speech he'd pick up on that same note. It sounded like one person was reading this whole thing so they had me change my voice and I played it in a strange—I don't know what I did, but I did it in a funny little voice. I don't know why I did that, but we kept it that way for a year on the air.

JASON: It was sort of a cross-over from a children's show and *I Love a Mystery*.

GEORGE: I never thought of it that way, but it was kind of a children's show. We had a lot of fun doing it. In those days radio actors were just marvelous. They were all part of a stock company. We had all the great names, Raymond Burr, Paula Freeman and Georgia Ellis played the other side-kick, the romantic end side-kick. It was kind of like a *Sam Spade* in the air with *Sky King* and *Sergeant Preston*.

It was one of those hybrid shows and as you said, very childish. Another wonderful show that I was the announcer on was *The Amazing Mr. Malone*. Frank Lovejoy was the star and again, the stock company, the announcers, the actors that you saw day in, day out every day. It was three blocks from Hollywood and Vine down to CBS. They were all there. You saw everybody every day during the week.

JASON: Another show you did around 1950 was another acting role for you. It was called *Too Many Cooks* with Hal March and Bob Sweeney.

GEORGE: I don't think I did much on that one, but the original *Sweeney & March Show* on radio was really fascinating, sort of an *avant garde* comedy show. Lud Gluskin—and there's one of the great names of all time—was the music director. Andy Williams and his brothers were the group on the show. All of the great comedy actors, Hans Conried; all of them played on the *Sweeney & March Show*, a comedy half hour. I was the announcer and I also did bit parts. I had one of the most awful experiences of my life on live radio on that show where I blew a line so badly it didn't make any sense to anybody. We had an audience too. I guess we've all had those moments. At the end of a sketch I had the payoff to the whole sketch. My line was, "Who's been feeding whiskey to the natives?" For some reason or other I put the script down and walked to the microphone without it to deliver this in dramatic fashion. I said, "Who's been feeding bananas to the natives?" It made no sense. Luckily, in those days you did two shows so I redeemed myself on the second show.

JASON: On live radio and also live television you really got

ACT II: SCENE TWO: KEEPER OF THE SECRET WORD

no chance for redemption. What was done was done.

GEORGE: It was really funny. Sometimes the second broadcast—there were three hours between shows, and if you heard the first one sometimes the second did not bear any resemblance because some of the great performers were known to take a drink or two in between times.

JASON: I remember a story that Sid Caesar told about live television. People would ask him about *The Show of Shows* and how long it took to do the 90 minute broadcast. He would say, "90 minutes." They wouldn't believe him. It was a simple answer to a simple question, but they just didn't understand that things were live in those days.

GEORGE: They were tough too at times. In some ways it was wonderful because you did get the adrenalin pumping. You did it and it was over. You couldn't go for innumerable takes. You didn't spend all day on a 30 second commercial or the one minute commercials we did in those days. I made a rule for myself never to take a drink when I was working. Some people obviously didn't. The teleprompter would be backwards. Lights would be knocked down, but it was live and we kept doing it, talking and pretending nothing had happened. It usually worked out pretty well.

JASON: There was such a thing with announcers in the earlier days, the things that people get away with now, they couldn't do. If you ever flubbed a word or line while doing a commercial or whatever, live, it was time to look around to see what was going to happen to you next. The ceiling was about to fall in. Isn't that true?

GEORGE: There was a great deal of emphasis put on perfection and maybe a perfection that doesn't even exist. When you think about it, we did a lot of work and didn't make many mistakes. That was part of the bigness of your job. That's why they paid you money not to make mistakes. The announcers then almost came out of a mold. Most of them were baritones. Most of them had over enunciation. Today, if you listen to commercials, they don't have announcers really as such, very few. They have voices. They use a voice like an announcer to throw in just a few words at the end of something or at the beginning, but usually they have people doing slice of life or a voice that wouldn't be hired, wouldn't win an audition at NBC 40 years ago.

JASON: Why don't we move on to more television? We will eventually get to *You Bet Your Life* with Groucho because most people remember you best for that one.

GEORGE: I think that's true. I think that the Groucho fifteen years made the best of my whole career.

JASON: I wonder how many people remember a spin-off from *You Bet Your Life* called *Tell it to Groucho*?

GEORGE: I don't know. I wasn't connected with that show because at the time I had a show of my own called *Anybody Can Play*, and probably did. I never had great success with my own shows. Then I had another show on daytime on CBS while he was making *Tell it to Groucho*, a show called *Surprise Package* It was interesting because the producer-director of the show was a fellow named Alan Sherman, you know "Hello Mudda, hello Fadda!"

JASON: That was a kind of early Monte Hall where you

had a big unidentified box and people had to figure out what was in it.

GEORGE: Kind of, yeah. We played for laughs because CBS, at the time, was terrified of any stigma because of the quiz show scandals. As a result our only prize had to be worth under $100. It was pretty tough. We were on against *Concentration*. They were giving trips to Europe for two and we were giving like a trip to Tijuana for one, one way. We had wonderful clues. The game itself was kind of fun. In fact, Harpo Marx came down with his son Bill to play piano. He brought his harp. One of the surprise packages was one of his paintings. Harpo wore that wonderful raincoat with all the table silver in it—dropped it all on the stage. When Harpo's near you always end up holding his leg. Did you ever see him do that? You're talking away and suddenly you realize you're holding this man's leg below the knee. Just out of friendship he donated his services and came down to the show with his son and his silverware and his painting. He was a very good artist, by the way.

JASON: Yes, I know. I guess it's also true that he was the funniest of the Marx Brothers and the most stable.

GEORGE: I don't know about the funniest. He was a different kind of funny. Groucho had the words, certainly. He said a lot of funny things. Harpo was probably the nicest of the brothers if you had to pick a nice person. He was a character too. They were all characters.

JASON: What I meant was not his stage persona, but as a person to meet. He was actually a pretty funny guy.

GEORGE: Oh yes, oh yes, and he did speak. You knew that, of course.

JASON: Of course.

GEORGE: I'm amazed at the number of people who ask me if Harpo was able to speak. Yes he did and very well. He was a member of the Algonquin Round Table. They were some pretty good intellects back in New York where the Algonquin is, people like Alexander Woollcott, Dorothy Parker, Perlman and Kaufman. I don't know if Harpo held his own, but he was certainly in there punching.

JASON: How about working with Donnie and Marie Osmond? That had to be a kind of strange experience.

GEORGE: Working with them was not a strange experience at all. That family was outstanding, marvelous people and nice to work with, I mean really nice. The strangest thing, because I was the announcer on the show, I was also responsible for the warm-ups. I did pretty well over the years with warm-ups. Now, here was an audience of frantic young people, really young people and I realized that I had not a heck of a lot to say to these youngsters. They weren't terribly interested in what I had to say. They were looking for Donnie and Marie and were talking, but as the shows went on I found more rapport. It was a fabulous show to do. On that show I did the announcing and had some walk-ons, little bits and pieces that were kind of fun.

JASON: You just brought up something that has not been touched on, on any of my shows. That is the fact that there was, in most every case on any radio show a warm-up announcer. People like Bert Parks got their start doing that. For anyone who has never seen a live radio show, they don't necessarily know what that was all about. Maybe you could explain it.

GEORGE: What the producers figured was that the audience that was sitting there would not know how to respond to being in a radio studio. So first the announcer, and this was very unfair, was responsible for literally doing a kind of comedy routine with the audience. We all had a bunch of dumb jokes and things we knew kind of worked, so we'd go out and warm up the audience, going under the assumption that they were cold when they came in there, and telling them when to applaud and how to laugh. It did seem to work. As it got more important that audiences react the studio then started to hire guys who did nothing but warm-ups. They didn't announce the show. They just came in and were sometimes better than the show the audience had come to see. Warm-ups for television are tougher because there is so much going on behind this person who comes out to warm up the audience. The set is out there and they're working and hammering and building the sets. They're still rehearsing. It's tough to warm up a TV audience.

JASON: You also worked on *The Mickey Mouse Club* on a thing called Secret of Mystery Lake.

GEORGE: You really find out things that I—not that I want to forget because it was an amazing period. I made a movie with a fellow named Larry Landsberg who worked as a producer for Disney off and on. This time he found these two fellows who had this marvelous wildlife footage of a place called Reelfoot Lake in Tennessee, of birds, egrets and swans, all these wonderful, wonderful birds. So he put together this story about the hermit at the game refuge and I was this naturalist who is sent there by Edgar Bergen, who I think had some money in the original picture. It wasn't a very good picture, but the stuff with the animals was great. I was the star. I was THE guy. It played a few nights somewhere and then Disney, when it didn't do well in the theatres, bought it and cut it up into seven episodes of fifteen minutes each and put it on *The Mickey Mouse Club.* I made more money in one day going over to do the openings and closings for those seven episodes than I made in the weeks when we shot the picture. Working on the Disney lot was so wonderful because it was such a clean lot. There was a kind of camaraderie there. I did a lot of narration for Disney films, one was *The Horse with the Flying Tail.* That won an Oscar as a matter of fact, the show itself, not me.

JASON: I think I've stalled long enough. Let's talk about Groucho and *You Bet your Life* on both radio and television. Groucho always looked like he was ad-libbing, but I understand that a lot of it was not ad-lib at all.

GEORGE: I think what you're saying is that he knew. Say for instance if you were going to be on the show, our staff would have completely—they'd have done background on you, more than you've done on me. They would have known everything about you and as a result they would have it all written down and Groucho would go over it with them. So he would know ahead of time what you did for a living, how many times married; all these things about you. They might even suggest a joke or two, but when you got on the show, who knew what you were going to say? He didn't, but he had at least a kind

	of a road map to know there was some story about your marriage or your kids or whatever. He knew what hot buttons to hit. He'd try to get you to talk about that so he could then use some of the jokes that he'd thought about. The good stuff, believe me, was absolutely extemporaneous. It was stuff that grew out of those little trails that were laid ahead of time.
JASON:	Things like asking a car salesman how many times he'd been indicted.
GEORGE:	He would do that. He did that to everybody. In the beginning when I first started on the show, I felt that when he said these things he really meant them. Maybe he did because I guess he was one of the first iconoclasts to make it big on radio and television. When General Bradley was on the show he told the General exactly what was wrong with the army, from the food up to the master sergeants. He was fearless. It was all kind of fun. Nobody ever really got too angry on the air; I don't think. Nobody hit him, certainly not during the fifteen years we did the show. He said some pretty scurrilous things about people, very often they were deserved.
JASON:	He could get away with things on a format like that, that he may not have on a more serious venue, even though he skated close to the truth.
GEORGE:	I think people expected him to say those things. Some would say, "I don't want to be on that show. He's too cruel to people." I pointed out that nobody twisted anyone's arm to get them on the show. They all wanted to be on it for several reasons. Some wanted the money, meager as it was in those days. Some wanted the fame. Some wanted to sell something. They had a book or something else to

sell or they wanted to be able to tell their friends that they traded jokes with Groucho, which was a dangerous thing to try. I always felt sorry for anyone who thought they could top Groucho. Groucho would never let that happen.

JASON: You might get the first one in, but after that . . .

GEORGE: I was able to get a couple in off and on. I learned not to try too often.

JASON: There's something I've always wondered about, not just from that show, but from a lot of others as well. You worked with Groucho and you always managed to keep a straight face no matter what he would say. It's a situation that arises on many shows. What was said may have been hilarious, but the side men always continued on with their lines as if nothing had occurred.

GEORGE: I didn't always. Now, there's an interesting point. We were on film and then we went to tape. As a result we could do anything. That was the secret to the success of that show, in my opinion. The fact that John Guedel, the producer, realized that on all of the things that Groucho had done prior to our show, he had been constrained by the format. The fact that he was live and he had a script and he had to get off the air at a certain time. He was never a big success on radio because of the restraints. If he ad-libbed he threw off the other actors. The director had a few years taken off his life because he had to get them off the air on time. We got a special dispensation to allow our show to be recorded in 1947 to go on prime time. In those days you weren't allowed to have recorded shows on prime time radio. That was the secret and the shows were the evidence. We did forty-five or fifty minutes of

	show and out of that came the half hour used on the air. He could say anything he wanted and often did. They had guidelines. They had things you couldn't say, things you couldn't do. They were much stricter than today.
JASON:	And through the blacklisting era, which was such a bad joke in many ways, not at all funny to the people involved.
GEORGE:	It ruined lots of lives. It was really, really terrible.
JASON:	There were so many things you couldn't say and you wouldn't even know that there was anything wrong with them. The ad agencies were very much responsible for that.
GEORGE:	Oh yes, in those days the agencies were literally in charge. Many of the shows were produced by ad agencies, not handled by networks. Our agency was Batten, Barton, Durst and Osbourne, or as we would say, B. B. D. & O. They handled DeSoto, which Groucho and I put out of business in eight or nine years.
JASON:	We had a couple of DeSotos. They were nice cars.
GEORGE:	They were great cars. I'll tell you why they were great cars. They used to give me one every year.
JASON:	From the DeSoto-Plymouth deelahs!
GEORGE:	Tell'em Groucho sent ya!
JASON:	Well, George, we've talked about the present and the past. Is there anything on the horizon for the future that we should know about?

GEORGE: Well, no. I have my star on the Boulevard. I'm very proud of that. It's been a good life in this business. I can think of nothing I'd rather have done, maybe been an architect or something like that. I've been able to work all those years and I'm still working long hours and arduously at times for Home Savings. Life couldn't be better. Our kids all grew up well. My son is associate producer on *Dallas*. I have a daughter who works for Home Savings. I have another daughter who is a pathologist, married to an artist, Jeff Kohl. I have a wonderful wife. We're going to be celebrating our 45th wedding anniversary, same people, we've been married all that time. Pretty good!

****

As is the case with so many of the people in George Fenneman's profession, there was altogether too much to talk about in the short time we had to do it. Why, we never even talked about the Secret Word, which if you said it on *You Bet Your Life*, you could earn a quick $100. Groucho often referred to him as the perfect straight man and also said he was like a male Margaret Dumont, who was the brunt of his jokes in several Marx Brothers pictures. They may have been caustic on the air, but in real life they were good friends until Groucho's death in 1977.

Another landmark show on which he worked was radio's long running version of *Gunsmoke*. He did the commercials and often, at the end of the show, did brief interviews with its star, Bill Conrad, about the virtues of the sponsor, L & M Cigarettes. Just a small note here, I spoke with Bill on several occasions, but he only wanted to talk about the future, which doesn't fit the format of this show.

We could have also talked about George's involvement with the U. S Office of Information during World War II, but that too went by the wayside due to time constraints. All in all, George Fenneman was an always busy, very interesting man and a quick wit to go with it. He passed away at the age of seventy-seven in 1997, a victim of emphysema.

Act III: Utility Men

In any sport, and in fact in many walks of life, there are people who do not always play a major role in the overall picture, but who are necessary to have handy to fit into a particular situation. These people are usually called utility people. In the business world we refer to them as temps. Without them the whole enterprise could fall flat.

The four subjects of this act, while often they played major roles, could at times fit this description. They were always available to take on almost any challenge, which they did with gusto. I'm talking about the character actors we all remember so well. Sometimes they were the only bright spot in an otherwise dreary scenario. Quite often they became better known than the stars of their particular shows.

All four of these show business personalities played important parts in the industry's past, each in their own particular way. There were many others who fit this mold, but this is a good cross-section of talent.

ACT III:
SCENE ONE
OSGOOD CONKLIN

Using that *sobriquet* is just a quick way of letting any older radio listener or television viewer immediately identify the man who is the subject of this interview. On radio as well as on the tube he played a variety of those sort-of blustery, confused characters as well as many other roles. Usually, but not always he was a memorable second banana, the type of roles that remain in our brains after the shows are over.

So, here he is as himself. He was Gale Gordon. We had our chat during a time when he was working in a stage play in Vancouver, British Columbia on May 25, 1986.

****

JASON: Gale, tell me a little about your background leading up to your radio career. What led you into that field?

GALE: I was actually between jobs as it were, in pictures, which I was definitely trying to get into, and theatre, which I started out in. I was in Hollywood at the time and somebody suggested, "Why don't you try radio? They seem to be looking for people." I called a radio station and talked to a young lady. She said, "Come on down at ten o'clock. I have a part for you." I went down to Warner Brothers at ten o'clock the next day on Hollywood Boulevard where they had their radio station in those days. I sat in the office for an hour or two. Someone said, "What do you want, young man?" I said, "I called Miss van Rieper yesterday and she wanted me to come down and do a part." She said, "Well, I'm Karen van Rieper, who are you?" I said, "Gale Gordon." On the phone I sounded like a middle age Englishman. She didn't expect to see a twenty-five or six year old man sitting in her waiting room. That was my start on radio. I worked with her for a long time. The fee in those days was two dollars and fifty cents for a commercial half hour show. Warner Brothers took twenty-five cents out as commission for hiring me.

JASON: I know that in those days money wasn't exactly flowing. Sometimes they paid talent with the sponsor's product, bread, meat or whatever. Did you ever run into that?

GALE: No, the only thing I ran into was, in California in those days the going rate for any show was $2.50 and every radio station was its own agency. They all took out twenty-five cents. I know that I wasn't allowed to work at one station because I had the temerity to ask for three dollars. They said, "Who does he think he is to ask for that kind of money?" They wouldn't employ me. I didn't work there for years.

JASON: In the thirties one of your earlier shows was this one:

****

ANNCR: Presenting the Amazing Interplanetary Adventures of Flash Gordon and Dale Arden. These thrilling adventures come to you as they are pictured in the *Comic Weekly*, the world's greatest pictorial

ACT III: SCENE ONE: OSGOOD CONKLIN

supplement of humor and adventure. The *Comic Weekly*, now printed on thirty-two tabloid size pages, each page in full four colors, is distributed everywhere as an integral part of your Hearst Sunday newspapers. (*music up and out*)

For the benefit of those who may not have heard the earlier episodes, here is the story to date. Flash Gordon, internationally famous American athlete, and his beautiful American sweetheart, Dale Arden and Dr. Zarkov, a great scientist, left the earth on a rocket ship. They crashed on the planet Mongo and were captured by Ming, the merciless, the cruel Emperor of Mongo, who commanded Dale to marry him and ordered that Flash be killed. But Flash escaped through the help of the Emperor's beautiful daughter who became deeply in love with him and proposed marriage. This, Flash refused, saying that he loved Dale Arden. Flash then met Prince Vultan, the huge bearded prince of the Lion-men and Prince Baron, a former member of Ming's court. Joined by Dr. Zarkov, these four friends promised to overthrow the government of Emperor Ming and rescue Dale Arden. They were almost successful, but at the last moment, with victory practically within their grasp, they were recaptured by Emperor Ming's soldiers and the four friends, together with Dale Arden, were condemned to a fate far worse than death. Securely bound, they were put on a gyro ship and sent as slaves to a prison city. Now, we continue the story.

****

GALE: Ah, Flash, yes, I was the Gordon who played Gordon, an odd coincidence. Many of the things on that show that were beyond belief are now

	reality, except for Emperor Ming, I hope. It was a whole new concept in those days.
JASON:	At about the same time you were doing a show called *Stories of the Black Chamber*.
GALE:	That was so long ago. I think I was a master spy named Paradine on that.
JASON:	I know too that you were in some way a part of the *Tarzan* series.
GALE:	Yes, it was directed by Edgar Rice Burroughs who also wrote the series. His real-life daughter was Jane. We made a series of records, 80 or 90 of them. I think we got $7.50 which was big, big money in those days. I played Cecil Clayton.
JASON:	I have a couple of those records. That was before the other two shows we talked about, around 1932.
GALE:	Yes, directed by Edgar Rice Burroughs and the leading man was his son-in-law.
JASON:	That son-in-law was James Pierce making the show a real family affair. A little later, in 1937, there was a Christmas series that I remember well. It was called *Cinnamon Bear* and consisted of twenty-six episodes that were played every day, leading up to Christmas. I play it here on this station every year and always get a good response from it. The main characters were Paddy O'Cinnamon, the Cinnamon Bear and the Barton kids, Judy and Jimmy. You appeared on episode two as Weary Willie, the stork and on episode sixteen as Oliver, the ostrich. Here's a small bit of you as Willie done with a very snooty British accent.

ACT III: Scene One: Osgood Conklin

****

WILLIE: Hello there!

JIMMY: Did you hear somebody call?

PADDY: Yes, over there. Oh, me, it's that awful stork!

JIMMY: Stork?

PADDY: Yes, Weary Willie. He's a terrible nuisance. Always going around in sharp hats and bragging about his wonderful travels. You know, he writes books. Don't pay any attention to him.

WILLIE: I say, hello and cheerio.

JIMMY: He seems friendly enough.

PADDY: Oh, very well, but I have to warn you, he's no good at all. No good at all. Hello Willie.

WILLIE: Greetings my friends, greetings. Could you perchance accommodate a weary wayfarer in your airplane? I've wandered many a mile and I'm most fatigued.

PADDY: Of course not, silly. You're bigger than our airplane is. You leave us alone. We're busy.

JUDY: Jimmy, isn't he funny? He's wearing short pants like a mountain climber.

JIMMY: Look at those enormous glasses and look at that silly hat with a feather in it. He's the funniest stork I ever saw.

WILLIE: Oh well, far be it for me to intrude where I'm obviously not welcome. Of course, I cannot expect people to be magnanimous or sensible.

JIMMY: What in the world is wrong with him, Cinnamon Bear?

PADDY: Don't pay any attention to him. He thinks he should talk that way because he has a diploma and writes books.

WILLIE: I don't like your insinuations, Paddy O'Cinnamon. If you cannot help me in my plight, perhaps you, my young friends, have the way-with-all to assist me in my ravenous need.

PADDY: He means he's hungry.

****

GALE: I'm afraid I don't remember that at all. The only Christmas show I remember was with Ronald Coleman. We did *A Christmas Carol*. He played Scrooge and I was the Ghost of Christmas Yet to Come.

JASON: In 1939 we heard *The Shadow of Fu Manchu*. He was a diabolical scientist referred to as the Prince of Evil. Featured as good guys were Hanley Stafford as Nayland Smith and Gale Gordon as Dr. James Petrie, but the two Gale Gordon shows that most people remember best were *Fibber McGee & Molly* and *Our Miss Brooks*. You played similar, but different people on both of those, Mayor LaTrivia and Osgood Conklin. Your ability at the double-take was incredible. Did it take long to perfect that?

GALE: In the case of *Fibber McGee & Molly*, that was a part that was written just for me by the creator of the show. His name was Don Quinn. I appeared on the show as a one shot, an ex-boyfriend of Molly's who had made it very big in business. He came to Wistful Vista. The Great Gildersleeve was suckered into playing their butler. They were trying to put on the dog for this visitor. I played that part and they decided, after one appearance with them, they seemed to like what I was doing and I got along very well with Jim and Marian, so Don Quinn wrote the character Mayor LaTrivia for me. Don gave me those wonderful illiterate things where I'd stumble over words the more flustered I got and then finally blow up. That established me as bumbling blowhard who finally collapses in the midst of his own muttering.

JASON: Since you are talking about muttering let's tune in on the sort of situation that get your character, Mayor LaTrivia into that sort of mood. This is from an episode called "McGee, the Fire Marshall."

****

MAYOR: Good day McGee. How do you do Mrs. McGee? (*big cough*) What goes on, fumigating?

MOLLY: No, the fireplace backed up, Mr. Mayor.

MAYOR: That's good to know. I'm just here on a matter of business. Mr. McGee, you're a public spirited citizen. I'm sure you'd be glad to give the city the benefit of your executive experience.

FIBBER: Why certainly, your honor. What do you want me to do, run for your job next year? Shucks, I'd be glad to. All I gotta do is profit by the mistakes you've made and . . .

MOLLY: McGee, let the Mayor talk.

MAYOR: Mr. McGee, the office of Mayor is not under discussion.

FIBBER: Oh, you think not? You should hear what people are saying about . . .

MOLLY: McGee! Let the Mayor talk.

FIBBER: Okay, go ahead trivial.

MAYOR: To be brief, McGee, one of our officials is making a nationwide survey. He'll be out of the city for a week or ten days. His office is too valuable and too important to remain vacant during that time. I want you to fill the vacancy until then.

MOLLY: Oh, what job is it, Mr. Mayor?

MAYOR: Fire Commissioner.

FIBBER: Well Bud, you've come to the right man. With my experience in fire fighting . . .

MOLLY: (*another bigger cough*) Pardon me, it's the smoke.

MAYOR: Very well then, consider it done. Here's your badge and here's your official appointment.

FIBBER: Mr. Mayor, I accept with pleasure and I must say, for a city like Wistful Vista, a man like me is just what the city deserves.

Act III: Scene One: Osgood Conklin

****

JASON: Of course, you know what that all led to. We are discussing the blustery nature of many of your portrayals. Let's go a little further with that. That type of character certainly served you well throughout the years, even through the first time you worked with Lucille Ball as Rudolph Atterbury on *My Favorite Husband*, then later on so many of the *Lucy Shows* on television. I understand you're getting ready to start a new one with her in the fall.

GALE: That's right. I've signed an agreement to do twenty-two shows with her, which delights me. They will be seen this fall on ABC. I believe they will be on, on Saturday nights, but that's only what I've heard so don't quote me on it. We will start in July getting the pre-production things in order and then with the manufacture of twenty-two shows.

JASON: Even though the characters will be a little different it will probably be similar to the others.

GALE: I have no idea except that we will be co-owners of a hardware store. I will have a son who is married to a daughter of hers and I believe two grandchildren are involved. That's all I know about the general theme and premises of the new show. I haven't seen any scripts, but I'll probably be sent one in the very near future. She's not only a great, great performer, but a wonderful woman and a real perfectionist. I love the way she works. I like to work the way she does, that is, make it the best possible show ever, which is her attitude. Nothing is just good enough. It has to be as nearly perfect as it is possible to achieve. I admire that. That's why she has lasted so long and been so great.

JASON: I understand that she is not too happy with a recent TV movie in which she played a bag lady.

GALE: I saw it. I think she was great, but it was very badly directed. I thought the dialogue was very poor. The main criticism that I have is that they went under the assumption that everybody in the world knows what a bag lady is. In the Midwestern United States very few people realize that bag ladies are part of the existence of New York, particularly. I thought they failed to show that or to plant it, so you didn't know what was happening. I found that to be a grievous fault, but I also thought she was fine. Why wouldn't she be fine? Everything she does, she does well.

JASON: There was a radio show that you did in 1950 that peaks my interest. I know about it, but I've never heard it. The theme of it would be very familiar to later TV fans. It was called *Granby's Green Acres*. You were on it with Bea Benaderet and Parley Baer.

GALE: It didn't last very long. It was an interesting concept, people buying a farm, city people who always dreamed of having a farm. It was later done on television for years with Eva Gabor and Eddie Arnold.

JASON: That was the reason I brought it up. They even had a farm hand named Eb, the same name as the character on *Granby's Green Acres*. That show was a one season summer replacement so the broadcasts are not easy to come by. You did many roles which we won't have the time to pursue, Gale. You worked the *Burns and Allen Show* and also with Edward G. Robinson on *Big Town*, with Penny Singleton on

| | her show and a lot of television. *The Brothers* was one series not too well remembered and of course you were with Lucy for eleven years so far. You did *Our Miss Brooks* on both radio and TV and who can forget Mr. Wilson on *Dennis, the Menace*. If you could select one radio role as your favorite, or one that really stands out, what would it be? |

GALE: I don't have any favorite. I've never wanted to play Hamlet. I don't have any preconceived desire to do any particular part. I'm very, very happy to be a character actor. I enjoy working every part I do. I enjoy it because I always learn something. I meet different people. I work with different people. I just love my work, period! I cannot pick any show and say that, that was the outstanding moment in my life because they are all important to me.

JASON: The show you're doing now in Vancover is *One for the Plot*. That sounds like it would be an ideal part for you, a British comedy-drama type thing.

GALE: It's an English part, absolutely wild. It's complete slapstick. We have a wonderful leading man, a young man named Ian Clarke, who does four different parts. He meets himself coming and going. It's absolutely wild, frantic and the audiences love it. It's the only farce of this kind that I have ever done. No one in this show is going to get fat, believe me. We're all running so fast and meeting each other back and forth across the stage. It's a wild scramble, but very amusing. We're sold out for the run, in fact, we were sold out before we opened and have eight weeks of sell-out crowds to look forward to. We close on June 29th and then I'll be going back to Hollywood. We will start in July on the new Lucy series.

****

I feel that I must make a comment here. This was the first of the many celebrity interviews that I did and I do not feel that I did Gale justice due to a bit of stage fright on my part. I would really like to get another chance to talk with him, but unfortunately he passed away in 1995.

Gale Gordon was inducted posthumously into the Radio Hall of Fame and he also has a star on Hollywood Walk of Fame. He played far too many roles to have covered them all in one discussion, but I feel that he was too important to leave out of this book due to my own shortcomings. In spite of that, he did have a lot to say.

ACT III:
SCENE TWO
MAN OF MANY INTERESTS

Here we have a very complex man. Although he spent all of his working years in Show Business, his story can be told from many different angles, all of them fitting under that one huge umbrella title. We will talk mostly about radio and television, but there was so much more that could have been added to his saga.

You might say that he had four separate and distinct careers during the course of his six decades entertaining us in one or another of the performing arts.

His name was Sheldon Leonard. On September 16, 1986 we had this exchange.

****

JASON: I know you came to us originally from your birth place in New York City. Just to hear you speak, I have no doubt of that fact, Sheldon. Let me begin by asking you where and how you got your earliest experience in the business.

SHELDON: I got started in the legitimate theatre in New York City on Broadway. I plowed right into the middle of it way back in the early 30s, more than a half century ago.

JASON: That is probably the most difficult venue to work, live stage.

SHELDON: At the time there wasn't very much choice. Radio had not yet developed into an entity and obviously there was no television. There was a very definite isolation that existed between legitimate stage and motion pictures so there wasn't a great choice of media in those days. If you wanted to do acting and you lived in New York, you did it in the theatre.

JASON: Most of radio at that time came out of Chicago.

SHELDON: Radio really had not gotten a foothold in the early 30s. In the middle 30s it began to grow up and become a factor in the careers and the earning capacities of the acting population. Up until then it was just an oddity. I remember fishing around for broadcasts on a little crystal set where you had to move a hair like wire to find a sensitive place on the crystal. That's the kind of radio we had when I got started.

JASON: When did you eventually get into radio? What show would that have been?

SHELDON: I did some radio in New York, a very occasional spot here and there. Some with Orson Welles on *The Shadow*, which was being broadcast out of New York and *The March of Time* and a couple of other shows that were current in the late 30s, in that period, emanating from New York. When I came to California to start working in pictures at the invitation of Metro Goldwyn Mayer, I found myself with a lot of idle time on my hands so I accepted an invitation to do a radio spot on a show called *Meet Me at Parky's*, with a character called Parkyakarkus played by Harry Einstein. He was a brilliant interpreter of comedy. I played a character called Orville Sharp who preceded Norm Crosby in the mutilation of the English Language. I played that character on *Parky's* for the remainder of the run on the air and from that I was invited to do a variety of other shows. Ultimately, I played running characters with Ann Sothern on *The Adventures of Maisie* show, with Judy Canova on her show, with Jack Benny on his show, with Bob Hope on his show and with Ed Gardner on *Duffy's Tavern*. I also did *The Phil Harris-Alice Faye Show*. I had a very busy schedule on radio. As a matter of fact, it acted as my entering foot in the door for television.

JASON: Let's go back to *Meet Me at Parky's*. That was an offshoot from *The Eddie Cantor Show*. Was that where you first met Frank Nelson?

SHELDON: I worked frequently with Frank, although we very often appeared on the same shows, our regular meetings occurred on *The Jack Benny Show* on which I played a Tout character who always said, "Hey Bud, whatcha doin', whatcha doin'." He played the character who would always greet Benny with his well known, "Yeesssss!" It was his trademark. I deeply regret his very recent passing. He was a very talented actor and a very good friend.

JASON: I talked briefly with Frank about two months ago, but as you know, my timing was awful. Of course, I had no way of knowing his situation when I rang him up. All things considered, I feel very honored that he would take my call under the circumstances. Some of the other people you worked with on the Benny show have been previous guests on my own little show. Mel Blanc was one of them.

SHELDON: There was Mel, there was Phil Harris and there was Dennis Day. Almost everyone in the Hollywood acting community made an appearance with Jack at one time or another. Other regulars?—Of course the immortal Rochester (Eddie Anderson) and a few others, Frank, Benny Rubin. . .

JASON: Artie Auerbach as Mr. Kitzel.

SHELDON: Unfortunately Artie died during the heydays of *The Jack Benny Show*.

JASON: You did a character named Grogan on Phil Harris' show.

SHELDON: The character on Phil's show was an outgrowth of my appearance on Jack's show. His writers thought of a character not too far distant from the one I was playing with Jack would be useful on Phil's show. We tried it and it was well accepted. It became a regular part of the show.

JASON: One of your shows that I would always enjoy hearing on Saturday evenings was *The Judy Canova Show*.

SHELDON: I played Judy's boyfriend, a taxi driver character called Joe Crunchmiller. I was with her for the duration of the show. It was a very happy relationship.

JASON: There again we he heard a lot of the same people, Mel Blanc, Gale Gordon and Hans Conried was on that show as well.

SHELDON: Hans was on every show. He was an itinerate actor, that is to say, he didn't play any regular character on that show, but he was the utility infielder, so to speak. Any time they had a different part or something that required an exotic interpretation they would call for Hans.

JASON: He also appeared with you on the *Maisie* show.

SHELDON: Not as a regular, but he made frequent appearances on it. Ironically enough, when I got into television and began producing and directing shows, I was able to establish Hans as a more or less regular on *The Danny Thomas Show*. He played Danny's uncle from Lebanon, Uncle Tounousse.

JASON: I understand Hans was also a fine director in his own right.

SHELDON: I'm not aware of that. The one who became a good director and a good producer out of our radio colony was Elliott Lewis. Elliott is still functioning in that fashion here on television.

JASON: And while he really didn't particularly like acting he was a fantastic actor.

SHELDON: Oh yes, he and his wife were very busy, a very highly respected team.

JASON: There was a radio show for which you are listed among the credits. I'm referring to *The Lineup*. Was that just occasional appearances for you.

SHELDON: Yes, occasional parts. My fee was a little too high for most shows because it had been established on such prime shows as *The Jack Benny Show* and *Amos and Andy*. It was a little too high for the shows that had smaller budgets. Frequently, I made an appearance more or less as an accommodation for a friend of mine, shows like *Broadway Is My Beat* and Jack Webb's show. What was Jack Webb's show called?

JASON: Which one, *Johnny Modero, Pat Novak, for Hire* or maybe *Dragnet*?

SHELDON: Oh of course, *Dragnet*.

JASON: He did several others, but that was the one most people remember best.

SHELDON: That's the one, *Dragnet*.

JASON: Do you remember a show called *Johnny Fletcher* with Bill Goodwin?

SHELDON: I do indeed because it was written by the writers who became my personal writers on *I Spy*. Mort Fine and David Friedkin wrote it. It was a good show. As a matter of fact, it showed every sign of becoming a hit, but it was in the declining days of radio. We were swimming against the tide and just failed to make it a continuing series.

JASON: I can't quite picture Bill Goodwin in a serious role. Was it a semi-comedy? I'm sorry, but I don't remember it at all.

SHELDON: It was based on some novels written by a then popular mystery writer about a private eye and his faithful, muscular side man Sam, which was the part that I played. It was semi-serious and semi-comedic. We got into absurd situations, but they were all directed towards the private eye kind of category.

JASON: Maybe in the vein of *Simon and Simon* or something like that.

SHELDON: I think there was a distant resemblance.

JASON: There was another one that didn't last too long. The problem had more to do with the writing than anything else. You worked it with Cary Grant,

Betsy Drake and again, Gale Gordon. It was *Mr. And Mrs. Blandings.*

SHELDON: That was when Cary Grant was trying to help his wife, Betsy, get a start on her career. He volunteered himself, so to speak, sacrificed himself to radio in order to get her going. I had a regular part on that, but as you said, the show didn't survive.

JASON: I mentioned Gale Gordon several times. You worked quite often with him. There were so may people, particularly character actors who just jumped from show to show, from week to week and just showed up all over the place.

SHELDON: We had a very good colony of actors here. They all worked from one show to another. Frequently, we had it timed so that if you were doing a show at CBS and another one at NBC and if they were in conflict, you could determine whether you could get out the back door and make an appearance at CBS while you were on an interval of your NBC show and still get back in time to pick up your lines at NBC. Very often it was possible to do that, thus earning two fees at the same time.

JASON: In other words, there were not many exclusives in those days.

SHELDON: No, there were no exclusives.

JASON: Which meant a whole lot of rushing back and forth.

SHELDON: The two major studios, CBS and NBC were only a block apart on Sunset Boulevard.

JASON: That was not the case in Chicago. While a couple

	of them were in close proximity to each other, there were some that required some travel.
SHELDON:	Chicago had a very prosperous and very talented pool of radio actors.
JASON:	People like Don Ameche and his brother Jim and another recent guest here, Willard Waterman all came out of that market.
SHELDON:	Yes, there were a lot of them.
JASON:	Let's move on to television. I'm thinking now of a show called *Big Eddie* on which you played a former gangster named Eddie Smith and co-starred with Sheree North.
SHELDON:	That, unfortunately, got off on the wrong foot. I made a resolution a long time ago. By the time we did *Big Eddie* I had been functioning in an executive capacity for quite a few years. One of the things that annoyed me most was when the lead actor tried to dominate the construction and the policy of a show that was supposed to be the terrain of the creative people, the writers and the producers and the director. So I was determined on the Big Eddie show, playing the lead as I was, that I would keep my nose out of other people's business, let them do their job and not interfere with it. Perhaps that was a mistake because, as I said, we got off on the wrong foot. There was inherent in that show a very good, very worthwhile and very timely subject. Instead of that we chose to emphasize the Damon Runyon aspect which was by that time out of date and old fashioned. It was a bunch of Runyonesque characters with Runyonesque dialogue. That generation was gone. It was no longer around. What we should have done, I now realize, was to

ACT III: SCENE TWO: MAN OF MANY INTERESTS

emphasize the relationship between Big Eddie and his wife, an ex-burlesque stripper who was emerging into a modern woman. It was a very bold platform from which to examine the then young feminist movement, the growth of women moving into a position of equality. That's what the show should have been about.

JASON: Let's say a few words about the Damon Runyon type character that you often projected. I have copies of several of *The Damon Runyon Theatre* shows. It seems like that would have been a natural fit for you.

SHELDON: For very early television I directed and produced the pilot for what became *The Damon Runyon Theatre*. I never had any more to do with it because I accepted a more or less more durable assignment on *The Danny Thomas Show*, but I put the first *Damon Runyon Theatre* on the air for television.

JASON: I was thinking more of the radio version.

SHELDON: I was on that many times, but only intermittently, not as a regular.

JASON: I think that maybe there weren't too many regulars on that show. John Brown was the only one who was always there.

SHELDON: John was perhaps the busiest actor in the business.

JASON: And a very funny guy when he wanted to be.

SHELDON: He was a very versatile man.

JASON: You were talking about moving into directing and producing. Could you explain for our listeners what it means to be a producer or a director? I often get that question, but my answers don't satisfy anyone.

SHELDON: I'm not surprised by that because there is no single explanation. To be a director on one show is quite different from being a director on another show. To be a director on a pilot is different from being a director of an episode. For example, if you come on an episodic show in mid-season, let's say as the director, the actors know a great deal more of how they ought to function and what they can or cannot say, than you as the interim director do. Therefore, what you really have to do is not to try to mold characterizations or readings or interpretations. All you're supposed to do is be a traffic policeman to keep them from bumping into on another and to put the cameras in the proper positions to photograph them. That's really all you can do in that situation, nothing really creative. On the other hand, if for example you're doing an anthology show you can mold it the way a symphony conductor molds the orchestra, a fortissimo here and a piano there and put the accentuation wherever you think it should go. You can do that either on an anthology show or the opening episode of a series as the characters are taking shape. From the point of view of the director, there may have many different responsibilities. Some producers allow the director to influence the writing, to be part of the preparation and to say, "That scene won't play, it's not funny", or whatever other contribution he can make. Other producers say, "You do your job and I'll do mine. You stay down on the stage and I'll send you the words. You just make sure they get said and they get photographed. Being a producer is also very difficult to define because if you have a strong executive producer, the producer has relatively little influence on the shaping and the policy of the show. The producers that I used on my various shows, I selected almost always because of their writing skill and because they could reshape a script that had problems and solve those problems for me and present the actors with a script that was playable and interesting and worthwhile. My producers were of a nature like Carl Reiner and Aaron Rubin, both skilled writers. Some others were Jackie Ellington, Chuck Stewart, Artie Stander and several others who were all distinguished writers. I chose to make producers out of them because I felt the principle contribution they could make was to keep a flow of good scripts coming down to the stage. On some shows the producer's main function is to keep the costs down and supervise the construction of the sets, the casting of new characters and office work.

JASON: In other words, a high class coordinator.

SHELDON: That's right. They call him a line producer.

JASON: You mentioned Carl Reiner. Was *The Dick Van Dyke Show* the first chance you had to work with Carl?

SHELDON: Yes, but it wasn't the first time I met him. I knew him from our mutual involvement in the entertainment business, but that was the first time we worked together.

JASON: The big one that is still in re-runs around here now was *I Spy* with Robert Culp and Bill Cosby. There has never been another series quite like it.

SHELDON: *I Spy* was an ice-breaker in many respects. It was the first show that dared to go out on distant locations because that was considered, in the old studio days, too complicated. It meant traveling with a huge body of equipment and people, but with the aid of a young Egyptian named Faud Said, who was a brilliant cameraman, we simplified and modified. We took the fat out and found that we could, in fact, travel economically to distant places and make pictures. That was one innovation and it was an innovation that has affected television to this day. The second innovation was introducing a black man in a leading role on an equal level with a white actor. It was unprecedented up until then. Black actors had been used as cartoon characters like Stepin Fetchit and others who played exaggerated characters that bore no resemblance to reality. Cosby was as real as he is today and fortunately, he had the charisma that enabled the part to establish a precedent and open the door for many other black actors.

JASON: Bill Cosby is a guy who seems to be able to do something with nothing and come out looking good. I remember meeting him at a live show in Chicago. During his show he was doing one of his normal routines when a fly came in and buzzed around his head for a couple of minutes. He couldn't seem to get rid of it so he proceeded to do fifteen or twenty minutes about the fly. Some of the folks in the audience scoffed and said it was planned that way and there really never was a mysterious fly. I can only say that I was sitting close enough to the stage to know that theory didn't hold water.

SHELDON: I think he is most creative. Our friendship is very deep and very sincere. I spent most of this past summer with him as his guest at the Hotel d'Cor on the Riviera. I'm going to visit with him in New York this week and join him in Las Vegas next week. My relationship with Cos is still very close and it may have been a factor in my evaluation of him. I don't think it is because I believe, whether he is my friend or not, I would still regard him as one of the outstanding geniuses of our entire industry.

JASON: He has another unique distinction. He is one of a very few television actors who ever cancelled his own show several times just because he was tired of doing them.

SHELDON: Bill can do anything.

JASON: He never had a ratings problem on any of the shows he did.

SHELDON: He's got a best-seller book and he's writing another one. His book *Fatherhood* was the number one best seller for a long time nationally and I think he established the record for nonfiction books, hard cover nonfiction books.

JASON: What can you tell me about Andy Griffith? I know you were the executive producer of his show for a long time.

SHELDON: I created that show. I gave it a tryout, as it were, by having Andy do a guest spot on *The Danny Thomas Show*. On it he played a small town sheriff. We used that episode as a way of selling a series to the General Foods Corporation. It was the first spin-off. Since that time spin-offs have become relatively common. That was the first time an existing series was used as a platform from which to launch a new series. I did eleven years with Andy. It worked out very well, very profitably and satisfactory for both of us.

JASON: Did you ever step in and play some roles on *The Andy Griffith Show*?

SHELDON: I was not the type for a rustic background. I was more appropriate for urban settings.

JASON: For instance, Phil Arnold, Danny Thomas' agent on *Make Room for Daddy*.

SHELDON: Yeah, I did the Thomas show. I did many appearances in *I Spy* because we were in a distant place like Athens or Hong Kong and there was a part that came up that I could handle. It made better sense for me to do it than to ship an actor from Hollywood to Marrakech or Morocco for two or three days work so I was a frequent guest on my own show.

JASON: That was one way to save the budget when you knew you could do it well yourself.

SHELDON: That was the whole consideration. I was financially backing the show.

JASON: With the little time left to us let's move on to motion pictures. You were in plenty of them. One role I have in mind is that of Harry, the Horse in *Guys and Dolls*. Was that your last Damon Runyon character?

SHELDON: No, no, it wasn't. After that I did a character for Frank Capra in a picture called *Pocket Full of Miracles* in which I played the same kind of character. *Pocket Full of Miracles* was a Damon Runyon story. It was not called that in the original version. I think it was called *Apple Annie*. I played it that for Frank Capra after *Guys and Dolls* and then, again for Capra, I did a semi-Runyonesque character in *It's a Wonderful Life*. I was the bartender. That's the picture where Jimmy Stewart imagines himself never having been born.

JASON: That was a movie that became a true Christmas classic. You did work with Capra quite a bit.

SHELDON: He was my friend and still is. I was always happy doing whatever he asked me to do.

JASON: In *Guys and Dolls* you worked with another big name director.

SHELDON: I worked with Joe Mankiewicz who went to high school with me in New York and later became one of our most distinguished directors. Joe directed it and Sam Goldwyn produced it. I worked opposite Frank Sinatra in it.

JASON: There were also some people in it who didn't seem like they'd fit the genre. One of those was Marlon Brando who did a really good job as Sky Masterson.

SHELDON: I think, considering what his natural equipment was, he did a hell of a good job. I think Frank was not perfectly cast although he did a great job of accommodating himself to the part. It was not his kind of part to play a meek, self-effacing, rather timid character. That's not exactly the concept of what Frank Sinatra is.

JASON: I understand that you are now enjoying a well deserved retirement.

SHELDON: At my age it certainly beats the alternative.

****

Sheldon Leonard acted in many more pictures than the three we discussed. He did forty-seven of them in all. Two of the better known ones would be *To Have and Have Not* with Bogart and Bacall in 1944 and his most recent adventure, *The Brinks Job* with Peter Falk and Peter Boyle in 1978. He even did one with Abbott and Costello called *Abbott and Costello Meet the Invisible Man.*

In his early days, between 1934 and 1939, he played major roles on the stage in at least seven Broadway productions. Some of those had long runs.

As he said, during his radio days he was extremely busy. On many of those shows you would have to be familiar with his voice to pick him out because, as has been often stated throughout these three volumes, credits were seldom given with the exception of the main stars, sometimes not even then.

On television he did some acting, but he functioned mainly as the writer or producer or director. On some he was all three. Some of those on which he was the initial driving force, that we did not discuss, were *Lassie, The Real McCoys* and *Gomer Pyle, USMC.*

He died in 1997 at the age of 89.

To learn more about this media dynamo I suggest reading his autobiography *And the Show Goes On.*

Act III: Scene Three
Will You Ever Get a Real Job?

That was the question constantly asked by the parents on both sides of their families. None of them could ever understand how show business could be a genuine calling because they knew that somewhere along the line it would fail to produce a living wage. That was the question and we will talk about the answer as we go along.

Let me introduce you to the truly charming and devoted couple who were the recipients of that worrisome request. They met almost by accident when they were both in their salad days just trying to hold it together and make ends meet. He was a struggling actor and she was a Broadway Showgirl in the Earl Carroll Vanities and also a a gifted sculptress. While they were both living in the same down scale hotel in New York, he decided one day to knock on the door of his neighbor to ask her for a cup of sugar or some such thing. In truth he was just feeling lonely and a little depressed and wanted some human contact. When he knocked on the door he was greeted by an attractive young lady who was covered with what looked to him to be talcum powder. He was a bit taken aback until she explained that what he saw was the remnants of chipping away at a sculpture she was working on. As time went on and they got to know each other, he discovered that one of her many talents was Gourmet Cooking. This was a challenge for her in their present circumstances because the hotel had a rule against cooking in their rooms. She, however, had used her closet as a kitchen where, on a hot plate, she could prepare some wondrous meals. Life went on blissfully for them in spite of their financial woes and it was not too long before they were married. Of course, I am over simplifying, but that is the long story on a short page.

The couple I am referring to are Jim and Henny Backus, who became good friends as well as lovers until Jim passed away. On June 22, 1987 we talked and laughed our way through a long three way conversation.

****

JASON: Anyone who says that Hollywood marriages are short lived is obviously not talking about Jim and Henny Backus who have been together for forty-three years.

JIM: Forty-three years? I didn't know.

HENNY: Jim! You should.

JIM: I thought it was thirty-eight. Well, who's counting?

JASON: My records say forty-three. Am I wrong?

HENNY: No, you're not wrong. We were married twice in one week. Not everybody can make that claim.

JIM: Tell him why we were married twice in one week.

HENNY: It was such a mob. We couldn't get reservations for all the people at one time so we were married in Philadelphia on Tuesday near my family, then we went to Cleveland and got married for Jim's family on Friday. Jim always says. . .

JIM: We took our marriage on the road.

HENNY: That's why it lasted. We had a tryout.

JASON: That really isn't so strange to me, although the circumstances were different. I was also married to my wife of many years two times. In Holland that's

	how it's usually done, once in the City Hall to make it legal and then again in a church for the ritual ceremony.
HENNY:	That makes some sense.
JIM:	Ours made no sense whatever.
JASON:	But you kept both families happy. That's worth something. I know you were born in Philadelphia and Cleveland, but you were basically New Yorkers for a long time.
JIM:	Our temporal home is New York. That was home base for me and for Henny too. We lived there for a few years. We've been back there so often. We used to average maybe ten or fifteen times a year. For a while we kept two homes. We still have our Tupperware in some hotel.
HENNY:	We have it at the Regency. Their basement is full of our things, spices, canned goods, pots and pans, etc.
JASON:	You made a statement in your book *Rocks on the Roof*, the first biography of your lives together.
HENNY:	That's the first book we wrote. We're on number four now.
JASON:	We'll get to that one, but you said something that I really don't quite understand. You said that you became real Californians after a while when you finally got used to the idea that they served the salad first. I've spent a lot of time in New York and I don't remember it being any other way.
HENNY:	May I say that in Europe and back East, as I

	remember it the salad was always supposed to cut the fat and the heaviness of the entrée. It was always served after the entrée.
JIM:	Between the entrée and desert, in Cleveland anyway.
JASON:	I stand corrected. Now that I think of it, when I lived in Holland and Germany that was they way they did it, at least in the better restaurants.
HENNY:	They also served an important vegetable as a side dish, didn't they—like asparagus?
JASON:	Always, yes. That's something they've gotten away from here.
HENNY:	I know, and to stay in shape we must do that.
JASON:	The real beginning of your careers was out in California on radio, but there's something I want to get to before that. When you got out there your first house was a little strange, in fact, you called it Taj Mahal on the Half Shell.
JIM:	It's been some years. It's still standing. We drive by it every now and then with mixed emotions. When we came out here it was tough to get a house, any house, or even to get a room. It was tough to get a place to sit down. Beggars couldn't be choosers. We were very lucky to have had that place.
HENNY:	There was nothing wrong with it. It was perfectly beautiful except there were mysterious rocks being thrown at the house.
JIM:	That wasn't the first house, Doll.

JASON: That was the split-level in Beverly Hills.

HENNY: You're right, that was the second house.

JIM: You're two houses away.

HENNY: You're right. Which house do you want to talk about, Jason? The haunted house was more interesting.

JASON: Was that first house haunted? I didn't know that.

HENNY: The one in Beverly Hills.

JASON: Okay, I mean the one with the rocks.

HENNY: The first house was just plain ugly.

JASON: The split-level was split all over the place from what you said in the book.

HENNY: I barely remember it. I'm very lucky. It was really a kind of horrible house.

JASON: But you never did solve the mystery of the rocks that kept flying on the roof.

HENNY: That's the second house. That's not the house you're talking about.

JIM: You don't know which house it is, Doll.

HENNY: The Beverly Hills house?

JASON: I think we're jumping back and forth now.

JIM: Doing a little house dropping.

HENNY: Let me just say this about that house. Before we

moved in, for several years, there were rocks being thrown at it. One tenant after another moved out. We stayed there because we had to. There was no place else to go. It was very hard to find anything. We wanted to buy our dream house, which we later did. During the years we were there we finally got friendly with whatever was throwing the rocks. After a rock would hit I would go out and say, "Stop" or "That was a lovely rock" or whatever. We found them. They were earth rocks. They were not coming from another planet. We had them analyzed. The American Physic Society was there. The police were there. It's still going on and every time we drive by there, there is a for sale sign on it. One night, about two years ago, I was going to a party across the street and so was Merv Griffin. He stopped at the same time as I did and I said, "Merv, right over there is the house you always make me talk about." So we walked over and there was a sign. The government had taken it over. There was a big sign out front and strangely enough it said, "For sale, this house is possessed." Isn't that funny? They meant by the government.

JASON: I guess they could have meant it either way.

HENNY: Sure, but it was always for sale. People buy it and then move right out. They have no idea what it is. Obviously, it's still going on.

JASON: I understand you even did some tests with a baseball player standing at the top of a mountain near by and he couldn't throw a rock anywhere near the roof.

JIM: They tried everything. I think it was Sandy Koufax just starting out, one of his first paying jobs. He stood on the top of the mountain trying to hit our roof with a rock, but he couldn't do it.

HENNY:	He even tried it with a giant slingshot, remember?
JIM:	And they had helicopters come over to try dropping things on the house. It just didn't work.
HENNY:	Keenan Wynn and his motorcycle group sat in our living room and waited for rocks. Then they'd chase up the hill trying to figure out where they came from, but nobody knew. They never found anybody or any evidence. The people next door had a Spanish house with a tile roof. Imagine the expense. There were always tiles crashing down when he missed our house, whoever he was.
JASON:	That's a fascinating story, but I think we should move on. Since you published *Rocks on the Roof* you've done a couple more books, but I think we should talk about the new one.
HENNY:	We have one that is just out now called *Backus Strikes Back*. We also have another one that will be out at Christmas called *The Golden Years* and still another for the following year called *Where Did Everybody Go?* The other book that you missed from 1962 was called *What Are You Doing after the Orgy?* I wish we could think of another title that good.
JASON:	Let's get into your radio days. Someone that I had as a guest not too long ago, and in fact I talked with him again just last Saturday, was Alan Young. There was a character that you did on his show, Jim, Hubert Updike III, the richest man in the world. I understand that you and Henny had kind of a dispute going over that character before he was brought to fruition.
JIM:	That's right. Henny, you tell him.

HENNY: Oh golly, he tried that voice many times. When he got the script I said, "Why don't you try that stupid voice you do at party's right before you put the lamp shade on your head and I have to call a cab to get you home?" He said, "Well, no, I've tried that voice a number of times. It doesn't work." He did it as a favor to me and it caught on.

JASON: Here's what Alan had to say on that same story:

ALAN: I remember that Jim Backus had been auditioning as a fish monger, which was an incongruous conception, but very funny, so we blended his voice with our character and he became Hubert Updike, the richest man in the world.

JASON: Here's Hubert:

****

HUBERT: Look out the window. There he comes down the street now and the poor idiot doesn't know the war is over. He's driving a piece of junk for the scrap drive. He's parking it right in front of my car. I'll go out on the porch and put a stop to it. (Door opens and closes) Alan Young, get that collection of trash off the street.

ALAN: Trash! Street! It's my car. This is my car.

HUBERT: Did you get the number of the truck that hit it?

ALAN: By the way, Hubert, is it safe to park my good old car in front of the house here?

HUBERT: You're safe until two o'clock.

ALAN: Is that the parking limit?

HUBERT:	No, that's when they collect the garbage. Oh, that was a witty one, ya har, ya har! Alan, how dare you park that thing next to my car? My car is half Duisenberg and half Jaguar. It's a racer.
ALAN:	So what! My car is half Chrysler and half Jeep. It's a creep.
HUBERT:	Well, I'll have to be jogging along now. Oh my, I'll have to call my dealer and buy a new car.
ALAN:	Another car? What's wrong with the car you have outside?
HUBERT:	It's pointing the wrong way.

****

JIM:	That was Hubert Updike III who was the grandfather of Thurston Howell on *Gilligan's Island*.
HENNY:	Actually, he's the same character with a different name, isn't he Jimmy?
JIM:	Same character, different shows.
JASON:	Another character that was similar was Chester Fenwick on *The Sad Sack*.
HENNY:	I've never heard it.
JIM:	You really go back.
JASON:	I have some *Sad Sack* shows in my collection.
HENNY:	Do you really?

****

SAD SACK: Chester—It's Sad Sack. I'm back.

CHESTER: Sad Sack! You're back! How are you, boy? Let me look at you. Turn around. Oh, you look great, boy. The army's done wonders for you. Tell me about it Sad Sack. You've been in the thick of things. I wanted to go, but they wouldn't take me. Do you know why?

SAD SACK: Was it because your uncle was on the draft board?

CHESTER: Why, Sad Sack, you know how bad my back is, boy. I couldn't carry a gun. But forget about me, boy. You're the one who's been over there deep in the glorious fight for freedom. It must have been rough. Tell me about it.

SAD SACK: Well, the first place I landed—

CHESTER: Don't think it's been easy here. We civilians put up with plenty so you boys could have the best. When I think of the nights I've gone without steaks so you boys could have Spam.

****

HENNY: I don't remember that show at all.

JIM: It was with Herb Vigran.

JASON: And Patsy Morrison and Doris Singleton.

JIM: You really do your homework.

JASON:	And of course, you worked with Mel Blanc on *Mel's Fix-It Shop*.
JIM:	Ugga, ugga, boo, ugga, boo, boo, ugga.
JASON:	That's right. That's the show that came from. I remember it now.
JIM:	Hans Conried was on that show a lot and Frank Nelson. We had a lot of fun. Mel's a wonderful guy. Just before we went on the air I was watching television and I saw Mel doing a new commercial. He's just as vibrant as he was damn near forty years ago. The man is amazing. He used to do those shows at Warner Brothers. He was the only one in the cast. He'd do every part and you'd never know. The guy is still in operation after his terrible accident. He came so close. It's a miracle that he's still with us.
JASON:	You worked with Bill Goodwin and you did Penny Singleton's show for a while and I have a *Suspense* show from 1959 on which you played a guy named Poppy, a very serious role.

****

POPPY:	All right, so I've got a record. You want to hang me on it? I served my time. Ain't you guys ever happy? That's the thing about you cops. A guy tries to go straight, you don't care. But let him make one little mistake and you hound him until the day he dies.
COP 1:	Don't try to paint any pictures for me, Poppy. I know you. People call you the only man born without a conscience.

Cop 2: What's the price for fingering a man as big as Blocker, Poppy?

Cop 1: Who contacted you, Poppy? Give us a name.

Poppy: Now, what is all this? All of the sudden a poor newsie's in charge of who gets rubbed out on his corner. You're the police department. This is your job. You're in charge. It's getting so an honest man is afraid to walk the streets.

****

Jim: We used to do so many of those shows. We used to do three or four a day sometimes. The next day I couldn't tell you what I did the day before. I did a lot of *Gangbusters* and *The Jack Benny Show*, in fact, I played the used car dealer when Jack tried trade in his old Maxwell.

Henny: That was one of the funniest shows Jack ever did.

Jason: Moving right along, let's switch to television. There are a couple of shows that immediately come to my mind. They were *I Married Joan* in 1952 and around 1963 you did the first of the *Mr. Magoo* series. They were made for theatres, but they also ran on television. Here's a scene with Magoo getting ready to do an opera.

****

Magoo: I'll bet this mirror hasn't been washed in years. I can hardy see my make-up.

Director: I know it may not be proper on stage, Mr. Magoo, but I must insist that you wear your glasses.

Act III: Scene Three: Will You Ever Get a Real Job?

MAGOO: Now, now, now, Mrs. Stickney, don't you worry your pretty little head about it.

DIRECTOR: Mr. Magoo, if you botch up my opera I'll, I'll. . . (*door slams*)

MAGOO: Oh dear, what a fool I've been. (*beep-beep*) Curtain time, my spear—oh, here it is. Now my shield, oh yes. Now I'll make you proud of me, Mrs. Stickney. On with the show! I have a sinking feeling, stage fright. Well, as they say, take a deep breath. Actually this acting game is old hat with me. Egad, there's my cue.

****

JASON: I read somewhere that Mr. Magoo or Quincy Magoo is the heart throb of Princess Margaret.

HENNY: I just want to say one thing to you and that is that Jim has been interviewed by everyone in the world about Magoo. You're the first person who ever knew Magoo's first name. Do you know what college he went to?

JASON: Rutgers, class of ought seven.

JIM: Lovey on *Gilligan's Island*, what was her first name?

JASON: That one I don't remember.

JIM: Marjorie Wentworth, or was it Sheliah Wentworth?

JASON: I don't think too many people remember the last names of the characters Dawn Wells and Tina Louise played on that show either.

HENNY: I sure don't.

JIM: No, I don't either. The Captain was Horace, Horace McAdams. Dawn might have been Mary Ann Foster, I think.

JASON: Mary Ann Summers.

JIM: Right and Tina was just the lady. I never knew she had a name—Ginger—Snap?

JASON: It was Ginger Grant. Those are the only two people in the cast who weren't in the later versions, weren't they?—Tina and Dawn?

JIM: Dawn was, but not Tina. We had to get someone else for her part. I think she came back for the last show.

JASON: I thought Jane Edwards played that role in *The New Adventures of Gilligan*, the animated version.

JIM: Oh yeah, we did that down in the Valley.

HENNY: What's that got to do with it?

JIM: Because we'd go in and do three lines and go back a week later to do four more.

HENNY: Which means that you didn't work with the rest of the cast?

JIM: No. They couldn't get us all together at the same time. That's the wonderful thing about animation.

JASON: That was the main subject of a conversation I had with Janet Waldo, one of many I've had with her. She played the teenage Judy Jetson on *The Jetsons* for twenty-five years and never aged a day. That's the miracle of animation. What about *Blondie*?

	Both of you were in the second cast of that on television.
HENNY:	I was hoping everyone forgot that.
JASON:	That bad, huh? Sorry, but it's a part of your joint resume. It was the only show I could come up with that both of you were on at the same time.
HENNY:	It was the only one we did regularly together.
JIM:	I didn't think it was as bad as people thought it was.
HENNY:	I thought it was worse.
JIM:	The vice president of CBS is one of our dearest friends. For business he saved certain pens. You know how they do when a pen has signed certain acts of congress. He said, "This is the pen that personally cancelled *Blondie*," and gave it to us.
HENNY:	It was to hang on the wall, which we did.
JASON:	There are shows like that. Not everything can be a hit.
HENNY:	It's never the actor's fault. We were so embarrassed because it was so badly done, in every way.
JIM:	It didn't have to be. The cast was very good.
HENNY:	What I don't understand is, why do it again? They had a perfect show with Penny Singleton and Arthur Lake. It's still on morning, noon and night so why would they do it again? They do it all the time and they do it with movies too.

JIM: I did a remake of *Miracle on 34th Street* which was completely unnecessary. The original was one of those movies that can never be topped, Edmund Gwenn as Santa Clause and Natalie Wood as the little girl with Maureen O'Hara and Thelma Ritter. Those were immortal parts. They were gems. They tried to improve on them. I don't understand why. They did the same thing with *Lost Horizon*.

HENNY: You also did another version of *It Happened One Night*.

JIM: I can't even remember the title of it. We had a great cast, Jack Lemmon and June Allison. If you put a gun to my head, I couldn't tell you what the name of it was, *Chase Me When You See Me* or *Catch Me If You Don't* or something like that.

HENNY: Imagine, they did it badly, changed the title, nobody knows what it was. It was just a bad movie. Why would they do that? Do you understand? I don't.

JASON: No, and I also don't understand why they are colorizing so many fine old black and white prints.

HENNY: This whole town is up at arms about that. It's awful. They've taken beautiful things that look like sculpture—they're so beautifully photographed—nobody does that anymore—and they've simply just ruined them. Now they're nothing.

JASON: In the first place, you can't do with color what can be done in black and white and even worse, the colors they add are far from true to life. It's like a pastel horror show.

HENNY: They're two completely separate mediums. One has nothing to do with the other and they should be left alone.

JASON: Absolutely, computers have gone too far in this instance.

HENNY: Yes they have! Yes they have!

JASON: Since we're talking about movies and the name Natalie Wood was mentioned, Jim, you worked with Natalie and Sal Mineo and James Dean in *Rebel Without a Cause*.

JIM: *Rebel Without a Cause*, yes. That was not our first picture together. I did four pictures with Natalie before we did that. One of them was *Father was a Fullback*, which was a very good picture for her. She played a little girl six or seven years old. At the time she was about nine. Another time I played her father. Altogether, I did six or seven pictures with Natalie.

JASON: Father was a Fullback would have been the one with Fred Mac Murray.

HENNY: And Maureen O'Hara.

JIM: Beautiful girl! That called for color because it was kind of a candy box idea. The people were gentle and the colors were lovely. But to do that to other films—well. . .

HENNY: It's abominable and everybody's furious. Something should be done.

JIM: Just going through the records I found out they colorized over 350 major motion pictures.

HENNY: A lot of getting up at 4:30 in the morning.

JASON: The list goes on and on so obviously we don't want to get involved with all of them.

JIM: Just a few words about *Rebel Without a Cause*.

JASON: I think one of the intriguing things about *Rebel* is that James Dean, Sal Mineo and Natalie Wood all met with tragic deaths long before their time.

JIM: And Nick Adams, he died in not the most common situation. I have a picture of all of the people who worked on that picture and it's amazing.

HENNY: Don't forget Nick Ray, the director.

JIM: And there were more. It's kind of spooky.

JASON: The only other person who comes to mind at the moment from that cast is Ann Doran, who played your wife and Dean's mother.

HENNY: She and Jim and the writer, Billy Stern are still around.

JIM: And Dennis Hopper was in that. Do you remember Dennis?

JASON: He was the leader of the gang that gave Dean so much trouble. I know another movie that I'll bet you had a lot of fun making—*It's a Mad, Mad, Mad, Mad World*.

JIM: I made that separate from the main cast. I was in New York that summer. I came back and I was in the airplane scene. I spent six days in an airplane with Buddy Hackett and Mickey Rooney. We were

	thirty feet in the air in a dummy plane, like a Link Trainer so they could spin us around. If you think spending six days in a confined area with Buddy Hackett and Mickey Rooney is fun you've got another think coming. I still have the scars to prove it.
HENNY:	They were hardly serene.
JIM:	The people who were in the actual chase worked in Palo Verde. All that summer they had a rough time of it, but I did just the one week. About six months later they did the scene where they came into my house and I went flying out the window.
JASON:	I remember that scene. There were so many people in that movie that, at this point in time, it's hard to separate them anymore. I remember Peter Falk as the cab driver.
JIM:	And Dick Shawn played a whacked out guy.
JASON:	He always did. He was way out there as Adolph Hitler in *The Producers*.
JIM:	Yes, he certainly did, but he's dead now.
JASON:	Sid Caesar was in it. That wasn't the best period in his life at the time.
JIM:	But he got out of it. He looks great now.
JASON:	I read his autobiography recently. It's quite a story. He's very proud of what he's done, as well he should be.
HENNY:	He's got a wonderful wife, incidentally.

JASON: She must be, considering all they went through, through the years.

HENNY: Did you see the movie Jim and I were in called *The Great Man*? That's a pretty interesting story.

JASON: I'm afraid you've got me on that one.

HENNY: It ran in New York for almost two years. It was Ed Wynn's actual first movie, but they released *Requiem for a Heavyweight* before they did this so people think that was his first, but it wasn't. It was a brilliant movie directed by Jose Ferrer and starring him with Keenan Wynn, Ed Wynn, Jim and me. Help me with the cast, Jimmy. It was so long ago.

JIM: Julie London. It was right after *Rebel* in '56.

HENNY: It's a very good movie.

JASON: Is there anything you want to talk about that I didn't bring up? I know that there is.

HENNY: We'll do this again when our new book comes out. Would you like to do it again?

JASON: Of course I would. You know I would. It's been more fun than a barrel of monkeys. Tell me the name of the new book again.

HENNY: The one that's going to be available around Christmas is called *Up the Golden Years* and it will be published by St. Martin's Press. The one that's out now is called *Backus Strikes Back*.

JASON: That's the one I know you'd like to talk about.

JIM:	That's the story about my fight against Parkinson's disease.
HENNY:	A funny book about a terrible disease.
JIM:	With Henny I wrote a funny book about a disease that's very, very frightening. The only way to look at it is by laughing at it which at times gets very tough. I'm very proud of the fight. Tell Jason about the letter we got, Doll. This is what makes show business.
HENNY:	When we sent it to the publisher he wrote a letter back to us. I wish I had it in front of me. He said, "This won't need editing. It's the only perfect book we've ever received," and he went on in that vein.
JIM:	From two people who are almost illiterate.
HENNY:	And have no education.
JASON:	I read the oldest one, *Rocks on the Roof* and laughed all the way through it.
HENNY:	We're not the same people anymore.
JASON:	I realize that, but I can see a lot of humor in your style.
JIM:	We're proud of all of them, but especially proud of *Backus Strikes Back*. It's something I can look at objectively because it is happening to me. We got a letter this morning from the Parkinson Foundation. I sent out letters to thousands of people and the Foundation received over $72,000 for their treasury because of them.
HENNY:	No other celebrity has ever raised more than

$25,000 on a letter, but Jim's is still bringing more in. We average twenty letters a day from people who are so supportive, wonderful strangers who have read the book and are so great. The Parkinson thing is a great cause for anyone who's interested because they're so close to a cure and it's a hideous disease. We're not really sure if Jim has it or not. He's a borderline case. They can't diagnose it. They can only evaluate it.

JIM: It's very tough in the twilight of your life, when you look forward to a restful finish and you get stuck with something like this.

****

It was such a sad way in which to end an otherwise very upbeat interview. Jim left us on July 3, 1989 as a result of complications of pneumonia. Henny went on for five more years before she too passed away. We had many conversations over that short period of time and I miss them both as friends, even though I never met them face to face.

It would not be fair to leave these two wonderful people without a couple of anecdotes about them. First a little story about Jim and his long-time pal, Victor Mature. They were close ever since they were both ejected from the Kentucky Military Institute for spending more time performing than with their studies. Later on when they were both working in a movie called *Androcles and the Lion*, they took a break and went to a very up-scale restaurant for lunch. Since they hadn't taken time to change they were still dressed in the full Roman Armor that their roles called for. When they were greeted with disdain because of the way they were dressed, Victor said to the maître d, "What's the matter? Don't you serve men in uniform?"

After they had both made it big in Hollywood they sent a card to the director of their previous school saying, "Best wishes from cadets Mature and Backus. PS: What are your honor students doing?"

Here's a tale about Henny. When Jim was working for Intelligence in the army during the war she always wanted to keep in touch, no matter where he was on secret assignments. Jim called her a telephone virtuoso, Toscanini at his best, because she could always find him any time, no matter whether he was on a battleship or in some remote spot. He said she could cajole, wheedle, tease, command, shout or plead until she got what she wanted. She was an actress, after all.

If you noticed, they were perfectly suited to each other. He could start a sentence and she would finish it. That came from a long and happy marriage. They were so used to each other it was like talking with one blended voice.

ACT III:
SCENE FOUR
THE CUT-UP

Known to his friends, associates and co-workers as a man to be watched, he never quite got rid of the image. No, I'm not talking about a terrorist or someone who did other dastardly deeds. I'm talking about a guy with an extremely quick wit and the ability to deliver a prank with the best of them. People who were on a set, during a rehearsal and occasionally during a broadcast, were never sure what he might do next. He was good at creating some truly humorous situations at the least expected moment, sometimes without letting on who the responsible party was.

I'm not trying to cast aspersions on him. He was around for a long, long time for all of us to enjoy on the radio, on television and in some motion pictures. He just always had to be having fun. He was one of those numerous actors who usually performed anonymously because of the system I have often spoken of throughout these three volumes.

Jerry Hausner was his name. It is hard to say anything negative about him because, deep down he was an all-around nice guy. We conversed on July 3, 1987. You may notice that once you get Jerry started he is hard to stop.

****

JASON: Before we get into the radio, television and picture worlds, let's talk a little about your youthful enterprises. I know that you were born in Cleveland and that you worked for a newspaper there. Please tell me more about that.

JERRY: I didn't really work for a newspaper. I sold newspapers, like Bob Hope sold newspapers in Cleveland. They tell me I inherited his corner though I didn't know him at the time. I worked with him many years later. I had a little stand in the lobby of the Leader News Building. Leader published the paper I was selling. The owner of the paper was Dan Hannah from the illustrious Hannah family of Cleveland who owned the Hannah Theatre and a lot of other things. I sold papers in the lobby of this very elegant marble building. Every afternoon, Mr. Hannah, the owner of the newspaper, would come downstairs in the elevator and I'd have his paper ready. I would hand it to him and he never said thank you or anything. He just walked out with it. I said to the fellow who hired me, "When does this guy pay off?" The papers were two cents apiece and I had to pay a penny for each one. It was a long time ago. It must have been 1920 or something like that. So the fellow who owned the news stand said, "Don't worry. He owns the building and the paper and everything. At Christmas time he'll give you a handsome gift." Christmas time came and went, but I never got a nickel from that guy. That's how I managed to get rich. I went on to finish high school. We did some plays in high school. We did a play called *Tweedles* by Booth Tarkington, famous American author. It was a very small cast. I think there were five people in the cast. As it turned out, years later, every one of those five of those people ended up in show business. Then I worked in dramatic stock. I worked as an extra at the Ohio Theatre in 1927. We did a play called *Broadway* written by George Abbott, who is still around. He's 100 years old now, still directing on Broadway. In the cast were people like Spencer Tracy. A man by the name of Hobart Cavanaugh played the lead. He was a kind of a star in those days. Even you probably never heard of him. Lee Patrick, Pierre Watkins, Robert Barret were all members of the stock company, a very nice stock company. I think I got $15 a week as an extra. I was going to school at the time, art school—Cleveland Art School. In 1929, after I'd had a couple years of experience in the stock company, I also played in a theatre called Gordon Square, which was a neighborhood stock company. I was a kind of local Jack Lemmon. We did a whole series of what they called in those days, bedroom farces. I played the lead in every one of those plays even though I was not what you would call leading man material. I was short. I was only five foot two or three, but I was playing the parts that were originally created by a man named Ernest Truex, who later became famous. It was a Jack Lemmon kind of guy, the little guy who always managed to somehow win in the end. The man who produced those plays was a fellow named Lauren Wade. He eventually wound up in New York with John Royal. John Royal had been the manager of the Palace Theatre in Cleveland. John moved on to be a big executive for NBC in New York. He took Lauren with him. It might amuse you to know how I went to work for Lauren Wade at the Gordon Square Stock Company. I was working in a drug store. I was about eighteen years old and I had just gotten out of high school. I was working in my cousin's drug store washing dishes. The soda fountain was a square affair. It was leased out to another man. I worked for the druggist who leased me out to this soda fountain. He was paying me $11 a week to be the cashier, trim the windows and do other work around the store. At noon time he let me wash dishes. The man who ran the soda fountain paid my boss $12 a week so he was making a dollar for the dish washing services. There was this man who came in every day to have his lunch. He looked familiar, but I never knew who he was. He turned out to be Lauren Wade, the producer of the stock company. One day he took me aside, I was walking out from behind the counter with a stack of dishes. He said, "Have you ever had any experience in the theatre?" I said, "Yes, as a matter of fact I had some." He said, "Well, you look like you're going to be a successful actor one of these days. You want to go to work for me?" I asked him what it was all about and he told me he had this stock company on the West Side of Cleveland. So I said, "That's what I'd love to do. What kind of money are you going to pay me?" He said, "How much money do you think you ought to get?" I thought that I'd heard somewhere that I could get $50 a week, so I said, "How about $50?" Of course, I was making $11 a week from the job I was doing. He said, "Will you settle for $35?" I dropped all the dishes on the floor and said, "I'm with you!" We walked out together. I was with him for a whole season or maybe more than that. I can't remember anymore. When the company finally closed he still owed me $5. He and I remained friends until he died a couple of years ago. He still owes me $5.

JASON: Let's jump forward to your radio days. When did that all begin?

JERRY: I got involved with radio with *Lum and Abner* who had just started recently and needed some kind of help. My friend Lauren Wade was already the manager of the WTAM radio station in Cleveland so he called me in to work with *Lum and Abner*. We did a pilot radio show with them. We became very close friends. Later on they were signed by NBC. They needed a secretary so I introduced them to my girlfriend. She became their secretary and worked for them for twelve or thirteen years managing their office.

JASON: I understand you just came back from a *Lum and Abner* convention.

JERRY: They have a convention every year. It's "The Lum and Abner Preservation Society." There are three young men. The president is a young man who is twenty-nine years old, Donnie Pitchford, and the executive secretary is Tim Hollis. He's twenty-four. Why they should be interested in *Lum and Abner*, who are both dead, I don't know. The show ceased to exist in the late '40s. The only reason I was invited to be the guest of honor was because I'm the only one still alive who knew them from the beginning. I met them in 1933. We became friends and stayed that way. Two weeks ago I went down to their birth place, Mena, Arkansas and then visited Pine Ridge, which was the imaginary town in Arkansas that they made famous. They based their locale on a little country store which they called "The Jot'em-Down Store." It was an actual general store belonging to a man named Dick Huddleston. That store still exists. It has a kind of a museum in the back room. They sell lots of *Lum and Abner* souvenirs.

JASON: It was the kind of homespun humor that never loses its edge.

JERRY: I guess that's it. When they started out they were inspired by *Amos and Andy*. They were country boys. They really knew noting abut radio or show business. They were very naïve. They had this big American dream that if *Amos and Andy* could make it, they could make it. As it turned out they did.

They went up to Chicago and auditioned and they were put on the air, but they didn't write scripts. They went into the studio every day and sat down and just ad-libbed for fifteen minutes. They made it up as they went along and they had some very funny stuff. It was a kind of folk humor, very real, very legitimate. Then when they were finally signed by NBC for the network, NBC insisted on their writing scripts. For the first script it took them twenty-four hours. They were used to just going in and improvising every day.

JASON: One of the funny things about *Lum and Abner* was the fact that Chester Lauck and Norris Goff each played several characters.

JERRY: That's right. They did sixteen voices.

JASON: Once in a while they forgot who they were playing, but they always got back to square one. They always managed to overcome their errors.

JERRY: We were talking about that the other day down there. They had one of the recordings where I think Goff made a mistake and did the wrong character. Chet said to him, right on the air, "No, you're Abner, you know." There was one show that they played for me which I had forgotten. I was playing at the Palace in Chicago in vaudeville at the time. Between shows I went over to visit them and they were on the air. I walked into the studio while they were broadcasting. As I walked in Chet Lauck noticed that I had entered the studio. He immediately improvised a whole new thought. He said, "Here I'm talking about Jerry Hausner the other day and I wondered what ever happened to him. Now he suddenly showed up." So that was on the air as part of the show. It had nothing to do with the script. They just wanted to announce my presence. Somehow, I finally wound up in California and in California there wasn't much theatre so I went into radio. They paid $5 a show. That was before AFRA. Some of the shows paid a promise of $5 and then cheated you out of it whenever they could. I remember, on one particular show, there were two guys who became famous later on. Frank Nelson found fame with Jack Benny, the guy who said, "Yeesssss." The other one was Hanley Stafford who ultimately wound up with Fannie Brice as Daddy on *Baby Snooks*. Slowly, we got to know each other out here. A lot of it is social in California. I managed to make a living. While I was doing the play *Of Mice and Men* in 1937 my girlfriend and I decided, since we'd been going together for ten years to take a chance and get married. So we did and that marriage lasted forty-two years until she passed away. We were very happy and fairly successful. I did a lot of radio over the years until 1942 when I enlisted in the army. I was in the Armed Forces Radio Service. We produced shows like *Command Performance, Mail Call, Jubilee* and *Yank Swing Sessions*. I produced that show. We did *Personal Album* using stars as emcees. I did *Personal Album* with Shirley Temple as mistress of ceremonies. June Allison worked on that show. It was all started by Tom Lewis, who became a colonel in the army. He was married to Loretta Young. He was a big executive at Young and Rubicam advertising for many years so he had great background for radio and he requested a whole group of men who were now in the army to be transferred to him. People like Howard Duff, Elliott Lewis, who was a terrific actor, myself, Bill Conrad and a number of guys who were not only actors, but writers as well. Sherwood Schwartz, who did *The Brady Bunch* and *Gilligan's Island*. So there was quite a group of talented people.

JASON: There were a couple of people you left off the list. I'm referring to Jerry Lawrence and Bob Lee.

JERRY: Of course, of course.

JASON: You worked on a show that Bob Lee wrote called *Young Love* with Bob's wife, Janet Waldo, a lady who does a lot of cartoons these days. It also had Shirley Mitchell and Herb Butterworth.

JERRY: All good people.

JASON: Someone that you did mention with Armed Forces Radio was someone you worked with on another show, Howard Duff.

JERRY: Of course. I did *Sam Spade* with him.

JASON: You were Sid Weiss, his lawyer.

JERRY: That's right. I was on the original audition, the original pilot, but of course they didn't call them pilots in those days. It was called a radio audition. It was done by Bill Spier who also did *Suspense* which I used to work on with regularity. We were called for this audition and we sat down in the studio. There were Frank Lovejoy, Eddie McDonald, Wally Mayer, Elliott Lewis, Howard Duff and myself and a couple of others. Of course, there was also Lurene Tuttle. Lurene was all set for the show to play Effie, Sam's secretary. I was all set to play Sid Weiss, his lawyer. These other guys were all there to play incidental parts. They were the cream of the radio actors of the time. We sat there waiting. Bill Spier was up in the booth. We waited for him to say, "Let's get started." We waited for nearly an hour. We couldn't imagine what was going wrong. Finally we stood up and looked up in the booth and waved our arms as if to say, "What in the hell is going on?" He punched his talk back button and said, "We're having a little legal problem. The man who's supposed to play Sam Spade, Lloyd Nolan, is not available. There's some kind of legal technicality. There's litigation going on about something in his contract. We're just trying to figure out what to do with it. We have the studio and we're here so we're going to have to try it with someone else." So, what he did was, he let each one of those guys that I mentioned read a few lines of *Sam Spade*. Casually, he said, "We'll go with Howard Duff." It was that simple. Howard Duff became Sam Spade and became famous. That's how it happened. We did the show. We did the pilot. Then somehow I went to Las Vegas for a few days. I got a long distance call saying, "Get back here. *Sam Spade* is going on the air and you go to work on Sunday. It was of course, live. I rushed back. When I got back and went into the studio Bill Spier said, "I'm sorry I made you come all the way back here for this." I said, "Are you kidding? It's a running part." He said, "That's the problem. The script has been rewritten and the part of Sid Weiss has been cut out. However, you'll play a different part." I was on the show for a couple of years, but I never played Sid Weiss. Sid never came back into the scripts. So I've had a couple of near misses in my life, what with *I Love Lucy* and *Sam Spade*. In a way it's been very nice because I've had a tremendous variety of roles and lots of interesting experiences. I've gotten to travel around the world a lot, busy all the time and never unemployed for long. I worked in radio as a free-lancer. I was doing *Big Town* with Edward G. Robinson, *Silver Theatre* and *Screen Guild* and *Lux Radio Theatre*. So many of those things. I've lost track over the years. Then television came in. I worked on *Burns and Allen* and a lot of early TV shows, which were live until they started to film them. They realized that live shows were kind of shaky. Then I went into the movies. I was in about thirty movies. Didn't do anything too important. I did small parts in pictures called *Wake Me When It's Over* with Dick Shawn; *Off Limits* with Bob Hope; and one with James Stewart called *Jackpot*. Then, in 1955, I went to Munich to work at Radio Free Europe. I was deputy program manager for the Czechoslovak unit. While I was there, I got a call one day from a friend of mine who had arrived in Munich from Hollywood, a man by the name of John Palmer who was a unit manager with *The Loretta Young Show* that I had done on television. John Palmer was the son of Eric Palmer who was a famous German movie director before John was born in Munich. Now he was back in Munich as the unit manager for a big movie with Kirk Douglas called *Paths of Glory*. He invited me out to the studio to have lunch with him one day. While we were having lunch this young man came up to the table and sat down with us. I didn't get his name at first. It turned out the young man was the director and producer of the picture. His name was Stanley Kubrick. We got to talking and I complemented him on a picture that I had seen, that he had made. He was pleased and said, "Can you work in this movie? I've got a part for you." I said, "You'll have to do it on my days off." I had to arrange with Radio Free Europe to take some days off. So I worked in the picture. I played a part that was ultimately cut out. Then I was hired back and I played another part in the same picture. That was one of the great pictures of all time, *Paths of Glory*.

JASON: You mentioned Kirk Douglas. You did a movie with him not too long ago that everyone should be familiar with.

JERRY: That happened recently in 1985. That's already twenty-six years after *Paths of Glory*. It was nice to work with him again. In the meantime I did a whole lot of others. Somewhere along the line, way back in the distant past, I introduced Jim Backus to John Hubley who was looking for a voice to do a new character called The Nearsighted Mr. Magoo. Hubley was a friend of mine. I introduced him to Backus and Jim became Mr. Magoo while I played the voice of Waldo, his nephew.

JASON: I think one of the reasons your name isn't exactly a household word is due to something that didn't exist in the beginning. There were no credits before AFRA was formed.

JERRY: That's true. People like Hans Conried. He and I did several plays. We went on the road with a thing called *Generations*, which Henry Fonda had done in New York with Larry Haynes. We played that for a whole year on the road. Where ever we would go people would stop us on the street and recognize him, but always for just one part, Uncle Tonoose. One day we talked about that while we were on the road. He said, "You know, the interesting thing is that people always identify me with Tonoose from *The Danny Thomas Show*. I only appeared on that show four times a year for three and a half years. I made a total of fifteen appearances on that show and that's the thing people remember me for." He told me he was wearing a padded belly and a false nose and didn't even look like himself. He was a big collector of Japanese art. He had 500 little ivory carvings. Where ever we'd play he got me up early in the morning and drove me to a museum. We were in Philadelphia and at five minutes before nine we were standing on the stairs of the Philadelphia Art Museum waiting for the door to open. Finally it opened and we were the first ones in. The receptionist, when she saw us, looked at Hans and said, "Vincent Price! You finally got here." I thought Hans might be upset about that, but he was used to it. He and Vincent were often mistaken for each other away from home.

JASON: Hans did a ton of radio work on shows that anyone who remembers radio would recognize immediately. He worked with George Burns and Judy Canova and was a regular on *My Friend Irma* with Marie Wilson and Cathy Lewis.

JERRY: That's right. He played Professor Kropotkin. He's gone now as are so many others. I miss him. We were good friends for forty-five years. I'm sort of like an uncle to his children. A nice family. We used to have a group. I don't know if these names are familiar to you, Barney Phillips...

JASON: You're talking about the *Gunsmoke* group and many others.

JERRY: You're familiar with Barney Phillips?

JASON: Barney was also Jack Webb's sidekick on *Dragnet*.

JERRY: That's right, and Herb Vigran?

JASON: *Sad Sack* plus, plus, plus.

JERRY: Well, our intimate group consisted of Hans Conried, Herb Vigran, Barney Phillips and Howard Duff. Here's an interesting little sidelight about Barney. He was on *Dragnet* originally and they decided to lose him so they wrote him out by killing him off in the script. One day he and I were doing another show. We came into the lobby at CBS and he said,

"It was awful hard to get this job." We were doing a local show for almost no money. He said, "Since I left *Dragnet*, I haven't had a running part in anything. It makes it really tough." As we walked out into the lobby, there was Gisele Mackenzie. That name rings a bell?

JASON: Gisele was on many shows including *Your Hit Parade*.

JERRY: That's right. She was out in the hall. She was doing a show down the way in another studio. She looked at us and we knew her, of course. At least I knew her and she knew me. She looked at Barney and said, "I thought you were dead!" He said, "No, no, not really, that was only in the script I did." She said, "Oh, so glad to hear that you're still alive." He said, "It's not doing me any good because I'm not working much." We were going up to the Brown Derby to have lunch and as we walked up the street I said, "You know, maybe a lot of people think you're dead. Why don't you take an ad in *Variety*? Take a full page and have your picture in it and say, 'I'm still alive'." So he spent $100, which was all it cost at that time to get a full page with his picture on it. Immediately, his career came back to life. So that was one of those lucky things.

JASON: What's the old line they say about actors? They pick up the morning paper to see if their name is in the obituaries. If it isn't, they eat breakfast and go to work.

JERRY: That's what they say.

JASON: Well, Jerry, I would say your recall is pretty total when it comes to your career.

JERRY: I'm sorry I don't have any written notes here to keep the chronology straight. I've been skipping all over the place. I'm sure I left something out.

****

My response to that last statement would have to be, not very much. Jerry pretty much covered all of the bases along with some interesting trivia that I had no clue of. He always treated everyone as a dear friend and because of that, he was very well liked in the Hollywood community.

I have to add a small personal note to all of this. When we finished the interview we got to talking about our own backgrounds away from the business. It turned out that he was in the process of organizing a tour of Germany for a travel company and when he found out that I had some history of my own in Germany; he invited me to join him on that excursion, free of charge. Now, Jerry didn't know me from Adam, but his offer was just an indication of his true personality. Unfortunately, I could not go, but I was touched by his invitation.

Jerry died in 1993, leaving behind many, many people who will sorely miss him. I'm one of those.

Act IV: More Men of Music

In Volume One we heard from four people who were deep in the musical world, each from a different perspective. Now it is time to introduce you to three more. In each case, the person in question was known for areas removed from the musical genre, but deep down, they were all entrenched in that performing art.

Once again we will go in three diverse directions to present the views of three talented experts of that sort of endeavor. We will hear first from another leader from the Swing Era who may be better remembered for other things than his band. Next, one of the giants of ballads and folk music, and finally, a man who's abilities took him all over the world of show business. For all three, music was a driving factor in their lives.

These are not hidden virtuosos. You will know them all well at the first mention of their names, so let us get started down this marvelous highway of melody.

ACT IV:
SCENE ONE
PHILLY AND ALICE

You may think of comedy when this man is introduced, but his roots and his original fame came out of the Big Band Era. During that time he was also fortunate enough to meet and wed one of that time's biggest stars on the Hollywood scene. She was the top box office draw for several years until she decided to end her picture days over a dispute with Darryl Zanuck. Their marriage lasted fifty-four years until his death in 1995, once again, a tribute to long term pairings in a place where we hear so much about quick divorces. They had each had unfortunately short first marriages, but once they got together they stayed together on the second try.

The gorgeous lady that I am referring to was Alice Faye and her lucky husband was, as I am sure you know, Phil Harris. On February 27, 1987 Phil and I had this chat.

****

PHIL: It's nice to be on with you, Jason. My father used to play Madison, Wisconsin years ago when they used to go in with a show under canvas, in the tent business, you know.

JASON: You were more or less from this area. You were born in Southern Indiana, in Linton, South of Terre Haute, but your career seems to have started in San Francisco in the Big Band business. How did that huge move take place? How did it come about?

PHIL: My father was in circuses. He was with Hackenbach & Wallace. He was with Ringling Brothers and he was with Sal Flutto. So I was practically raised by my grandmother and grandfather because my mother traveled with the show. Later on my father got a job with the orchestra in a theatre in Nashville, Tennessee so I moved to Nashville when I was about eleven years old. While I was there going to school we organized a Dixieland Band. Some people from Honolulu heard us. They were opening a new theatre in Honolulu so we went over there to open the new Princess Theatre in Hawaii. I spent a year there. The rest of the guys went back home to go to school. I only got to the first year of high school. From there I went to San Francisco. I stayed in San Francisco where I was a side man with two or three of the big bands on the coast. I later—it's kind of a long story. A fellow came over from Australia to pick four musicians to go over there and augment a big band at Luna Park in Melbourne. We were all friends, but we were working in different spots, Frank Remley, Carol Lofner, a guy named Chuck Moh and myself. This guy picked us up to go to Australia. So we went to Australia and augmented with the band. We took a bunch of arrangements. It turned out very well. We stayed there for a year. When we came back the others all went back to Nashville, but I stayed in San Francisco. Then later on I played with quite a few big bands, Henry Halstead, Glen Oswald Serenaders, who were making time on the coast. Then Lofner started a band down at Balboa, down near Santa Monica, down that way, a little farther. He called me and said, "Do you want to go to work?" He had Chuck Moh. We had Frank Remley—the same group. I went down and joined them and that later became the Lofner-Harris Band. In 1929 we opened the St. Francis Hotel in San Francisco. We stayed there

|||through '29, '30 and '31. Then they came to me and wanted me to take my own band into the Coconut Grove. In '32 I left Lofner at the St. Francis with a group. I took part of the band and augmented it with some fine musicians in Los Angeles. I followed Gus Arnheim and The Rhythm Boys. That's the way I got started with my own band.

JASON: One of those early sidemen who played violin and guitar and was a great whistler was Muzzy Marcellino.

PHIL: I found him at the Galileo High School in San Francisco. When I left San Francisco to come down and start my own band at the Coconut Grove, I left Muzzy with Lofner in Frisco.

JASON: And then he moved on to be with Ted Fio Rito before he started his own band.

PHIL: Muzzy's a good boy.

JASON: You had another musician with you who later went off on his own, and very successfully, Xavier Cugat. He also played violin.

PHIL: Yep, Cugat was working with Anson Weeks at the Mark Hopkins in San Francisco until I brought him down. He was playing fourth fiddle with me. I had a full string section. I mean four violins and a viola or something at the Grove. They never allowed acts at the Grove. They might have a dance team once in a while, The DeMarcos or somebody, but they did have a rumba and tango band that alternated sets with us. In those days the rumba was very popular. So when I heard the rumba—I can't remember the guy's name—he should have been the rumba king. He kind of gave it up and Cugat came to me and said, "Can you fix it so I can put my rumba band in those spots?" I said, "Yes", and that was the way he got started. As you know, he became a tremendous hit all over the world.

JASON: I believe the name of the man he followed was Carlos Molina, right?

PHIL: Carlos is correct.

JASON: You mentioned Frank Remley. He was with you a long time and became a celebrity in his own right, but we'll get back to Frankie a little later. You had some other people with you who are worth mentioning, Nappy Lamar and Nick Fatool.

PHIL: I had a host of great players. I had Eddie Miller. I had Stanley Wrightsman. I had Jack Jennay. Even when I had my own house band in New York I had Goodman. I had Shaw. I had Butterfield. I had Manny Klein. I had some great, great players. I've been very fortunate. I had Bushkin. I had Buddy Cole. I've always tried to surround myself with the best.

JASON: While you were playing a gig in 1933 at the Lafayette in New York you met someone who has meant the world to you for many years.

PHIL: No, that was the Pennsylvania Roof. I followed Vallee in there.

JASON: But your first meeting with Alice Faye was kind of an inauspicious event, wasn't it?

PHIL: She was singing with Rudy when I took his place. They came up to my opening night. That's when I first met her, but I didn't see her again until, I don't know exactly, I'm bad on time, but she had a home near me in Encino. She was pretty big in pictures when I met her. She was a major star when I saw her again.

JASON: And in time you were married in 1941. By my figures that's forty-six years now.

PHIL: Forty-six years and we have two daughters, four beautiful grandchildren I'm very proud of and everything's going fine.

JASON: While you were in the band business and also later on, you got to be known for your unusual singing voice and the type of songs that you did. Your trademark song was "That's What I Like about the South." What was the origin of that little ditty?

PHIL: We were in Cincinnati. We had big books in those days. The books would be a foot thick. I never called a set set when we'd go on, like a lot of musicians did, the leaders. I'd call one tune and then while they were dancing around I'd ask the people, "What do you want to hear," because we had a tremendous catalog. You had to in those days. So, invariably, when I'd call a tune the second trumpet or somebody would lose it, couldn't find it—it's hung in there someplace. The people are standing out there on one foot, one leg, don't know what to do. So I started to have the rhythm play an eight bar turn-around. While they were playing it we started making up dirty lyrics, stuff I can't repeat on your air. It was just an eight bar play so they could kind of keep dancing. They'd be crowding around the stand. They all wanted to hear what those lyrics were, so, me coming from the South, because Linton is just about as much South as Nashville. I was eating turnip greens and corn bread and sow belly before I moved to Nashville and loving it. Anyway, I'd start making up lyrics myself and all I could think of was food. So we started fooling around with those and that's how "That's What I Like about the South" got started.

JASON: You're right. I know Southern Indiana. That's about as Southern as you can get.

PHIL: Oh yeah, they still go out on the railroad tracks and pick those dandelion greens, turnip mustard greens. Wish I could get some of them out here.

JASON: Jack Benny, when he started on the air in 1932, had a different band every year until you came along. He had George Olsen, Ted Weems, Frank Black and then Don Bester. Then along came Phil Harris. You were with him for eighteen years.

PHIL: I met Jack when I had my own radio show, my band show. I was staying at the Essex House in New York and he and Mary were living there. I met him and we became very good friends. You know, his whole thing was kidding the product. He had a program back then sponsored by Canada Dry ginger ale. They told him they didn't want him to kid the product so that didn't happen. They he went with Chevrolet and that didn't happen. Then he went with General Foods, with Jell-O. The guy used to complain about Jack kidding him about his spats, the band leader you just named, Don Bester. I'm standing next to him one time in the men's room at the hotel and he said, "I wish he'd stop talking about my spats." I said, "I wish he'd start talking about anything about me.", not knowing then that I was going to be with him. I was seventy-eight weeks on my own show and then I had the circuit. I was playing for the National Hotel chain, Ralph Hintz. I played New Orleans. I played Galveston. I played Dallas. I played Cincinnati and I played the New Yorker. So I'm on this tour of my own. I had no worries, but then my program was discontinued. Jack called me, or rather, George Burns called me. I was in New Orleans. He said, "I'd like you to work for me." They were very big on the air too, as you know. So I go to my boss. I had a contract. He said, "Certainly, Phil. I'd like to see you get it." That was Seymour Weiss, who at the time owned the Roosevelt. So I get out to California and for some reason or other, Music Corporation had booked Wayne King. So I'm without a program now and I'm without a job. Jack Benny was in town and he invited me out to the Trocadero. That was one of the top clubs on Sunset. During the course of the dinner he said, "What program are you on this year?" I said, "Well, I haven't got one. Mine's expired." He said, "Then you're with me." I just happened to be in the right spot at the right time.

JASON: Money was never an object to Jack, was it?

PHIL: Oh, no, no, no, no. Jack Benny was one of the most generous guys in the world. That's why the gag played so much. He once said to me—we were on the train, on the Chief that we used to use all the time. It was a tough ride too, two or three days. So a bunch of us, we used to sit back in the observation car and have a few belts. Then we'd go to our compartment and read or lay around because we had nowhere to go. The only place it stopped was Pasadena and then you're on the way to Chicago. I'm walking through the cars and I get a tap on my back. I turned around and Jack was there. He said, "Hey kid, you keep drinking like that and it won't be funny." You see, what he used to do was take some little thing and magnify it. He used to come to me, I don't know, maybe every two or three months. We had a manager then who was married to Mary's sister. His name was Myrt Blum. Jack used to say, "Go tell Myrt to give you some more money." I said, "Gee whiz, I've finally got a home. I'm off the road. I'm doing great and all I'm doing is saying, 'Hello Jackson, here comes Rochester'." He said, "Go ahead and ask for some more money." In the same breath he'd say. "Have you got a quarter? I want to get a couple of Robert Burns cigars." That's the kind of guy he was. I'll tell you something. He was as close to me as any man ever got. He was one of a kind. All of his people were personally contracted to him. You couldn't do another program unless he said so. He was the first—I guess the only one who did that. If you wanted Don Wilson or if you wanted Mary or you wanted Rochester or you wanted Dennis Day you had to get his permission because we were all exclusive to him. All those guys were getting very good money. Then he started some of the others like Mel Blanc and Sheldon Leonard. He put a lot of actors in business. I'll tell you something. It really busted me up when he went.

JASON: Just for fun I want to insert one of those cheap jokes from a program where you and Dennis and Jack were having lunch. You'll have to wait until the end of the bit for the quick punch line.

****

JACK: What are you going to have, Phil?

PHIL: I don't know, Jackson. What are you having?

JACK: I don't know. Oh, waiter, there's lipstick on my glass.

WAITER: There's water in it too. Wash it off.

JACK: Well! Phil, have you decided yet?

PHIL: I'll have a roast beef sandwich and a fifth of milk.

JACK: Phil, milk doesn't come in fifths.

PHIL: How do I know? It's the first time I ordered the stuff.

JACK: Dennis, Have you made up your mind yet?

DENNIS: Yeah, waiter, bring me a scoop of ice cream with a strip of bacon in it.

JACK: Dennis, ice cream with bacon? That's ridiculous. Why don't you have it with chocolate syrup?

DENNIS: Okay, waiter, bring me some bacon with chocolate syrup on it.

PHIL: Yeah, that's what I meant. What are you going to have, Jackson?

JACK: Oh, I don't know. Waiter, what would you suggest?

WAITER: How about lamb stew?

JACK: No.

WAITER: Veal cutlet?

JACK: No, I'm going home soon. I just want something to hold me together.

WAITER: How about some scotch tape?

JACK:	Just get their orders and I think of what I want. Dennis, how do you like having two shows?
DENNIS:	And I get more money too
PHIL:	Great, they just picked my and Alice's option for another thirteen weeks. Holy smoke Jackson, haven't you made up your mind yet about what you want to eat?
JACK:	How can I think when you fellows are always talking? I've got two shows! I've got two shows! I've got two shows! It's all I hear.
WAITER:	You should be happy. A lot of people are out of work.
JACK:	I haven't got two shows. They've got two shows.
WAITER:	Can I have your order—please.
JACK:	I think I'll just have a hamburger. Do you have hot chocolate?
WAITER:	No, but I'll give you a Hershey bar and a match.
JACK:	Oh, nuts!
PHIL:	I'll have that too.
JACK:	Look at that beautiful blond coming in. I'll move over. Maybe she'll sit between us. (Crash) Oops, I forgot I was sitting on the end. Help me off the floor, Phil.
PHIL:	Well, there's a switch, me picking you up.
JACK:	Look fellas, I've got to go home now. I'll see you later.

PHIL: Wait a minute, Jackson! What about the check? What about—. After eleven years you'd think I'd know better. How tight can a guy get?

****

JASON: A couple of character actors who were on that show were Artie Auerbach and Frank Nelson, who recently passed away.

PHIL: Yes, we just lost Frank, but my guy who played Remley on my program is still with us, Elliott Lewis. He's a very talented boy. I don't have to tell you that. And Sheldon Leonard was the tough guy, the tout. He went on to be very successful in the producing business.

JASON: Since you brought up your own show, *The Phil Harris/Alice Faye Show*, I think it may be appropriate to give everyone a taste of that before we move on.

****

ANNCR: Phil has decided that it's about time his children saw their daddy at work and so he and Alice are taking them to watch the band rehearsal. Now, as we look in, we find the Harris family entering NBC.

ALICE: You girls are going to be proud of your daddy when he's standing there leading his orchestra.

PHYLLIS: Does daddy have a good orchestra, mommy?

ALICE: Well . . .

PHIL: I'll answer that. Kids, your daddy's got a terrific outfit, twenty-six different kinds of instruments and I stand in front and lead then all.

Phyllis: Do you use a podium, daddy?

Phil: Naturally. I got the best podium player in the business. Hey, come on kids. We're rehearsing in this studio right here.

Alice: Phil, Do you think it's wise to take your children into your band room?

Phil: Sure, why not. I want them to see all the boys in the band.

Alice: Yes, but do you think they're old enough to stand the shock?

Phil: All right! All Right! The boys in the band are all right. They're perfect gentlemen and they have a lot of respect for me. They do just as I tell them to do. Don't worry about a thing. Come on everybody, let's go in.

SFX: (*Discordant loud mixture of instruments*)

Phil: Hold it! Hold it! And keep holding it! Keep your heads down and don't breathe. Hey fellas, come on, let's keep it down and quiet in here. I got a surprise for you guys. I want you to meet my daughters. Kind of cute, ain't they?

Arnie: Yeah, the one on the left is beautiful. Mind if I kiss her?

Phil: Go ahead, Arnie.

Arnie: Okay, pucker up, honey and I'll lay one on you.

Phil: Arnie! That one's my wife!

ARNIE: How was I supposed to know she was your wife?

PHIL: Why didn't you ask? Go back there and sit down. All right everybody, let's get ready to play. Girls, anything in particular you'd like to hear? We can play any song at all. You see, we got a big reservoir. What would you like us to play, Phyllis?

PHYLLIS: How about "Farmer in the Dell?"

PHIL: Ha, ha, ha, ha. Oh, baby, this is silly. These men are accomplished musicians. Pick out something hard.

PHYLLIS: How about Rachmaninoff's prelude in c-sharp minor?

PHIL: You heard her boys, "Farmer in the Dell."

PHYLLIS: But daddy, I said . . .

PHIL: Okay, we'll play that.

ARNIE: Play what?

PHIL: What she said. Now come on, let's play it. I'll kick it off.

****

JASON: You mentioned Frankie Remley played by Elliott Lewis. The story of how that came about is interesting.

PHIL: Frankie never talked on the Benny show, but the mention of his name always started the laughs and he was the greatest audience Benny ever had. I happened to meet him when I was going to Honolulu. These guys were playing on the boat. They had a little four piece thing. That's when I first met him. That was back in the '20s. We became friends and when we came back over here we went to Australia together. Then we came back and he was a member of the Lofner-Harris band. When I went to the Grove he went there with me. Naturally, when I went to New York he was with me and he was with me on my radio program and also when I went to the Benny program. He was with me practically all my life, a nice guy.

JASON: He was a good left-handed guitar player.

PHIL: He was all right. He was a good rhythm player. He couldn't run all over like these guys are doing now, but he was a good rhythm guitarist.

JASON: The character of Frankie became the second major role on your show with Alice. It was you and him for the bulk of each show, getting into trouble, with Alice bailing you out at the end, or trying to. Here's a cut from one of those shows where Remley was trying to be a sculpture and you were introduced to his new girlfriend and model.

****

PHIL: All right, Remley, I'm letting you use my house to do this sculpting in. Where's this model you called?

REMLEY: She'll be here soon. She's real class and she's crazy about me.

PHIL: Why? What can this dame possibly see in you, Remley? She must be after what little dough you have.

ACT IV: SCENE ONE: PHILLY AND ALICE

REMLEY: I resent that. She don't need my dough. She told me she's from a very wealthy family, but she gave it all up to be an artist, never asked for anything. Boy, you're a cold guy. The only thing she ever asked me to buy for her was a mink coat to keep her warm.

PHIL: And you bought her a mink coat just to keep her warm?

REMLEY: Not exactly. I talked her into red flannel underwear.

PHIL: Frankie, I don't know. I can't understand how you can go for a dame like that. They don't think of anything but themselves. They have—

REMLEY: Here she comes now. Come on, I can't wait to introduce you to her.

SFX: (*door opens and closes*)

CYNTHIA: Frankie!

REMLEY: Cynthia!

PHIL: Tennis anyone? Shall we have a go at it? Gad, this sounds like a weekend with no hotel room.

REMLEY: Come on in, Cynthia. I want you to meet my pal, Phil Harris. Curly, this is Miss Cavendish.

PHIL: How do you do, Miss Cavendish? I'm very happy to meet you.

CYNTHIA: How do you know? How can you say you're happy when you don't know anything about me at all and I don't know anything about you? I might decide we'll be enemies later.

PHIL: Why wait?

REMLEY: You two are going to learn to love each other.

CYNTHIA: Oh, I doubt it. I can't stand men with curly hair.

PHIL: Frankie, what's cooking here? Did somebody slip barbed wire into her corset stays?

REMLEY: You just don't understand her yet, Curly. She's really very much in love, especially with me. Watch this. Cynthia, aren't you going to kiss me hello, dearest?

CYNTHIA: You know I can't kiss. Kissing is vulgar.

PHIL: Oh, this kid's as warm as a penguin's instep.

REMLEY: I agree with Cynthia, kissing is vulgar.

PHIL: You mean that, Frankie?

REMLEY: I do.

PHIL: And you feel the same way about it, Cynthia?

CYNTHIA: I do.

PHIL: I now pronounce you man and wife. Rub noses and get lost.

****

JASON: There were others on your shows that bear mentioning.

PHIL: Of course. There was Julius Abbruzio played by Walter Tetley. He was the grocery boy. The show

ACT IV: SCENE ONE: PHILLY AND ALICE

did very well. We were on for seven years. Our ratings were good. I'm proud of that show.

JASON: Another man on your show and many, many others was Gale Gordon. He was Mr. Scott, the sponsor's representative.

PHIL: Gale was great.

JASON: And still is.

PHIL: He's a beautiful man. My God, look at all the years he spent with Lucy, and Lucy's a perfectionist. She was like a female Benny. What Jack used to do—he had an office in Beverly Hills with a big conference table. Those writers had to come in there and sit with him. I used to go in with them because Jack and I were very good friends. They'd come up with a line for me that would break the building down. Jack would say, "I can't use it. It doesn't fit his character. I've spent so much time building that character up and I'm not going to tear it down." Lucy was the same way. You'd have the toughest time in the world changing one line in the script with Lucy. You'd go through it and through it and through it. I used to go to her and say, "Do we have to read this thing four times a day?" She'd say, "That's right. Give me a few minutes." Then you'd start right over again from the top. Then on the night when you did the show you'd actually know it. You'd been through it so many times. She used to pass me in the wings and say, "Isn't it nice to know what you're doing?" On every show that she did I can guarantee that the actors didn't need the script. I had one line in there one time that I was struggling with. I was supposed to be a drunken piano player. She had a line that somebody was using for me. I was back of the bar at the piano. I couldn't get the line. It was just worded like something I would never use. I said, "Look, we're going to stop the whole works because I know I can't get that line." She said, "The night when the camera rolls you'll get it." So I told her I would gamble with her. That night I'm staring at the bar and she's got it pasted on the bar in letters about two inches high. I just read it off the bar.

JASON: Gale said pretty much the same thing about her when I talked with him last year. He said she was she's a real perfectionist, but a pleasure to work with because of it.

PHIL: One of the greatest.

JASON: Jack Benny, after the Jell-O era, went with Lucky Strikes.

PHIL: That frightened me too. That's another thing that will never happen again. That was when we were at Hollywood and Vine, while he was still on NBC. I met him in the parking lot one Sunday and he said, "We're leaving Jell-O." That was like a bomb. Jell-O was like a household word, like Pablum, everybody's got to use it. I said, "Wait a minute, Jack. Don't ever leave that. What're you going with?" He said, "I'm going with Lucky Strikes." In those days they used whoever was hot, those cigarette people. They would use you for thirteen weeks and they unload you. In other words, if you went on a cigarette program, after thirteen weeks, look out, because you're dead. I said, "Please don't do it." He said, "I have to do it." I said, "Why do you have to do it?" He said, "I can't get any more money from Jell-O. They can't make it fast enough." That's how well it was selling. Not only that, if you were to go to a movie theatre on a Sunday night,

	the manager would have to promise you he'd stop the picture and run the Benny show.
JASON:	That used to happen with *Amos and Andy* too.
PHIL:	The two of them, that's right.
JASON:	On your own show the sponsor, Rexall, never had a center commercial as such because Gale Gordon, as their rep would weave them into his part.
PHIL:	I insisted on that because I didn't want to break the thread. I said you can put a commercial at the front and you can put one on at the back, but I don't want a commercial in the middle. We'll work it like having Alice's brother going down to Rexall every once in a while. I didn't want to break the thread because we had a story show with the kids and everything. I was lucky to get by with it. I insisted on that and I still wonder today how I got away with it.
JASON:	That could never happen today.
PHIL:	No, they wouldn't let you do it today, however, we had in there where the grocery boy would stop by the Rexall store to pick up this or pick up that, but not a cold commercial because I thought you'd lose the story line. I said I'd try it and I got by with it.
JASON:	Some of those stories were really great. I remember one where Remley talked you into buying some cut rate meat, half a cow, and it ended up costing about twice as much as it would have through the normal channels.
PHIL:	We had a lot of funny shows. Connelly and Mosher started that thing. Then Ray Singer and Dick Chevillat

picked it up and did a tremendous job too. That's when Connelly and Mosher went with *Amos and Andy*. The show ran for seven years. I have all of those programs. I have a little library in my home town of Linton. We have those seven years of records of those shows. We play them once in a while, not because we were in them, but because they were good shows.

JASON: Your show was often a continuation of the Benny show and sometimes flowed out of it since you followed him on the air.

PHIL: That was another thing I insisted on because, without any problems at all, you can imagine the ratings I inherited right off. If you don't get ratings, I don't care how good your show is, you're gone.

JASON: Let's move on to Phil Harris on the big screen. There were some pictures in which you were a musician, but you were also an actor in quite a few.

PHIL: The first one was a three reel feature that won an Academy Award for Mark Sandrich. Mark is the one who became very famous with Astaire and Rogers later. I did a thing called *This is Harris*. Then after that I did a feature on a boat, *Melody Cruise*. It took me eight years to live that one down because Mark Sandrich wanted Fred Astaire, but Fred was in a Broadway play and couldn't get out of it to do the picture. My manager at the time, Mina Wallace, Mike Wallace's sister, came to me and said, "Phil, don't take it.", because I'm supposed to dance on tables and up on the wings and on the railing. That's the kind of picture it was so she said, "Not that you can't act, but this is not for you. You've got to be able to move. You've got to be able to dance. You're not a dancer." They couldn't find anybody else so Mina Wallace kept talking, kept talking. I never will forget Mark. He said, "I'm sorry. It's either you or me. I'm going to come out on this picture, but you're not." He was right. After that, *The High and the Mighty* was one of the best. I did that with John Wayne. I was nominated for an Academy Award for that. Then I did *Wheeler Dealers* with Jim Garner who is a hell of a guy. I mean that I a good way. I fooled around in pictures, but I never got to do what I actually wanted to do because they type you. In those days they made a pretty boy out of me. They always had me with lots of girls around so, like the actor says, I never got a part I could really get my teeth in. Today I'm sorry for two things. I always wanted to do a Broadway play, which I never did, and then I always wanted to do a good, solid character part in some picture, but after all, the business was good to me and I can't complain. It treated me beautifully. I've got a beautiful family. I don't have to go looking for work. I've been very fortunate. As we talk I'm sitting outside by the pool. I've got my Labrador sitting next to me. I've been throwing his ball into the pool to exercise him. You should see Palm Springs right now. The mountains are completely covered with snow. There isn't a cloud in the sky and the sun is beating my brains out sitting here right now. People ask, "To what do you attribute what success you've had?" I say it was because it was always fun for me. I looked forward to going to work. I always loved to meet the people and I loved what I was doing. That contributed a great deal to what little success I've had. Right now, when I want to get my kicks I go to New Orleans. I spend a couple of days with Pete Fountain or I go up North and get with two or three of the great players up there. I make trips out to these Jazz Festivals, Dixieland, which was my racket. I know most of the guys who are left and I enjoy myself. I enjoy what I'm doing. That's why I feel so good. That's why I'm grateful that my health is all right and that my family are all healthy. What else could you ask for? I don't have one thing to complain about. I don't have a bad day.

****

Quite obviously, Phil Harris was a very happy and contented man, taking one day at a time and making the most of each one as it came along. Here is a little side note that bears mentioning. During this whole conversation Alice Faye was also present making a few comments here and there, but she asked me not to include them in the final product so I have honored her wishes. If you were there listening with me you would have been able to hear the closeness between those two people. They seemed to be very well suited to each other.

As I mentioned at the beginning of this piece, Alice was a top box office draw for several years working mostly in musicals. Some that you might remember were *In Old Chicago, Alexander's Ragtime Band, Hello Frisco, Hello* and the original *State Fair*. Her dispute with Zanuck was over a part she did that was cut out because he wanted to promote his new protégé, Linda Darnell. She got in her car, drove off the lot and never came back. Zanuck had second thoughts, but her mind was made up so she never returned to pictures.

They are both gone now, Phil died in 1995 and Alice in 1998. He was a rare breed. No one will ever match his style.

ACT IV:
SCENE TWO
WAYFARING STRANGER

I guess I already gave away the identity of the next guest included herein. He was very much a wayfarer for many years while trying to promote what he did. Hardly anyone could see the value of his talent until he finally found his slot in show business. While he did later earn an Academy Award for his work in pictures, he is best remembered for his ability to deliver a folksy ballad. He had a tremendous repertoire of songs and could bring up any one of them at the drop of a hat. His book *Wayfaring Stranger* chronicles his early years struggling to make a name for himself when the public did not seem to be ready for him. He finally made it and we are all happy that he did.

Burl Ives is the person I am describing. On April 22, 1987 we had this talk.

****

JASON: Today I'm talking to the recipient of numerous awards in several different facets of the performing arts including a Donaldson for his work on the stage, an Oscar for his work on film and a couple of Grammy's for his music. Burl; before we explore the past let me ask you about the tour you just completed, that I understand was very successful.

BURL: Yes it was. I started this season by going to London to do a movie that will be on this fall called *Poor Little Rich Girl*, which features the great Farrah

Fawcett. I played her father, F. W. Woolworth. I enjoyed that very much. We came back, did a couple of benefits and then we went on a tour. I think we did six or seven countries. Now I'm back here, getting ready to go on vacation.

JASON: Getting ready to go to Mexico, I hear.

BURL: Yes, but then I have a thing to do for the Kennedy Center for the Arts and Education down in Orange County in their beautiful new auditorium. They're having a 'Do' down there. In about two weeks I'll have to come back from Mexico to do that.

JASON: You're the spokesman for that group?

BURL: Yes, I have been for three years.

JASON: Let's go way back to your early youth in Hunt Township, Illinois, Jasper County, near Effingham or in that general area.

BURL: It's about twenty-five or thirty miles from Effingham, about forty miles from Terre Haute and about fifty miles from Vincennes, Indiana. That about situates it.

JASON: Your singing career goes back to your roots. Your family was a singing family.

BURL: (Big laugh) I know your point. My grandmother was really the fountainhead of the folk lore that I learned.

JASON: We can't really count your first singing job as professional.

BURL: Yes we can. I got a dollar for that. Was that the

ACT IV: SCENE TWO: WAYFARING STRANGERS

Old Soldiers Reunion? I got a dollar.

JASON: The story I have is that you were promised a quarter, but you never got it.

BURL: Oh no, that is not so. I was promised a dollar and I got it. It was the first one I had ever seen.

JASON: So much for research, but you did sing "Barbara Allen", which you've sung many, many times since then?

BURL: I sing it at about every program I do.

JASON: Somewhere along the line you played professional football.

BURL: I did that in Terre Haute, Indiana. It was sort of the beginning of professional football. That was in '29, I think. What it was—was a group composed of high school and college football players that didn't want to give up the game. They got together a team in Linton, Indiana, the place where Phil Harris was born, and Indianapolis and various other places. I played on the Terre Haute team for three or four games. It was a terrible thing because the referees had no authority. There was no organization. It was really just a bunch of people from a town, like they'd pick a baseball team in the old days. They decided they were going to have a football team. That's how it started. It was called Independent Football. Each game would usually end up in a riot. It was really a dangerous place to be. After three games I said I've had it. I'm going to stick with my guitar.

JASON: Let's get into your early years and how you got into singing, of course, you always were a singer, at least in your own mind, or wanted to be. You spent a lot of years on the road.

Burl: I did a stint with a carnival, but that wasn't singing. I did it as a wrestler. That was for a couple of weeks. It was a terrible life. I appeared on individual nights at a tent show. I never was a part of the tent show *per se*. They'd have things like an amateur hour. I'd appear in those situations. I liked it very much.

Jason: Is it true that you got into some trouble for singing "Foggy, Foggy Dew" one time somewhere out west?

Burl: Yeah, I was in a park out west some years ago, in Mona, Utah and a policeman came along. He said you don't want to be around here. He let me sleep in the jail. He was very nice. The story has been sort of embellished for the writing, so I just put that in, but later, which is absolutely true, the song was banned. It was considered somewhat risqué and was sung in fraternity houses, places like that. CBS banned it and wouldn't allow me to sing it. That was in 1939, I guess. I felt terrible. Arthur Godfrey was a very powerful man in show business at the time. In the '40s and the '50s he had tremendous clout. I met him in the hall and he said, "They tell me they won't let you sing 'Foggy, Foggy Dew'." It was one of his favorite songs. I said, "That's true." He said, "I'll fix that." So he went on the air and he said, "Now I'm going to sing "Foggy, Foggy Dew." He sang one verse and then he stopped and said, "And then they wed." The objection was that there was a child born and it sort of alluded to the child being illegitimate. That was the objection. Can you imagine that with what is going on today?

Jason: No, a lot of things changed in that respect. Now

ACT IV: SCENE TWO: WAYFARING STRANGERS

some things are reversing. I'm referring to the recent FCC rulings.

BURL: I heard a song yesterday on television that astonished me.

JASON: Tell me about your first professional acting job.

BURL: Jason, that is very difficult to pinpoint. We moved into a little town of one hundred population. We were sort of isolated there because we had no roads. In the winter you couldn't get in or out because of mud holes. In that little village of one hundred population we had a theatre group. We put on plays for the people and I was in them because I was in grade school. I was always performing so I always got a part in those shows. I was acting as a child as well as singing. Then I'd go to school and I was acting in the drama things and singing and dancing, all that activity. I did it in college as well and then I stopped off in Terre Haute on my way back home from a jaunt east. I stayed in Terre Haute at a fraternity house and I got a job on the radio. That was the first truly professional job I got at WBOW.

JASON: Your career on the network must have begun in 1941 on CBS.

BURL: The first job—now I can answer you. The first job I got on radio was on NBC. There was a program with a man they called "The Hymn Singer." The reason he was on was because one of the mothers or grandmothers in the organization was partial to this man, so they put him on the air and he sang hymns. He went on vacation and I substituted for him with my guitar, singing ballads one summer. That was the first job I had on NBC. Later in the fall, Alex Lomax put on a show on CBS called *Back Where I Come From* on which were Josh White, The Golden Gate Quartet, Woody Guthrie and a whole string of ballad singers.

JASON: You did some work with a gentleman I consider to be a good friend. I talk with him with regularity, Norman Corwin.

BURL: My first acting job on the air was given to me by Norman. It was a very high class show. There's nothing like that on the air now. He did really beautiful and esoteric and meaningful programs.

JASON: I believe the one you're referring to was "The Log of R-17" from his series "26 by Corwin."

BURL: I believe it was.

JASON: A couple of years later, again with Corwin. At the time of the broadcast he was sick. This one was called "Lonesome Train" written by Earl Robinson and Millard Lampell.

BURL: Yes, yes, that was a marvelous work.

JASON: You were the narrator, the singing narrator. The show was based on the travels of Lincoln's funeral train back to Illinois where he is buried. About a year later, Eleanor Roosevelt remembered the lyrics. That was at the time when her husband Franklin died.

BURL: You know, Corwin is really an unusual, and I think, tremendously important kind of talent. When radio became mostly music and TV became the focus, I think we lost a lot of important stuff because sound does not make the mind shut down. The mind is free to go where it wants to go. The imagination of man is much greater than the eyes where the focus is what you see and so the two, what you see and hear, become one. If the mind is set free to roam you get a much greater impact. I think that's the kind of programs that Norman Corwin did. It was a cultural pity that we lost him because his most powerful medium no longer exists.

JASON: One of the greatest assets of his approach to radio was that he always had history in mind. Things that may have seemed trivial in a script at that time are very important now.

BURL: I remember once he did an absolutely beautiful program from the Bible, "The Story of Esther." Oh, my goodness! That Esther was so—well, talk about color, that program had color. Your eyes saw the color of that program and it was light purple. (Laugh) That's crazy! I would like to see a revival of a few hours a week, an hour or two a day, to the kind of attention that those programs, the serious programs on CBS, brought to us. There was also a lady by the name of Nila Mack who came out of vaudeville and did some remarkable children's programming on the radio.

JASON: Let's talk about your movie career. You've done some very big ones and a couple of them that I'm not too familiar with, but you reached the top of the acting business when you were awarded an Oscar for your role in *Big Country* in 1958.

BURL: Like all good westerns it was built on the business of the cattle or sheep controversy and water access. Those are the basic elements of the western story, or bad guys against good guys. That was a very fine script. We had certainly one, if not the greatest director I ever worked for, William Wyler.

JASON: Your co-stars in that one were Gregory Peck, Charlton Heston, Jean Simmons, Carol Baker and Charles Bickford, but it was Burl Ives who walked off with the Academy Award.

BURL: Well, I guess I was lucky.

JASON: Earlier on you worked with a well remembered actor who only did three major roles before he was killed in a tragic car accident. I'm speaking of James Dean and the picture you had in common was *East of Eden*.

BURL: There was a part of that film where Raymond Massey asked James Dean to read from the scripture. Now, Massey was a fine gentleman from the old school. When I say old school I do mean OLD school! He was an aristocrat from Canada. He had the finest schooling. He was a wonderful man. James Dean was not out of his quality. He was from the generation that was kicking their heels up. This was an immovable object hitting up against this flashy satellite. So Elia Kazan, who was another great director, said to me, "Do you think I could get Massey angry?" I said, "I suppose you could." He said, "How would you do it?" I said, "You have two opposite elements here. You don't have to do much to get it going." Jimmy Dean pretended to be completely undisciplined, but he wasn't. That was part of the rebel influence in his life and the thing that he sort of created around himself. So what happened was, Kazan went to Dean and said, "Now, I want you, when he tells you to read from the Bible, I want you to needle him. See if you can get him mad, but don't tell him what you're doing." So James Dean started playing the scene and he began to use—you know those seven words that aren't supposed to be used now—well, he used them all as he read the scripture. I thought Massey would blow up. We could see he was just fuming. Elia was shooting while all this was going on. Finally Massey stood up and said, "I shall go no further with this scene!" It was terrible. He really gave a speech. As he walked off the set he muttered, "Language like that before ladies and gentlemen." He just walked off the set, but Kazan got what he wanted.

JASON: I remember that scene well. Dean would read a verse and then say, with a vengeance, "Selah." You could watch Raymond Massey start to boil. So it wasn't just acting, it was real? I assume they cleaned it up for the final print.

BURL: Oh yes, it was real. Dean was picking on him.

JASON: Another character you played in 1958 was Big Daddy Pollitt. I enjoyed that picture. It was *Cat on a Hot Tin Roof* with Liz Taylor and Paul Newman.

BURL: That was at a time when Elizabeth Taylor had just lost her husband, Mike Todd, in a plane crash. She was very upset at the time, but she did her job in spite of it. I admired her for that. She's a lady with a great deal of steel in her spine. She performed very well under very tough circumstances. Paul, of course, is a sweetheart.

JASON: He is exactly what he seems to be, isn't he?

BURL: Yeah, that's the way Paul is. He's all there. He's steady, just like his driving. I do have a story to tell you. This takes in James Dean. I was at some kind of a party where there were several people from the cast of *East of Eden*, okay? Jimmy was sort of holding forth as the focus of attention because he was interested in race cars and was going to buy one. I was introduced to a young man who sat sort of back from the circle, a very handsome young man who was doing a film at Warner Brothers, some religious film. I don't think he liked it. That's where I met him. He was there and we were all listening to James Dean expounding on this racing car. Here was this quiet, handsome young gentleman listening. He was Paul Newman. Later on, I thought how unusual it is that that scene comes back to me because Paul has become a champion in that field and is very much respected by all the great drivers. That is quite a feather in the hat of an actor who got into racing at the age of forty. I always wonder if that day, listening to James Dean, had anything to do with it.

JASON: That's a good point. We always think of James Dean as young because he died so young, but we forget that Paul wasn't much older than Dean at that time. I think the religious picture we're referring to was Paul's first flick, *The Silver Chalice*. He's still very much with us now.

BURL: He's still the same in most ways. Of course he's matured, but I think he's even more handsome than he was and certainly more effective. He's grown into a wonderful actor. He should have had that prize many, many years ago, but those things are funny. They didn't give one to Bogart for a long time either. When he finally thought he was going to get it, Bogart said, "If they give it to me I'm going to make one statement. It's about time!" But he didn't. He did like everybody else when he won.

JASON: I want to bring up one more picture. Then we'll move on to some other facets of your career. A gentleman who just recently passed away was in this one with you. He was Rock Hudson. The movie was *The Spiral Road*. You were a kind of crusty old doctor in the jungle. I saw it again not long ago on late night TV.

BURL: I'm glad you did because that was a good film. I enjoyed playing that old doctor and I enjoyed working with Rock Hudson. I thought he did a great job in that picture. His reviews said he didn't cut it, but I thought he did. His performance was excellent. That was the first time he got a role with a little meat on it. I don't think the critics like it when you step out of bounds until you do, away from the sort of parts you've been playing, then when you do they have to accept it, which they often don't.

JASON: There's a phase of your career that many people are not aware of, because it is more of a local type of audience thing. I'm referring to Broadway and regional stage performances going all the way back to '33 and *The Boys from Syracuse*.

BURL: I had tried out for another show. I had failed to get it. I was down to my last dollar at that time. I took that dollar and took a ride to Central Park. I got out and sat down of a bench. I was flat broke. Some guy came along that I knew. He said, "I'm going to a chorus call. Why don't you come along?" I said, "Where?" He said, "At the Alden Theatre. They're doing *The Boys from Syracuse*." I said okay, picked up my guitar and went with him. It was the end of the audition. This friend of mine said, "There's a guy here with a guitar. Would you like to hear him?" He said that to the people out front doing the audition, who were Richard Rodgers and Lorenz Hart, George Abbott and Ezra Stone. They said, Okay, let him come out." I came out and sang one song. They liked it and wrote the part of a tailor's apprentice for *The Boys from Syracuse*.

JASON: You won a Donaldson for your role in *Sing Out, Sweet Land*. I don't know what a Donaldson is.

BURL: At that time they gave out a plaque for best performance in a musical. I don't know much about it myself except that I won one. I think it's still in existence.

JASON: You did quite a bit of work on Broadway and across the country on the stage. You did Big Daddy in *Cat on a Hot Tin Roof* before it was on film. You also did Captain Andy in *Showboat*.

BURL: I did fourteen months of Big Daddy at the Morosco Theatre.

JASON: The first thing most of us think of when we hear your name is "The Wayfaring Stranger," in other words, you're singing.

BURL: That was the first thing I did on television. I got a job at CBS after *Sing Out, Sweet Land*. I was one of those sustaining artists. I was on at six in the morning and nine at night plus two in the afternoon. When ever they needed my I was the fill, which was a very good thing for me. I didn't realize it at the time, but I had a different audience each time. They'd hear me and then try to find me. I was coming on at various times each day, each with a different audience, which was good for me.

JASON: You cut so many, many albums.

BURL: I had a certain number of ballads and folk songs, but when you sign a contract to do two albums a year, you run out of material. Then you've got to start doing something else, so they sent me to Nashville and I did all kinds of different things. I didn't have enough ballads.

JASON: You've done Australian folk songs. You've done Irish folk songs. You've done at least a couple of Christmas albums.

BURL: And a lot of hymns.

JASON: Yes, and you also did an album with the Korean Orphans Choir.

BURL: Oh yeah, I enjoyed that tremendously. Those kids were just wonderful. Incidentally, I ran into a couple of those kids recently, both in one town, I can't remember where. They came back and they are now music teachers in schools.

JASON: You've written and published a number of books. Some of them were song books. You also wrote an autobiography about the early part of your life, published way back in 1948 called, naturally, *Wayfaring Stranger*. Another one was called *Wayfarer's Notebook* which sounds like it too could be autobiographical.

BURL: *Wayfarer's Notebook* was not an autobiography. The idea of it was to present literature that I liked. It's an omnibus kind of thing. It was a nice book. It was well received critically, but it didn't sell very well. It was my pick of things that I enjoyed. I'm not a book reader. I'm a dabbler. I pick up a book and read a little bit here and a little bit there. I wrote the introductions and the comments afterwards.

Jason: What was *Albad, the Oaf?* It sounds like a children's book.

Burl: *Albad, the Oaf,* yeah. That was basically Albert Haig, who is now famous as an actor, and I. I wrote the story, the libretto, and he put the music to it. It was originally a children's opera which Margo Jones in Dallas was thinking of doing. It never got off the ground. Later I turned it into a children's story.

Jason: Well, Burl, I'd like to go on all day. There're so many things we missed, but the clock says no.

Burl: I could tell you stories for years, Jason. Please give my best to Norman Corwin when you talk to him again.

****

There is little doubt that Burl could have gone on. As is the case with many folk and ballad singers, they can be fantastic storytellers. After all, isn't that what that form of music is in essence, a story to be told? I just wish there was room here to include all that he told me after we exhausted our radio time, but continued our conversation. He was in no hurry to say goodbye.

Folk songs, Sea Shanties, Ballads, Hymns, Christmas Songs, and Children's Music, all of those and more were part of his catalog. He spoke of running out of inventory, but when that appeared to be happening he left no stone unturned looking for more songs and more diversity all over the world. He had a few top ten hit singles and he recorded many, many albums, ninety-three of them to be exact. His work on the stage spanned over thirty years. He did twenty-seven movies. He was very much in evidence in the '40s and the '50s on radio, including six shows for Norman Corwin on "The Columbia Workshop" and "Columbia Presents Corwin." On television, among his many performances were *Miracle Worker* and a much later one called *Caravan of Courage: An Ewok Adventure.* He did concerts around the globe and was still doing them when we did this interview.

All in all, you would have to concede that he was a busy, busy man.

The one major downer during his career was in the 1950s when he was named in the egregious yellow sheet, *Red Channels* as a suspected communist. He was no more a communist that Mickey Mouse, but all it took, to be accused in those trying days, was to have a little pity for the refugees of World War II. The Black List was a horrible thing and it destroyed those not strong enough to fight its damage. Burl did overcome.

He died in 1995 due to complications of mouth cancer and is buried in his native Hunt City Township in southeastern Illinois.

ACT IV:
SCENE THREE
SOUTH RAMPART STREET PARADE

When you see that classic Dixieland song title it is not likely that you would immediately think of the humorous, but also very deep man who is the subject of this segment. He not only wrote the lyrics for "South Rampart Street Parade," he also wrote over 8500 other songs. That certainly qualifies him to fit into the group that makes up Act IV of this book.

He is best remembered for his years on television, but as you will soon see, that is not what he was doing at the time of our discussion back on June 22, 1987. Here is what Steve Allen had to say about many things when I caught up with him at his hotel in New York. He was on a very tight schedule, but he was so easy to interview that he got a great deal of information out without my having to cut and paste to assemble it. What you will read is almost the entirety of our conversation from end to end with no need for editing. In that respect, he kind of took the fun out of my task.

****

JASON: *I live with eight men, a published writer of earthy prose and poetry, a deep thinker, a comedian, a pianist, a composer, a crusader, a motion picture star and a tender father.* That statement was made by Jayne Meadows, who for the last thirty-three years has been happily married to my guest, Steve Allen.

STEVE: Jayne did say that, didn't she? How nice.

JASON: For all you've done through the years, I find it interesting that what you're doing now is a throwback to your beginnings when you first started on the media. You're back to working on radio now.

STEVE: Yes and it's almost eerie in that the same process of evolution is taking place. By that I mean that back in '48 after I'd been doing comedy for some time I took a job on a radio show playing records. Within a few weeks I had gotten rid of most of the records and turned it into a comedy show. That again is happening now. About six months ago I started to do, along with my TV work, a program that had been called *Make-Believe Ballroom* for many years. On my first day on the job I did a four hour tribute to Jerome Kern with a great deal of music, obviously. Now we play scarcely any music and many days, none at all. It's about 98% comedy now.

JASON: *Make-Believe Ballroom* goes all the way back to 1935. Has it been continuous through all those years until now?

STEVE: The fellow who actually started the show with that name—the program was no different than 47,000 other record shows. It was just a guy saying, "And now here's Frank Sinatra doing 'Stardust'." The name was created, as far as I know, by a fellow named Al Jarvis, a Los Angeles disc jockey. Then it was copied by a New York disc jockey named Martin Block. He did it for quite a few years and then a fellow named William B. Williams did it for thirty years or more. He, unfortunately, died several months back. For now they've stopped using that title because we're not playing records. Now they're just calling it *The Steve Allen Show*.

JASON: Steve, early on you did a talk show out in Los

ACT IV: SCENE THREE: SOUTH RAMPART STREET PARADE | 175

	Angeles, or I should say, a music show that turned into a talk show. That was on KMX, right?
STEVE:	Correct, yes.
JASON:	And that would have been the real beginning of your career after a couple of years in Phoenix or maybe less than that.
STEVE:	There were a number of other things. I had already done a coast to coast radio show, a comedy show for two years called *Smile Time*, those two years being 1946 and 1947. That was after the Phoenix thing. I had been working for the CBS station there.
JASON:	In 1949 you were doing a show called *Earn Your Vacation*. I must confess that I don't know anything about that one.
STEVE:	It was rather like *You Bet Your Life* that Groucho later did. In fact it was done by the same production people. I was sort of playing the utility infielder position for CBS radio in those days, doing programs of various sorts in addition to my regular nightly show.
JASON:	Actually, your early radio career wasn't long prior to television for you because of the timing.
STEVE:	That's right. I worked on radio for about seven years. Then in about 1950 or '51 I moved on to TV.
JASON:	You were the host on many early television shows and a panelist on a couple of others, but the big one was *The Steve Allen Show*, with a lot of people we all know. The one prior to that was *The Tonight Show*. Many of the people who got their start on that show are big names today.

STEVE: Some of them worked with me on *The Tonight Show* and then, quite a long list, worked with me on the Sunday night show. Both of those shows were at NBC.

JASON: We're talking about Don Knotts and Louis Nye and that group.

STEVE: Wonderful gang of funny people.

JASON: Speaking of funny, I have your latest book, *How to be Funny*, which was kindly sent to me by your agent in L.A. I'm about half way through it and my cohorts here tell me that I haven't gotten very funny yet. Maybe when I finish it?

STEVE: You never know. It could happen at any minute.

JASON: I like the way it's written. You wrote it like a school text with assignments at the end of each chapter.

STEVE: It has something of the text book structure to it, although much less formal than a traditional text book. It does, as you've already noted, reveal a lot of the tricks of the trade of joke writing and joke delivery and sketch construction, that sort of thing.

JASON: You're known as a great ad-libber and there's no question of the truth of that. I'm just wondering who might have influenced you most as a comedian when you were very young.

STEVE: I suppose it would have to be my mother. She was a professional vaudeville comedienne, who Milton Berle was kind enough to refer to as the funniest woman in vaudeville. Actually, she wasn't any different on stage than she was off. That was the normal mode of discourse in her family and since I grew up in that family, my father having died when I was an infant, I just talked the way the Donohue's talked. Years later I was very surprised to find out that I could make a living that way.

JASON: You wrote a play for Broadway called *The Wake*. I know it was semi-autobiographical. Would that have had anything to do with your Uncle Steve, Steve?

STEVE: I did a play on Broadway called *The Pink Elephant*. I just appeared in that. *The Wake*, while it was written and produced for Broadway, hasn't yet been seen in New York City. It was produced as a play and also published as a novel. It is very largely autobiographical. All of the characters, with one exception, are actual members of my mother's family. It's the story of what happened one day in the lives of this particular family at the wake. That's when they hang around the body in the living room and shed a few tears, have a few laughs and quite a few arguments. It's a typical story of what happened in an Irish family of the 1930s.

JASON: You referred to your show on KMX and the fact that you did music in the beginning with some talk and then it became mostly all talk. I believe something else came out of that because of one occasion when Doris Day was to be a guest and at the last minute couldn't keep the date.

STEVE: That was a very significant breakthrough and like most breakthroughs in the field of science or the arts it was just totally a matter of happenstance. Before that I had done the traditional thing in radio comedy. First you wrote a script. Then you held it in your hands and sat next to a microphone and read the funniness off the paper. That's how all those great shows, you know, Benny and Hope etc., were done. I worked mostly in that way too on the program we were talking about. Then one night, Doris Day, my would-be guest, didn't show up. They had forgotten to tell her about it, I later learned. So I was on the air live and faced with about thirty minutes of dead air. I had already used up the few pages of written material I had prepared for the evening. The only thing I could think of to do was to grab one of those big, heavy stand-up microphones and lug it around the audience. Fortunately, I got more laughs doing that than I had ever before with the written stuff, just ad-libbing of course. I had nothing prepared. I soon realized that I had stumbled onto something very effectual. As I said earlier, I didn't realize you could make a living just talking the way my family had, but that's what I was doing with the audience. I've done that sort of thing ever since, working studio audiences, that is.

JASON: Your many books cover a wide range of subjects. You're obviously much more than a comedian. Everyone should know that, but if they don't I think we should go over some of the things you've written about. You wrote a book about the migrant workers.

STEVE: Farm workers, yes.

JASON: Right, it was called *The Ground is Our Table*. I will get it and read it.

STEVE: Back in 1952 I had seen a television documentary written and narrated by Edward R. Murrow who perhaps, eighteen year old people today should be told, was one of the best things about early television. He was with CBS, a newsman. I was angered by the show because it revealed, first of all, the dreadful injustice and the conditions under which most American farm workers lived in those days. That was the early '50s. And secondly, I was angry at my own ignorance. Until that night I'd never even known of the existence of that problem so that started my interest in it. My book was published some years later in 1966.

JASON: The Murrow piece was *Harvest of Shame*.

STEVE: Exactly, a really fine think piece.

JASON: You wandered about quite a bit in your youth, but you grew up mainly in Chicago.

STEVE: That's about as close to a home town as I have. I was born in New York City. I have lived in New York and Chicago and Des Moines and Phoenix and Los Angeles.

JASON: You've also done books on subjects like China and of course, you documented in print your series that you did for Public Television a few years back called "Meeting of the Minds." That was an extremely intelligent series and also very educational for anyone not too familiar with many of the great, and some not so great, people in history. It was a series that you wrote and produced and hosted. Of the people who appeared on those shows, I think the most consistent name was Mrs. Allen, Jayne Meadows.

STEVE: I offered Jayne all of the women's roles. She turned me down on three of them, but she did play all of the other parts. It's hard to remember all of the people she played from history. Some of them were Cleopatra, Marie Antoinette, Susan B. Anthony, Florence Nightingale, Elizabeth Barrett Browning, Margaret Sanger and Catherine the Great of Russia.

JASON: I think that may be all of them.

STEVE: I believe so.

JASON: You wrote somewhere in the neighborhood of 8000 songs over the past thirty years or so.

STEVE: Longer than that because I started as a child, but yes, several thousand songs.

JASON: I'm going to surprise you because I have my own favorite Steve Allen song one that not too many people have ever heard or even heard of, which I find unfortunate.

STEVE: I hope I remember it.

JASON: I'm sure you will. It was from a show that was on Broadway for just a quick wink based on Sophie Tucker. The song is "I Love You Today."

STEVE: Oh, thank you. Yes, I do recall it well. There've been a number of lovely recordings of that song. Those who write music for shows, Broadway and other productions of musicals, enjoy an advantage over the guys who write the books, in fact, all of the other participants. Even the major musical writers of the century, Cole Porter, Irving Berlin and those fellows, have had their share of shows that were not successful, but they didn't really matter as much as the success of the songs. Some of the greatest songs of all time have come out of shows that closed on the road before they even reached the major markets. It is a very fortunate thing for me that a number of the songs from Sophie have been recorded by a number of people.

JASON: I was introduced to that song by a very beautiful

young lady who came into my recording studio a few years ago to cut an audition tape. That was her feature song and I must say she did it justice. Another person who played it every time I went to see him at his piano bar on Rush Street in Chicago was Les Tucker. You probably never heard of him, but he was a fixture there for years and he told me it was one of his favorites as well. He won over a lot of his regulars to it. Just a few of your other well-known songs were "Impossible," "Pretend You Don't See Her," "The Theme from Picnic," and one that I didn't realize was yours, "South Rampart Street Parade."

STEVE: I wrote the lyric for that in 1952, I think it was.

JASON: And "Gravy Waltz," of course. I won't go through a list. We don't have that much time. You worked with someone on *I've Got a Secret* whom I spoke with in the recent past. He had nothing but good things to say about your ability to ad-lib and he was certainly your match in that area. That was Henry Morgan.

STEVE: Henry was a guest recently on my radio show, very funny, very witty fellow.

JASON: He hasn't lost any of his edge.

STEVE: No, he was just as amusing when he was on with us a few weeks ago as he was thirty years earlier.

JASON: Rather than have me ask all of the questions, is there any other area that you'd like to talk about that I may miss?

STEVE: One of the odd things I find—I should mention that *How to be Funny* is my twenty-eighth book so

I'm often interviewed about the various books I've written. It's expected these days, especially if you're a public figure that you will take part in the promotion and publicizing of your words. Publishers are constantly trying to get writers on the various TV talk shows and that sort of thing. One of the oddest questions that's ever put to writers is this, "Say, I've heard about your new book, heard you talking about it on *The Today Show* or *The Tonight Show*. Where can I get a copy of that book?" I never understood that question. I have various stock and allegedly funny answers like, "I know this is going to sound like the craziest suggestion in the world, but you might just try, on the outside chance, try a book store. I wouldn't waste too much time at Midas Muffler or your neighborhood meat market because they may be out of copies right now, but a book store could possibly have it." Kind of a sarcastic way of making a point. I don't know why people wonder where they would buy books. Where would you go?

JASON: You don't really want me to answer that, I'm sure. I think one of your first books was *Bop Fables*.

STEVE: It was indeed. That came out in the early '50s.

JASON: The reason I brought that up is because, not too long ago, you released a recording of *More Bop Fables*.

STEVE: They first came out in recorded form in the early '50s and then, a couple or three years ago they were recorded in different form. I recorded some of them in the old days, but recently with a fellow named Jazbo Collins—He and I got together and did the stuff over, but this time we had Slim Gaylord, the great bass player and jazz entertainer and singer, do an alleged translation in double talk Spanish.

	There was an added layer of craziness in that version and they did come out about three years ago.
JASON:	Ala Jose Jimenez, Bill Dana.
STEVE:	Well, not quite, but it was funny.
JASON:	Everyone knows you play piano, jazz piano or pop piano, whatever style you choose at a given time. I don't know how many people know about all of the other instruments you play. In *The Benny Goodman Story* on the big screen you played Benny and did some clarinet work. How well were you trained for that? I know that you did some work with Paul Yagatti for that.
STEVE:	I never played the instrument before I did the picture. I had to take some formal instruction in it, so that I could play it. The playing was obviously done by Benny himself. The music in musicals is pre-recorded. When you think you're seeing Bing Crosby sing, you aren't. He sang it three weeks earlier so he's just moving his lips in synchronization with his earlier recording. So, as I say, Benny did the playing. There was one scene where I did play, when Benny was nine years old and he was practicing his scales on his first instrument. Benny himself was not able to make the mistakes that a beginner makes. I was just starting to learn clarinet at the time so when you're hearing Benny at nine you're actually hearing me doing pre-recorded scales. I later learned, not to fool people, to play a few little things, but I still haven't gotten down with the instrument. It's very demanding. It's not as easy as some others.
JASON:	Does that go for the sax and the other reeds? They probably use similar fingering.

STEVE: The saxophone is easier to play than the clarinet. I'm not sure why it is as difficult as it is. It's a lot of fun to play and a great jazz instrument in the hands of the right players, but the number of good saxophone players is much, much larger than clarinet jazz players. There have never been very many statistically.

JASON: That was probably the one movie that people remember with you playing a starring role.

STEVE: Yes, I'm sure.

JASON: You did some others as well.

STEVE: Not terribly many. Most of us who worked on television for thirty or forty years concentrated on that. It's possible to write a song in your car or a short story at night at home, but you can't really have a television career and a movie career at the same time.

JASON: That brings up another point. You write your songs just about anywhere and everywhere, don't you?

STEVE: Yes, anywhere my brain happens to be at the moment. They all come out of that source so it doesn't matter at all where I am. It's more convenient if I have access to a piano at those moments because I immediately record the songs on tape. If I don't quickly record them I can't remember them just a few minutes later.

JASON: But you have tape recorders just about everywhere you go.

STEVE: I have a little pocket size machine that I carry with me for word dictation. What I do when a song occurs to me, let's say on an airplane where I have no piano, I will make up what is called a dummy lyric and at least for a week or so that dummy lyric will enable me to recall the melody. If much more time than that passes, not even a dummy lyric is of much help. I've probably forgotten at least 150 songs through the years. They felt great at ten in the morning, but an hour later I couldn't remember them at all because I had maybe a dead battery in my tape machine and no piano at the moment.

JASON: I think the most amazing part of all this is the fact that you've written enough songs to be in *The Guinness Book of Records* for that accomplishment and most of them are good ones. I'm sure that some of them weren't, but who's counting? You don't read music, do you?

STEVE: No, I'm music illiterate. So is Earl Garner who wrote "Misty." There's no necessary connection whatever between the gift of composition on one hand and the ability to read on the other. That applies to both composing and playing. Art Tatum was the king of the piano, but he was blind and obviously couldn't read music. George Shearing was another blind virtuoso.

JASON: Did you ever play any of the jazz houses in Chicago that I knew so well? I'm thinking of The Blue Note and The Brass Rail and a few others.

STEVE: I played The London House on one or two occasions. I should remember if I played the other jazz clubs there. I played quite a number of them around the country. At the moment I don't recall what other Chicago clubs I played.

JASON: The one connected with The London House was Mr. Kelly's which is no longer there.

STEVE: Right.

JASON: Why do you think comedy is such a hot item these days? Why is it doing so well?

STEVE: I think the answer to that is certainly obvious, but there's some little mysterious part of it that isn't exactly clear, which is the way it is. The obvious part has to do with the fact that today's generation is the first generation in the history of the world that has been brainwashed by comedy since infancy. In earlier days, through most of history, there was no such thing at all in terms of public art. Even going back to the '30s, '40s and '50s you could maybe go to a comedy night club or see three or four comedy movies or maybe you'd hear comedy on the radio, but you weren't brainwashed with it morning, noon and night. Today's generation has had that since infancy. So if anyone has some natural talent or eccentricity or funny teeth it enables them to get easy laughs. They have a tendency to gravitate toward that as we might gravitate towards Basketball or car repair or some other field. Then they see this constant example and they are instructed by that example. There are so many easy avenues of employment. There are scores, hundreds I guess, of comedy clubs all over the country, even sometimes in relatively small communities, so it's easy to get work. In some ways it's the equivalent to the vaudeville circuits of the '20s and '30s. There are a great many of these and they concentrate exclusively on comedy. The young people who perform there sit back and have a beer and watch each other so they can learn from each other. There's an audience now. Not only do we have the performers, but we have a generation that itself may not be specifically interested in performing comedy, but like to see it. There's an audience for comedy albums, comedy films and comedy TV concerts.

JASON: There's so much comedy these days that we really don't need to hear and I really don't know why it appeals to anyone. I'm thinking of a recent special on one of the cable networks and I won't mention any names. It was nothing but foul language and racial slurs from end to end. I see no logical reason for that. I turned it off and went back several times to see if someone truly funny was coming on, but it didn't happen.

STEVE: I deplore that. I have not yet heard from anybody who, when that stuff comes on says, "Well, you folks can sue me, but I love filth." I never heard anyone say that. Everybody seems to ignore it so I guess the question is who are these idiots who are laughing at it? I think it's disgusting, but some very funny people do it. You might say some of them are no talents who can't get a laugh any other way, but that's not true. Some of them are major talents like Eddie Murphy, Richard Pryor and Buddy Hackett. There are people who specialize in filth. I guess they can always find an audience, but somebody ought to tell them that most people don't like that. It has nothing to do with the times. There were old time comics who worked dirty and recent comics who work clean. I think Steven Wright is one of the cleverest of the new comedians, those who came on the scene in the last six or seven years. He never does dirty jokes, but he sure is funny.

JASON: I think a part of the problem, especially in live situations, is mob influence. The comedian throws off a punch line and then waits for a laugh. Someone starts it and before long many others join in. Pretty soon most of the audience is laughing and many of them don't know why. It's almost like they're afraid not to react when people around them are laughing.

STEVE: That's true. If you're in a club and 30% of the people who are laughing find a joke personally repugnant you'll probably go along and laugh because it's perfectly possible for a given joke to be utterly filthy and yet very funny. You can't say that something is disgusting and therefore, under no circumstances, is funny. Sometimes it ain't. Sometimes it is. It's one more sign of the deterioration of our entire culture, our entire civilization. There are a lot of bad things statistically along with the problems that brought us to this point. We were talking earlier about the show about when Fred Astaire died. I had no idea he was going to pass away so I had prepared nothing. I was just speaking out of my affectionate respect for him. I said this is the measure of how our society has deteriorated. We have gone from gentlemen and gifted artists like Fred Astaire to the punk rock version of music. That folks is deterioration.

JASON: I think there's a little bit of a trend going on back the other way, don't you agree?

STEVE: There are signs, but they're on the edge of the mainstream. There are young people who work in a classy manor. There's Michael Feinstein, who's the toast of New York with his emphasis on the music of Cole Porter and George Gershwin and people like that. There's a fellow named Steve Ross who does the great music of the '20s, '30s and '40s. There's the Blue Bird Society Orchestra who play the arrangements of the '20s and '30s. You could make quite a long list of encouraging signs. North

Texas State University has had a superb jazz program for many years. A lot of great jazz musicians come out of that particular college. They're all eighteen, nineteen or twenty years old. They are never the less, not interested in schlock rock. They are interested in the Benny Goodman sound, the Count Basie sound or other more modern jazz sounds. These are plus signs. They're signs that civilization is somehow preserved. Unfortunately, what sells eight million albums is mostly garbage. When I say that, I'm talking mainly about the material. I'm certainly not against rock and roll. I like some of the performers very much. I'm a big Michael Jackson fan and I love his sister's work. I love Stevie Wonder. I could give you the names of fifty-seven performers who I think are very talented, but the songs are simply not as good as those written by Irving Berlin or Johnny Mercer or dozens of others I could name.

JASON: I think it's mainly because the audience listening to them isn't actually listening to the songs at all.

STEVE: They're buying what the drum player does chiefly or what the bass player does. Rock music, at least in the rhythm section, really swings so they're buying a beat and a sound. They usually have no idea what the lyrics are until they've heard the song about forty-seven times, whereas, when you hear a Frank Sinatra lyric you've got the whole story right up front. You don't have to listen to it eighteen times and argue with your friends as to what the last line is—that kind of nonsense.

JASON: Although they may not know it, they're working with something pretty well established. Unless I'm speaking out of school, I believe that most of the patterns used in rock music are based on the circle of fifths theory written by Nikolai Diletskii (Nikolay Diletsky) way back in 1679.

STEVE: And some of it's the blues and some of it is boogie-woogie. There are perfectly legitimate elements in much rock. Jerry Lee Lewis, who made his first appearance on my show back about the time we had Elvis on, was a good boogie-woogie pianist so boogie-woogie is one of the legitimate elements of rock and it's still there. It was one of the reasons why, when I first heard Elton John, I liked his work. He had some boogie-woogie elements, or eight beats to the bar for those who don't know what that term means. It goes back to the black piano players of the late 1920s. It is nothing that Elton or Elvis or Jerry Lee or any other more modern person created. They are just performing it well.

JASON: What lies in the future for Steve Allen? I know you have a couple more books coming out soon.

JASON: At the moment I'm working on various books. I'm doing one called *Adventures in a Vast Wasteland*, kind of a casual history of television sprinkled throughout with personal observations and anecdotes. Then I have another book about the music business for which I don't have a final title yet and a book about the collapse and erosion of intelligence in the American population. Also, one of the networks is talking to me. It might happen a year in the future or it may not happen at all. At least we're discussing the possibility of a comedy show. I keep writing a lot of musical scores. I'm writing two at the moment for Irwin Allen so it's more of the same old stuff, a lot of fun.

****

Andy Williams called Steve Allen a renaissance man. He once said that he was a man with so many talents that he could be listed on every page of the *Yellow Pages*. Although we did not talk much about it, Steve was the originator of the very long running *Tonight Show*. During his tenure on that show he began many of the humorous type of skits that became the substance of his programs and many that followed it through the years. He provided the spring board for the careers of so many young comedians and singers who have since made their names so well known to us.

By reading his words you should have been able to realize that he was a very deep thinker whose opinions should be listened to and heeded by us all. When he was not writing and delivering jokes or songs he was taking on more serious issues, some of which got him into problems with some very nasty people. One such occasion was when he took on the mob...He saw one day a copy of *Life* magazine with a picture in it of a man who had been beaten within an inch of his life by enforcers from organized crime families simply because he had publicly objected to the installation of pin ball machines in a candy store near an elementary school. Steve went on the air and explained, off the cuff, that these people were not Damon Runyon characters. They were animals willing to resort to arson, terror and even murder. The mail he got in response was mostly favorable, but he also got the attention of some pretty unsavory elements. This so infuriated Steve that he asked the station he was working for to let him do a special half hour show to go further into the background of the mafia connections to our everyday lives. He dug up film clips of some of the more heinous gangsters in the New York area. He prepared a script with the aid of the New York City Anti-Crime Committee and was ready to do the broadcast. Not long after he submitted his script to his bosses he received an anonymous call from someone who recommended that he not do the program. When he asked why, he was told that he would be casting aspersions on a very fine family man named Benny Levine and that it would not bode well for him if he did what he planned. Steve was then offered all kinds of bribes to prevent him from doing what he wanted to do.

It is a long story, but the offshoot of it was that the whole thing got his Irish up and he went ahead with the broadcast. The result was that his tires were slashed right there in the studio parking lot and he got a variety of mysterious death threats from unidentified callers. They even went so far as to release stink bombs in the studio just before an ensuing show. As a foot note to the whole affair it should be noted that four years later seventeen of the mobsters were held without bond for a plethora of alleged crimes.

On the lighter side it should be noted that he developed some very odd characters who earned their own claim to fame by merely showing up in his studio audience with regularity. One of them was an oddly clad elderly woman who was obviously not too well off. Steve used to interview her as often as he could, but all she wanted to do was compliment him on what a swell guy he was. Finally he asked her why she was really there and she said, "I want one of them Pomeroy cameras." She got her wish many times over and received several Polaroid cameras as time went on along with many other gifts because she was an asset to the show, whether she knew it or not. She always identified herself as Mrs. Sterling. No one ever learned her first name.

There were so many incidents during his long career that could be brought up, but I'll leave it to you, the reader to do some more thorough investigation of his life. One source of information would be his very entertaining autobiography called *Hi-Ho, Steverino: My Adventures in the Wonderful, Wacky World of TV*. It is just one of the nearly fifty books he wrote during his lifetime.

In the year 2000, Steve was driving to his son's house when he was involved in what seemed to be a minor traffic accident. When he got to his destination, he said he was not feeling quite right and decided to take a nap. He suffered a massive heart attack and never awoke from that nap. The autopsy showed that he had ruptured a vessel in his chest causing blood to surround his heart. They also determined that he had fractured four ribs in what had seemed to be an innocuous accident. As Phil Harris said about Jack Benny, Steve Allen was also one of a kind.

Photo Gallery

The Children's Hours

Is it too late to join?
(Blue Network)

THE CHILDREN'S HOURS

Terry & his gang (Terry and the Pirates)
(King Features)

THE CHILDREN'S HOURS

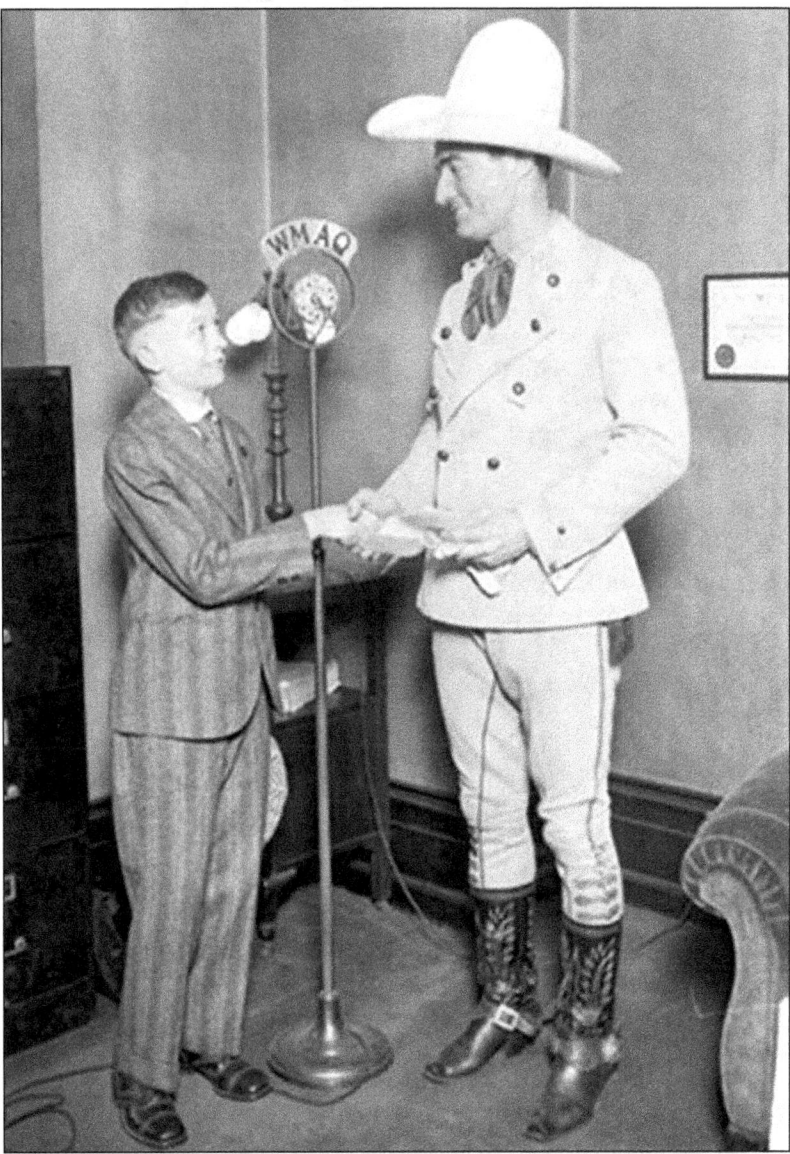

Tom Mix with a young would-be Ralston Straight Shooter
(Mutual)

More for the Kids

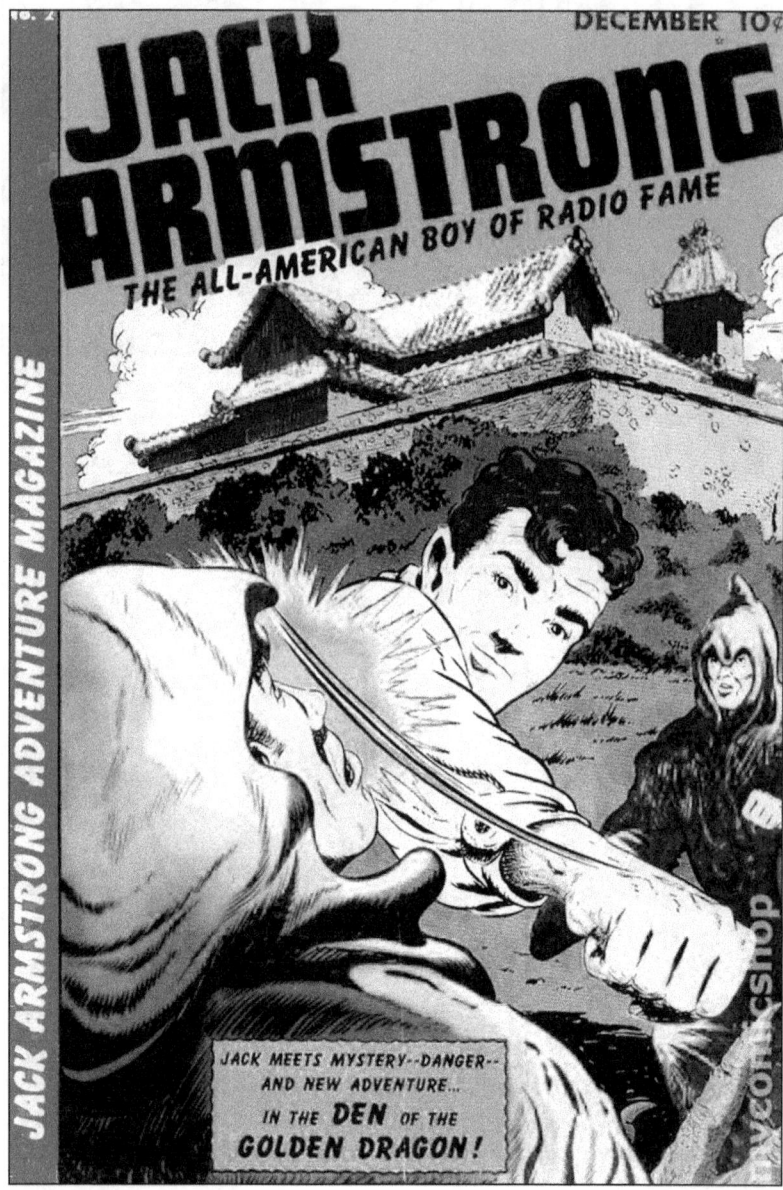

Take that—you evil doer!
(Parents Magazine Press)

More for the Kids

Even on the ground, the bad guys were 'done for.'
(Mutual)

MR. HIT PARADE

André Baruch at his best
(Bing image)

Mr. Hit Parade

The very refined, Mr. André Baruch
(André Baruch collection)

Keeper of the Secret Word

George Fenneman "Tell'em Groucho sent ya!"
(George Fenneman collection)

KEEPER OF THE SECRET WORD

George with Groucho Marx—the perfect foil on *You Bet Your Life* (NBC)

OSGOOD CONKLIN

Gale Gordan and Wiliam Shakespeare
(Bing image)

OSGOOD CONKLIN

Gale as Mr. Conklin and *Our Miss Brooks'* Eve Arden
(CBS)

Man of Many Interests

Sheldon Leonard—He and Frances Bober were married for sixty-six years
(Bing Image)

Man of Many Interests

***It's a Wonderful Life*—Nick the bartender (1946)**
(Republic Pictures)

WILL YOU EVER GET A REAL JOB?

Jim & Henny Backus—a pair for 46 years
(Backus collection)

Will You Ever Get A Real Job?

Jim
(Backus collection)

The Cutup

The Prankster—Jerry Hausner
(Hausner collection)

THE CUTUP

Jerry in *Paths of Glory*—pictured with Christiane Kubrick (1957)
(United Artists)

Philly and Alice

Phil Harris
(Phil Harris collection)

PHILLY AND ALICE

Alice Faye with Phil Harris on *The Phil Harris-Alice Faye Show*—yet another long Hollywood marriage
(NBC)

WAYFAIRING STRANGER

Burl Ives
(Burl Ives collection)

Wayfairing Stranger

Burl—winning an Oscar in *The Big Country*—pictured with Chuck Connors and Gregory Peck (1958)
(United Artists)

South Rampart Street Parade

The Thinker—Steve Allen
(Universal–International)

SOUTH RAMPART STREET PARADE

Steve and Jayne Meadows—forty-six years together (1955)
(New York Daily News)

VIC AND SADE

The cast of Vic and Sade—Bill with Bernardine Flynn and Art Van Harvey (CBS)

VIC AND SADE

Bill as Herman Glimpscher with Bernard Fox on *The Dick Van Dyke Show* (CBS)

Soap Queen

Betty Lou and her husband, Louis Lauria
(Betty Lou Gerson collection)

SOAP QUEEN

Betty Lou speaking for Cruella Da Vil in *101 Dalmations*
(Disney Studios)

WRITER AND PUBLISHER

Carlton E. Morse. . . doing what he did best
(Mutual)

Writer and Publisher

The cast of *One Man's Family* (1945)
(Bing image)

From Blondie to Jane Jetson

Glamorous Penny Singleton
(Penny Singleton collection)

From Blondie to Jane Jetson

Penny 'Blondie' with Arthur Lake 'Dagwood'
(ABC)

SERIOUSLY FUNNY

Eunice Mary Quedens (Eve Arden)
(Bing image)

SERIOUSLY FUNNY

Eve, Zachary Scott and Ann Blyth in *Mildred Pierce* (1945)
(Warner Brothers)

MCGEE'S NEIGHBOR

Shirley Mitchell
(Bing image)

McGee's Neighbor

Shirley with Vivian Vance—*I Love Lucy*
(CBS)

Philo Vance

One of Jackson Beck's favorite cartoon voices, 'Bluto,' from the *Popeye* series
(King Features)

PHILO VANCE

Jackson Beck, the announcer of *The Adventures of Superman*
(ABC)

Sam Spade

"The" Sam Spade, Howard Duff
(ABC)

Sam Spade

Howard with his spouse, Ida Lupino in *Woman in Hiding* (1949)
(Universal)

The Saint

Mr. Price—host of PBS *Mystery!* (1981–1989)
(PBS)

The Saint

The Saint
(CBS)

THE SAINT

The Fly — Vincent in the original movie version (1958)
(20th Century Fox)

ACT V
THE SERIALS

Under the umbrella of radio and television programming called serials there are many variations of many themes. The first things that may come to mind are the ever present soap operas or serial dramas, as they were often called. However, there were other directions these masters of serialization probed over the years. As we have already discovered, many of the kid's shows were produced in that format, but here we need to consider other uses of that ever popular genre. We will look in on serial adventure, serial comedies and of course, we will visit the soaps.

Each of the three people I will use for examples of this style was among the best at what they did. We will hear from two actors who whose work went in mostly different directions even though both of them did some cross-overs into each other's specialties. We will also hear from one of the most prolific writers in the field.

This was a valuable part of the radio days and it still is on the small screen during the daytime hours and sometimes into the evening. Life is always a little easier when we can hear and see the kind of problems the characters in these programs have to encounter and not have to experience them ourselves. They were not necessarily meant to be your typical next door neighbors, but there were often some elements that we could relate to.

The programs we will talk about constitute some of the longest running series on the air.

ACT V:
SCENE ONE
THE GOOK FAMILY

This is the story of a very peculiar family dubbed "Radio's Home Folks," and their even more peculiar friends and neighbors. It will be told by one of the family members who constituted a big part of their success on our radios every day during the week for a long period of time. Although, in a true sense, it could not be called a serial because it was more a series of vignettes, but it had much of the serial format in it.

The person we will hear from did much more work than just this one show, but it was the one that he is best remembered for. When he started to play his character he was a very, very young man, which was exactly what his job called for on the series. When the last of the broadcasts was aired he was in his late twenties, still pretending to be a kid. That was the miracle of radio.

On October 21, 1986 I had a long talk with this gentleman. His name was Bill Idelson and the show in question was *Vic and Sade*.

****

JASON: Bill, I know that the rest of the regular cast from your long running show, *Vic and Sade*, was from this general area, but I don't know a whole lot about your own background other than that you are from Illinois. Tell us a little about those early years.

BILL: I was born in Forest Park, Illinois, a suburb of Chicago, about ten miles west of the city, but was very much like a small town. What made Forest

Park famous was that it had more cemeteries than any other town in the world. It was in *Ripley's Believe it or Not* for that, something like 1500 cemeteries. I think it was the burial ground for Chicago. My dad ran a tavern, as it was called in those days, for about forty years, all through prohibition. I was kind of proud of it. That's my background, small town boy.

JASON: What got you into radio? Chicago was certainly the right place to be for that then.

BILL: My sister was interested in drama and went to Sherwood Music School in Chicago. She taught a little drama group for children in her home. She was current with what was going on in radio. She heard that there was an audition on for the part of Skeezix on *Gasoline Alley*. She took some of her students down there and she also took me as an afterthought. I got the part. That was the start of my career.

JASON: You worked there with Irna Phillips?

BILL: Irna was the first Auntie Blossom on *Gasoline Alley*. It was on WGN, which was the *Chicago Tribune*'s radio station. They did all their own comic strips, you know, *Harold Teen, Little Orphan Annie* and *Gasoline Alley*. Most of the comics that appeared in the *Tribune* were done on WGN.

JASON: You worked with Carlton E. Morse on a couple of his shows. You played Pinkie for a while on *One Man's Family* and Clay on *The Woman in My House*.

BILL: A lot of things were a direct result of working on *Vic and Sade*. Carlton was a *Vic and Sade* fan. That was one of the reasons he called me in. I did have

	to audition for the part of Pinkie, still in all, doing *Vic and Sade* stood me in good stead throughout the rest of my career, even on television.
JASON:	You worked with a couple of my recent guests on this show. I'm referring to Will Waterman and Parley Baer on *Those Websters*.
BILL:	Right, with Eddie Firestone. Eddie became a very good friend of mine. As a matter of fact, we lived together at one time when he was between marriages and I wasn't married yet after the war. We were both veterans. We had a house in West Hollywood for a while.
JASON:	Let's move on to *Vic and Sade*. That was the show that you are probably best remembered for and as you said, it was the key to much more work. That was a very interesting show. It was very down to earth, but at the same time, a little strange.
BILL:	That was the uniqueness of it. It appeared to be a very naturalistic kind of show and yet, the people were almost surrealistic in a way. The people were just a little weird. It was satiric. That's what it was. It was Paul Rhymer's view of a small town.
JASON:	Paul was himself a small town boy from that same area.
BILL:	From Bloomington, Illinois.
JASON:	Your co-stars were Bernadine Flynn from here in Madison and Art Van Harvey who was from Indiana.
BILL:	Bernadine's father had a men's clothing store in Madison. I met him. He was a wonderful fellow.

	He used to come down to the show every once in a while to see Bernadine and I met him.
JASON:	The names of the people on *Vic and Sade* were a story of their own, people like Rishigan Fishigan from Sishigan, Michigan and the twins, Robert and Slobert Hink.
BILL:	Who rode on a power lawn mower from Mobile to someplace, but never knew exactly where.
JASON:	Even the locations were odd, to say the least. Do you remember the name of the social club that Vic belonged to?
BILL:	The Sacred Stars of the Milky Way, wasn't it? And Dismal Seepage, Ohio and several other places. You may be interested in Vic's job before he became Vic. He sold advertising space for the *Hog Breeder's Journal*.
JASON:	Can you tell us something of Art's personality when he wasn't Vic?
BILL:	He was a very funny man. He was a kind of down to earth, middle of the road kind of guy. He and his wife used to come and drink in my father's tavern. This was directly responsible for my getting the job on *Vic and Sade.* The show had just started and Van, as I called him, was in my father's place talking about the fact that they were looking for a boy to be on the show. It started out with just Vic and Sade, but no Rush. After about ten days they decided they needed another character. My father said, "My son has done some radio." Then they hired me without an audition or anything. It was an 8:30 in the morning show, a sustaining show and it wasn't very important so they didn't even

JASON: take the trouble to audition me. They hired me on the spot.

JASON: They brought in your character, but they never really explained him very clearly.

BILL: It was explained on just one show, but they went over it kind of quick. It was depression time and Sade's friend had several children she couldn't support. She was going to have to farm out one of the boys. That one was me. Sade decided to take me in to help out her friend.

JASON: All of the sudden you were there for the rest of the run except a couple of years you were in the service.

BILL: When I arrived on the scene I had very little to say. In the first script I just said, "Hello." That was it.

JASON: It lasted for a long time after that.

BILL: Twelve years.

JASON: But after that initial appearance you did have a lot to say. Here's a segment from one of the odd situations you found yourself in. You have just come home with an assortment of bottles and boxes. Vic and you are in this scene, but no Sade.

****

RUSH: Hello Gov.

VIC: Whatcha gonna do—start a drug store?

RUSH: No. I got a job.

VIC: Job?

RUSH: Gonna spend this evening over at Grandpa Snyder's house givin' him his medicine.

VIC: Does all that junk comprise his medicine?

RUSH: Lot of it, ain't there? Well, he's a pretty old geezer. Needs lotta stuff.

VIC: How come ya got his medicine here at home?

RUSH: I'm studyin' up on the different doses. Got his chart, see? The way I got the job, Grandpa Snyder's two daughters are going to an entertainment at the High School tonight. They hired me to come over from six-thirty till ten an' take care of Grandpa. Pretty good job too. I'm gonna get fifty cents.

VIC: What's in this box?

RUSH: Pills, I expect. What's it say on the lid?

VIC: Yamilton's Drug Department, H-97-Z-124.

RUSH: I'll look it up on the chart, H-97-Z-124?

VIC: Yeah.

RUSH: (Reading) Give Grandpa two of these with a glass of water twenty minutes after eating and at half hour intervals after that.

VIC: Hmmm, what's this?

RUSH: I dunno. It's just called blue stuff on the chart. (Reading again) Give grandpa a level teaspoon of blue stuff every two hours beginning at six-thirty.

Act V; Scene One: The Gook Family

Vic: I suppose this villainous lookin' brew in this bottle is referred to as yella stuff?

Rush: Uh-huh. (Looks at chart) Give Grandpa a tablespoon of yella stuff at twenty-five minutes to nine.

Vic: Looks to me like there's enough junk here to doctor up an army.

Rush: Plenty of it, all aright. Well' you take an old guy like that, they hafta have...

Vic: What's this thing?

Rush: It's just kind of a flat dish.

Vic: Grandpa Snyder gonna swallow it with a glass of water at midnight?

Rush: (Laughing) Naw. See this box?

Vic: Yeah.

Rush: It's got powder in it. I put the powder in a pan with water. Then I heat the water. Then I pour the water in that flat dish and Grandpa inhales the fumes.

Vic: Grandpa must put in some lively evenings.

Rush: Yeah. I wouldn't wanna hafta take such a bunch of medicine. Maybe when I get old enough I'll—

Vic: I dunno. (Reads chart again) Give Grandpa one pinch of black stuff twelve minutes after he has his egg.

Vic: What time does he eat his egg?

Rush: Ahhh. (Reads) Give Grandpa one raw egg at nine-fifteen.

Vic: What if he don't feel like an egg?

Rush: I thought of that myself. If he turned down the doggone egg it'd throw the whole works off. Some other things I gotta find out about too. Look here for instance: Give Grandpa pink stuff at hour-and-a-half intervals beginning at six fifty-three. This here is the pink stuff, ya see?

Vic: Uh-huh.

Rush: Well, an hour an' a half from six fifty-three would be an hour plus six fifty-three plus a half hour makin' it eight twenty-three. That's the first interval, OK. Eight twenty-three plus an hour an' a half would be an hour plus eight twenty-three or nine twenty-three plus a half hour, makin' it—

Vic: Holy Smoke!

Rush: See how mixed up it is?

Vic: You better take an adding machine along, an' a private secretary.

Rush: An' another thing. I hafta give Grandpa his X-26-Y-14 pills at eight twenty-four. That'd only give me a minute gangway between the pink stuff an'—

Vic: I think you better resign from that job.

Rush: Oh, no. I can use that fifty cents. Anyway, pretty soon I'll call up one of the Snyder girls an' get everything straight in my mind.

Act V; Scene One: The Gook Family

VIC: Here's a bottle that says, "Take two or three pills every three or four hours."

RUSH: Yeah. What's a guy gonna do about that?

VIC: Why dontcha mix all the stuff up in a jug an' give it to Grandpa in one big snort?

RUSH: He'd probably blow up.

****

JASON: I think we should leave them to work it out. Wasn't it true that at one time you were on NBC and CBS simultaneously?

BILL: Yes, and Mutual too, all three networks at the same time.

JASON: Which you could do in those days.

BILL: They were all within a few blocks of each other. We'd just run from one studio to another. You mean as far as the legal aspect was concerned and all that?

JASON: Right. *Ma Perkins* was another show that was on two networks at the same time.

BILL: They just bought the time. There were no rules against it.

JASON: There was no exclusivity then either.

BILL: No. At one point we were on as many as six times a day, on all three networks.

JASON: How much of that was live?

BILL: All of it was live. There was no taping in those days. It's hard to remember that the tape recorder or even the wire recorder hadn't been invented yet.

JASON: I know there wasn't any tape at that time, but I also know there was a lot of use of ETs in those days. A lot of shows were recorded in that manor.

BILL: But it was cheaper to just have the actors come over and do it.

JASON: Cutting an ET was sometimes quite a project as a matter of fact. It had to be perfect or you'd have to start all over from the top.

BILL: Exactly. I've been on recordings where we were down to the last line and everybody's knees were shaking. Somebody would fluff the last speech just from the pressure and we'd have to go back to the beginning and do the whole thing all over again.

JASON: In one case that Don Ameche told me about they were doing a segment of *Jack Armstrong*. The sound man tripped over a bucket of water just as they were finishing up, after about fifteen takes. They had to start over.

BILL: They probably put that sound man's head in that bucket afterwards.

JASON: Tell us more about Bernadine Flynn.

BILL: Bernadine was a woman I dearly loved. As you said, she was from Madison. As a young girl just out of college she went to New York. She did some work on Broadway where she met Don Ameche. It's interesting that you just mentioned him. Things got slow in New York. She heard that things were going well on radio. Radio was just starting up then in Chicago. She came back to Chicago and was very busy. She called Don in New York and said, "Get out here. There's work for actors. Come to Chicago." She got him to join her in Chicago. Bernadine was a very, very kind of aristocratic, intelligent sort of lady, but she could still do the down home, small town kind of stuff. She was married to a very well known doctor in Chicago. She was really upper crust. Her best friend was Edith Davis, Nancy Davis' mother. She traveled in rather high society. She had two aspects. She was a society lady, but she was also a Wisconsin small town girl.

JASON: She had quite a sense of humor, didn't she? She would start laughing and then couldn't stop ala Jack Benny.

BILL: Bernie was wonderful. I just loved her.

JASON: There was another character that was added to the cast later on and became a fixture on the show. He was Uncle Fletcher played by Clarence Hartzell.

BILL: Clarence came into the script because Van had had his second heart attack. No one knew how much he would be able to do after that. The network people decided to bring in another male character. They held an audition and Clarence won it.

JASON: He was the only member of the cast not from the mid west. He was from West Virginia.

BILL: He was? That's the first time I've heard that.

JASON: Huntington, West Virginia.

BILL: He lives in Arkansas now. He's very happy there. I visited him not too long ago and stayed with him for a week. He's quite a guy. You know, when he started doing Uncle Fletcher he was not much older than I was. He was a young man, but he had an old voice.

JASON: That was the kind of thing that was do-able on radio, but not on TV.

BILL: Clarence was marvelous. It was strange because we had the illusion that nobody could fit into our cast. We were so attuned to one another and to Paul Rhymer, the writer of the show. We thought we were unique. Then when Clarence came along he became just one of the *Vic and Sade* people. It was amazing to us that anyone could just step in and be a part of it.

JASON: It must have become like a real-life family.

BILL: That's true. We got pretty close. We all respected one another a great deal.

JASON: The characters that were brought into the dialogue were only spoken of, but never actually appeared on mike until the later part of the run. One of those late comers was Johnny Coons.

BILL: When I went into the service, Paul, very lovingly decided not to have another Rush. He had a boy in there called Russell. Then he brought in other characters, but that made a change in the show that a lot of people didn't like. Part of it was because of the disruption of the regular characters. If any one of us had left the same thing would have happened. It just broke up the team.

Act V; Scene One: The Gook Family

JASON: Johnny Coons did play your part after you were gone for a while.

BILL: That was much later. The show was off for a while and then came back in the evenings as a fifteen minute show. That's when he played Rush. Then when I got out of the service I took it over and Johnny played Mr. Sprawl. He was a kind of senile old fellow who was retired. Paul invented that character just to keep Johnny around because he was giving the part of Rush back to me.

JASON: Even later Johnny Coons became known to children in Chicago as Uncle Johnny Coons on his own kid's show.

BILL: I wasn't aware too much of what was going on in Chicago by then because I had moved out here to California. Johnny was a wonderful actor, very nice guy and a good fly fisherman. He made fly rods. That was his hobby. They were too expensive for me to buy.

JASON: Let's go back to some more of the people and places that were talked about, but never heard. It was a weird *Vic and Sade* rogue's gallery. There were places like the one Sade used to frequent, The Little Tiny Petite Pheasant Feather Tea Shoppy.

BILL: And the Thimble Club.

JASON: And Uncle Fletcher lived at The Bright Kentucky Hotel.

BILL: Paul went on and on with The Bright Kentucky Hotel. I don't know if you remember one show where this guy Hank Gutstop complained because he also lived at The Bright Kentucky. When the

> trains went by his bed walked across the floor from the vibration. He complained because one night it walked across the room and out the door and into someone else's room.

JASON: Good old Hank Gutstop.

BILL: He was enraged.

JASON: Down the street was the garbage man, Jake Gumpox.

BILL: His horse had a sister named Bernice, but I forget the horse's name—oh, yeah—Howard, Howard was the horse. Howard stopped dead in the middle of the alley one day and stood still for three minutes. The thing was that at that moment Bernice had suffered a heart attack and died while pulling another garbage wagon on another street. I'll never forget her.

JASON: Let me insert one more bit from a show that was about Jake Gumpox indirectly. Sade was preparing to give him a birthday present, but she had a very peculiar way of doing it.

****

SADE: Got the socks?

RUSH: Yeah. They're in a Christmas box though. Mr. Gumpox might think—

SADE: Before you sit down go in the pantry an' get that cigar box on the shelf.

RUSH: I planned to make somethin' outa that cigar box.

SADE: Do like I say. Where's the things from the library table?

Act V; Scene One: The Gook Family

Rush: Here.

Sade: All right. Go get the cigar box.

Rush: I been savin' that cigar box.

Sade: Look out an' see if the garbage buckets are still there.

Rush: They're there.

Sade: (To Vic) What shall I write on the envelope, Happy birthday, Mr. Gumpox?

Vic: Yeah, better still—"Bright star, would I were steadfast as thou art, hung aloft the dark canopy of night."

Sade: (With disgust) I'll fix it. Person could break their back doin' favors for a person an' a person'd never give a care.

Vic: You misunderstand. The relations between Mr. Gumpox an' myself—

Rush: Maybe I could get this cigar box back again, Mom. After Mr. Gumpox gets his socks he won't have any use for it.

Sade: Lay it down.

Rush: Whatcha writin'?

Sade: Note.

Rush: Gonna put the present in the garbage?

Sade: Sit down and eat your dinner.

Rush: Gov, is Mom gonna put the present in the garbage?

Vic: I couldn't say.

Rush: Know what'd be funny?

Vic: What?

Rush: Give Mr. Gumpox a piece of pie for his birthday an' put it in the garbage. He wouldn't know which was his present and which was—

Sade: Some people can be just awful silly over nothin'.

Vic: Ya hear that last crack by the doctor here?

Sade: Yes I did—ridiculous nonsense for a great big boy in the eighth grade.

Vic: Sure is. I got an idea, Polo.

Rush: What?

Vic: Say Mr. Gumpox is fifty years old.

Rush: Yeah?

Vic: How about stickin' fifty candles around the garbage bucket?

Rush: Make it look like a cake, huh?

Sade: Oh, stop that foolishness for goodness sake. Vic, how's this? Dear Mr. Gumpox, just a little remembrance on your birthday. Good luck an' many more of em, The Gook family, All right?

Vic: Fine.

ACT V; SCENE ONE: THE GOOK FAMILY

****

JASON: The ones who were on quite a bit on the phone and much later as real characters were the Brainfeebles, Dottie and Chuck.

BILL: Yes, and Ruthie Stembottom and Fred. They came over all the time to play rummy and eat tutti-frutti ice cream

JASON: Nothing could be normal at the Gooks. Other people might have vanilla or chocolate. At their house it had to be tutti-frutti.

BILL: There was a big discussion. Vic was always disgruntled when Fred and Ruthie came over. Sade would always be bright and bubbly on the phone. Then she'd say, "The Umptydumps are coming over. What kind of ice cream should we have?" He'd say, "Tutti-frutti, okay?"

JASON: There were a lot of relatives around too.

BILL: Bess, the sister in Carberry that Sade went to visit when she was having a real-life baby. Bernie had a couple of children while she was doing the show so she always visited Bess in Carberry for a week or so when that happened. Paul would write her out.

JASON: Can you add anything interesting about the production? Maybe some funny thing that happened on the set?

BILL: Well, I'll tell you, you know, people who were fans of *Vic and Sade* I don't think realize that the show was on for like two and a half years as a sustaining show at 8:30 in the morning. I don't believe anybody heard us. At least, it was our conviction that nobody heard us. I got twenty-seven dollars and fifty cents a week for doing the show. I think Bernie and Van got thirty five. We had fun because we thought we were doing it just for ourselves. We were in a big studio where Walter Blaufuss played the morning serenade. They would stay in the studio and play our theme song, "Oh, You Beautiful Doll." At they end of it they would put down their instruments—clink—clank—clunk—and go into the hall for a cigarette while we were on the air. While we were doing the show you'd hear these instruments being dropped on the floor. They'd come back after fifteen minutes and play the theme again. We did that for two and a half years before we got sponsored.

JASON: Did you ever run into a situation where they paid you in product instead of cash like some sponsors sometimes did?

BILL: No, but we did get product in addition to our salary. We got a three pound can of Crisco each month which we couldn't possibly use up. We used to give them to our neighbors. I know some people were doing radio for five dollars a shot because there was no union in those days. AFRA hadn't started so they paid you what ever they thought they could get away with. Some shows paid ten, but you'd have to kick back five to the producer. That was the reason that AFRA was formed, kind of for protection.

JASON: And of course, there were no credits and no royalties.

BILL: Absolutely right.

JASON: Let's switch gears. You have worked pretty heavily in television for quite a long time. What can you tell us about that?

BILL: I did some acting after the war and then things were tough so I went into the real estate business. While I was in real estate I wrote a script for *Twilight Zone* and they bought it. Then I started doing some writing. The first comedy show I wrote for was *The Dick Van Dyke Show*.

JASON: So you worked with Sheldon Leonard.

BILL: Sheldon and Carl Reiner. Then I segued into *The Andy Griffith Show*. I did a lot of those. The strange thing about Andy is that he confided in me that he was trying to do *Vic and Sade*. That was the essence of his show.

JASON: That was also from Sheldon Leonard.

BILL: That whole thing was all the same stable. It was *Dick Van Dyke*, *Andy Griffith*, *Gomer Pyle* and *Danny Thomas*, all done by one little clique, same studio, same people.

JASON: You did some production and direction as well.

BILL: I produced *Love, American Style* and the first year of *Bob Newhart*. I did *Anna and the King* with Yul Brynner and a show I'm sure you never heard of called *The Montefuscos*. That lasted about five minutes and then left the scene. I've done production and story editing and so forth.

JASON: I would guess your primary function today is writing.

BILL: Yeah, right now I'm working on a show called

Punky Brewster about a little girl. It was on NBC. Now it's on cable syndication.

****

Bill Idelson might have also mentioned that he wrote for many other shows on television, among them were *Get Smart, Happy Days, The Odd Couple* and *M*A*S*H*. He won two Writers Guild Awards along the way. When he talked about *The Dick Van Dyke Show* he did not mentioned that he played a recurring role on that show as well as writing for it. He was Herman Glimscher, Rose Marie's Casper Milquetoast kind of boy friend who had to bring his mother along when they went on a date.

During his time in the Navy he was awarded the Distinguished Flying Cross and four Air Medals for his work as a night fighter. You can read all about that period of his life in his book entitled *Gibby*. By reading that book and his other two books, *The Story of Vic and Sade* and *Bill Idleson's Writing Class* you can learn a lot more about him. All three are available through BearManor Media, which just happens to be my publisher as well. PLUG-PLUG! Sorry.

He died in 2007 due to complications from a hip injury. Norman Corwin was an admirer of his. In his comments to the *Los Angeles Times* after Bill's death Norman said, "He was a luminary. He stood out among radio comedians and he stood out because of very good writing by Paul Rhymer and very good acting by himself. I had nothing but admiration for this fellow." No one could be a better judge of such things than my friend, Norman Corwin.

ACT V:
SCENE TWO
SOAP QUEEN

It is now time to enter into the world of the Soap Operas with one of their busiest protagonists. That is not to say that soaps were her only artistic endeavor. It is simply a fact that she was so often employed by them in her earlier days on Chicago radio. As you will see, she was much more than a Soap Opera Queen, but that was an extremely important area of entertainment then and still is today on television.

So, let us hear what she had to say about the soaps and other facets of her career. The lady was Betty Lou Gerson. We had this conversation on May 1, 1987.

****

JASON: You worked on many of the soaps during the early part of your radio days and even some later on, Betty Lou. Before we go into your career why don't we talk a little about soap operas in general? You know as much about them as anybody.

BETTY: I certainly was on an enormous number of them. Most of them came out of Chicago because Chicago was the home of the soap opera. A few came out of New York, but the people in New York were mostly just waiting for parts in plays. They weren't really interested in the soap opera as a career. In Chicago we weren't really that interested in the theatre because radio was just so terribly important in those early days.

JASON: It was a good basic training ground for many actors who later moved on to other areas. It was a story telling medium.

BETTY: I remember working once with John Huston. At that time Johnny was very much of a Lincoln type of chap. I think he was doing Lincoln in some show when he also worked with me on another one. He said, "Why don't you come out and do Mary Lincoln with me? You're not interested in this radio nonsense, are you?" I said, "My goodness, do you expect me to give up all of my shows? For what, Equity minimum?" He just couldn't understand that this was the career we chose.

JASON: There were so many shows going on in Chicago at that time so you would have been giving up a great many things to go out to New York to do one role.

BETTY: As a matter of fact, the group of us in Chicago actually made *The Glass Menagerie* famous. It was just about to close and we just kept it going by telling everyone and throwing parties for the original cast. We, in Chicago, had more to do with the success of that play and therefore, the career of Tennessee Williams because we thought it was simply fabulous.

JASON: It was about '45 or '46 that the industry moved out of Chicago in two directions, east and west, but mostly to Hollywood.

BETTY: Sure, we came out in 1945. It was a question of either going to New York or to California. I just plain didn't like New York so we came out here. My husband was able to bring his shows out too. He was doing *Those Websters* and *First Nighter*. Irna Phillips brought *The Guiding Light* out here for me.

JASON: There's a question that I think most folks know the answer to, but maybe you should explain why those serial dramas were called soap operas or simply soaps.

BETTY: They were sponsored by soap companies. Procter and Gamble was one of the great sponsors. General Mills was big too, but Procter and Gamble probably had more of the shows on. That was why they were called soap operas. There were so many of them. *Road of Life* was sponsored by Procter and Gamble. *Mary Marlin* was sponsored by P & G. I think they had *Woman in White* and *Midstream* as well. I was the lead in all of those.

JASON: You were also the lead in a show done by a couple we were talking about the other day. They turned out soap operas like a factory. They were Ann and Frank Hummert.

BETTY: Oh, yes, they did *Arnold Grimm's Daughter.*

JASON: That was the one I was referring to.

BETTY: They were terribly important. They did dozens and dozens of shows. They made scads and scads and scads of money.

JASON: They managed to turn out some pretty bad things along the way as well as the good ones.

BETTY: I wasn't that familiar with most of their shows. Didn't they do *Betty and Bob*? That became a joke because the lines were like, "But Betty" or "But Bob."

JASON: Sounds like some commercials we hear today.

BETTY: Exactly, they made a big thing out of it, a comedy take-off. I think Bob White got started on that show. Bob had it first and then Don Ameche got it.

JASON: And then Les Tremayne.

BETTY: Was Les on that too?

JASON: Yes he was. The Hummerts also did some that lasted a long, long time. They did *Ma Perkins* and *The Romance of Helen Trent*, which between them ran over sixty years.

BETTY: They did *Ma Perkins* for George Fogle. Virginia Payne was simply wonderful on that show. She was absolutely marvelous.

JASON: She was also on *Lonely Women*, wasn't she?

BETTY: I don't know if she was on *Lonely Women* or not. That was a wonderful show. I'd forgotten about that. That was really a marvelous, marvelous show and Irna did that. I was on it with Will Waterman.

JASON: And Les was there also, Les Tremayne, and Barbara Luddy. That was sort of a continuation of *Today's Children*.

BETTY: Yes it was a continuation of Irna's *Today's Children*. I think it has something to do with the rights to the program. She got into a fight with somebody about it. I don't remember all the details.

JASON: I believe she ended up suing WGN over it because they wouldn't put it on the network. She ended up leaving and going to NBC. I think it was over *Today's Children*, but I'm not positive.

BETTY: I think you're probably right. I'll say one thing for

Irna Phillips. She sure had guts. If she thought something was right she'd fight tooth and nail for it. She was a very close friend of mine.

JASON: Okay, I was wrong. The show that I should have said was *Painted Dreams*. That's the one she brought suit over. It eventually did end up a network show. That was often said to be the first soap opera, started way back in 1930. It was not one of your shows.

BETTY: No, because I started in '35. It was so long ago I don't know what to say.

JASON: There's another name we should mention from *Today's Children* who became a big name on radio. That was Ireene Wicker.

BETTY: Yes, as a matter of fact I followed Ireene on many things. That's how I got started on *First Nighter* as Don Ameche's co-star. June Meredith went away on vacation. While June was on vacation Ireene decided she wanted to go on vacation. Because I had played the lead on *Talking Picture Time* the producer/director of *First Nighter* asked me to come and play the lead on that for a while, while Ireene and June were both gone. I said, "Certainly." When June left the show for good that fall they held auditions all over the country and I was the winner for the female lead roles on *First Nighter*. I came out to California with Don at the end of '35. We went off the air for the summer in 1936 so I went back to Chicago and got married. When they wanted me to come out to sign a five year contract I said, "No way, unless you give me enough to fly back to Chicago and be with my husband every week." They said, "Why does a little girl like you need all that money?" which I found rather insulting. So I suggested that they get with Barbara Luddy. Barbara was very good. I told Tom Wallace about her. So they talked to Barbara. You know how that worked out. She was with that show for years and years and years. She was a brilliant actress and a brilliant comedienne. Then seven or eight months later they called me back and asked if I had any objection if they offered the production and direction of the show to my husband. I told them I was making so much money doing soap operas that I couldn't care less about his show.

JASON: You worked on *First Nighter* for just about a year or so opposite Don Ameche.

BETTY: Ah-huh, and then I worked on *Grand Hotel* opposite Don's brother Jim for a number of years.

JASON: Those two guys were around Chicago radio for a long time before they moved to Hollywood. Sometimes they worked the same show at the same time.

BETTY: Actually, Jim and I worked together a great deal longer because Don became a star so very quickly out in Hollywood and went on to do much more than *First Nighter.* So when *Grand Hotel* came along they asked Jim because he sounded exactly like Don.

JASON: And if fact, that became a problem when they were both doing *Jack Armstrong* because they sounded too much alike. Jim was Jack and Don was his friend, Captain Hughes. The producer decided that the two of them didn't belong on the same show because no one could tell them apart.

BETTY: They were both lovely men. I saw Don not too long ago when he was honored by Pacific Pioneer Broadcasters.

JASON: Every time I call him he's in the process of starting another picture. That's been going on for a couple of years now.

BETTY: It's just wonderful the way his career has come back, just absolutely wonderful.

JASON: A couple of soaps that you worked that really enjoyed long runs were *Road of Life* and *Guiding Light*.

BETTY: I wasn't on *Road of Life* too long. Carl Wester was producing that for Irna. They took me off *Road of Life* and put me on as star on *Woman in White*. I was not on *Guiding Light* in Chicago, but when they brought it out here they took that title because I think Irna had the rights to that show.

JASON: *Guiding Light* is still running on television.

BETTY: Yes it is.

JASON: It started way back in 1937 on radio. Talk about a long run!!

BETTY: It was a very well written show. So many of the people who were on it could have gone on to television, but they wanted the television version to be out of New York for some reason, not out here. Our choice was definitely not to go back to New York. I couldn't imagine anything worse. I would never live in New York. I like the feeling of California much more and of course, I love Chicago.

JASON: I want to bring up a show that is not too well remembered because it came on late in the radio days when the fight with television had already begun and it did not run for very long. It starred a then big name in Hollywood. The show was *Box 13*. The man was Alan Ladd.

BETTY: Yes, I did many of those with Alan. He was such a nice man.

JASON: That was his own syndication for the Don Lee Network.

BETTY: And I did a great many of them because, in the first place, I wasn't much taller than Alan. I did have to wear flat shoes.

JASON: I thought everyone was taller than Alan.

BETTY: I won't dispute that. He was a very little guy, but he was a very, very nice guy. I really felt very sorry for him because he had a very unhappy life. His wife, Sue Carol was really a kind of dreadful person. She was so insanely jealous of him. You couldn't even have a kiss on *Box 13*. She cut them all out. You're reading from a script. You're not actually acting it out. If you're kissing anyone you're kissing your own hand.

JASON: Did the sound men do that part?

BETTY: No, they just weren't there. She had them cut out of the script. There was never a love scene, never.

JASON: That wasn't done with a live audience so anything could have happened with sound effects. People would never have seen it.

BETTY: She sat in the control room for hours. She wasn't just jealous of me, it was the same for any woman that got anywhere near Alan.

JASON:	There was a lady I always enjoyed listening to that you worked with on one of the later soaps on the west coast, *Aunt Mary.* The lady I'm referring to is Mrs. Davis from the *Our Miss Brooks* show, Jane Morgan.
BETTY:	Oh yes, Jane was lovely. What a really dear lovely lady.
JASON:	A while back when I was talking with her, Eve Arden told me that Jane was as much Mrs. Davis in real life as she was on the radio.
BETTY:	Yes she was. She was a dear, dear, dear girl. You know, I did a lot of things when I came out here. I did *Mr. President* with Edward Arnold. That really was a great deal of fun to do. Then I did some things for Walt Disney. I was the voice of Cruella De Vil in *101 Dalmatians.* They re ran that last year and I guess it broke all records. It brought in something like thirty million on the re-run of it.
JASON:	That was my wife's favorite animated character, Cruella. Of all the Disney productions that was the one she remembers best.
BETTY:	I have a big cartoon of me with all the dogs.
JASON:	Tell me a little about Wyllis Cooper. You worked on a show called *Flying Time* that he wrote. I understand he was quite a guy.
BETTY:	We called him Bill. He was just an absolute darling. I remember something that happened on *Flying Time.* Roscoe Turner was on the show. He was the guy who flew across the country or around the world or something. So we decided we were going to do Roscoe and Bill broadcasting up in the air. So we

went to do the broadcast. It was very, very bad weather. You could tell that Roscoe Turner was as nervous as he could be because he wasn't at the controls of the plane. Bill was nervous. I think Jack Knight, who was the first pilot to fly cross country with air mail, was a guest that day and he was nervous. Both men were absolutely white and shaking because they couldn't control the plane. They weren't flying the plane. They finally brought it down. They just couldn't stand being up there with somebody else in control. They did the broadcast on the ground.

JASON: Could it have been Paul Mantz doing the flying that day?

BETTY: I don't think so. I knew Paul. I met him when he was a guest on the show. No, I think it was just an ordinary pilot. Everybody else was just broadcasting. Roscoe was broadcasting. Jack Knight was broadcasting. They just didn't trust whoever was flying.

JASON: The reason I asked is because I used to work on loan to Paul Mantz. I know that very few people ever got nervous when he was flying.

BETTY: Well, these flyers were just as nervous as the devil at a revival meeting because they weren't in charge.

JASON: That would have been one of the first radio remotes.

BETTY: Yes, it would have been, sure, but we did it on the ground. It wasn't a remote. We certainly didn't end up doing it in the air. They said they could not do the show with somebody else flying the plane.

JASON: *Flying Time* was just stories about people in aviation?

BETTY: It was just fun to do it. I'll never forget. I had hay fever. Bill Cooper had a nasty little sense of humor. He wrote my character, Aunt Sue, in with hay fever so that he could create my sneeze. I'd come to the studio an hour early just to clear up my hay fever. I used to wear nose plugs that never were effective at all. Then I'd get on the show and the script had Aunt Sue sneezing, so God bless Bill for letting me sneeze.

JASON: In other words, you would have been in trouble if you lost your hay fever.

BETTY: I had to pretend it when I didn't have it. He was a wonderful guy. They used to say he'd turn off all the lights, write in the dark and scare himself silly when he was writing *Lights Out*.

JASON: Which was what we were all supposed to do when we listened to *Lights Out*. Most people think of Arch Oboler in regard to that show, but of course, Wyllis was the originator and did it until he got tired of it.

BETTY: And Arch's, I thought were third rate compared to Bill's. I really did. I thought they were very third rate. The real creativity, the uniqueness was Bill's.

JASON: Another of your shows that I remember well was one starring Brian Donlevy. Do you know which one I mean?

BETTY: Oh, yes, I even rode in the Christmas Parade with Brian. I can't quite remember the name of that show right now.

JASON: *Dangerous Assignment*.

BETTY: Yes, of course, *Dangerous Assignment*. Bill Kahn was the director of that. Brian was just a dear, dear man, an amazing man. When you saw him on the screen he didn't seem as short as he was. They'd photograph him in a way that made him look tall. Brian was a very short man. I don't think he was much taller than Alan Ladd. But, he was a nice man. I'd forgotten *Dangerous Assignment*.

JASON: You mentioned someone last night when I called you from my home that you feel was one of the best of the best soap writers, Jane Crusinberry.

BETTY: Jane was brilliant and creative and very, very sophisticated with her writing. *The Story of Mary Marlin* was a brilliantly conceived and written show. Jane wrote that and she never had any ghost writers. I don't really know if Jane is still alive. Anne Seymour would know because Anne was very close to her. The writing of *Mary Marlin* could match or beat anything, anywhere.

JASON: Writing for soap is a little different than any other type of writing. Usually they would make up a framework that would just cover a couple of pages and then write a whole year or two of programs from that.

BETTY: Certainly, and there were plots and sub-plots and sub-plots to the sub-plots. Actually, they were much better than the soap operas that are on today, which I think are boring, like *Dynasty* and *Falcon Lair* (*Falcon Crest*) and all that.

JASON: I can honestly say that I have never seen *Dynasty* or *Dallas* or any of those shows all the way through even once.

BETTY: I have watched, perhaps a few minutes of each. I think they're bull. I'd much rather have a good book than that.

JASON: The casts on radio and the plots on radio of these soap operas, or serial dramas, whichever you want to call them, were sometimes immense. There could be fourty or fifty or even sixty people woven into those stories. Some only showed up once or twice in a year.

BETTY: I know. It got so expensive that Procter and Gamble told Jane they simply couldn't carry that many people under contract, since she had all those complicated scenarios. I know that in the last year I was playing on *Mary Marlin* I would be guaranteed three times a week in the lead. I couldn't have five times because she had too many other plots for other people.

JASON: I often wonder how the writers were able to keep it all straight in their minds.

BETTY: They must have had graphs plotted out like you would for your ancestors. I don't know.

JASON: There are family trees available for shows like *One Man's Family.* Carlton E. Morse wrote that and it went on for many years.

BETTY: I had a part on that one when I came out here.

JASON: I think everybody showed up there at one time or another.

BETTY: But I do think Jane had more real talent for dialogue. She was very difficult to work for because she rolled around and the scripts were always long, but she had complete control over them. You couldn't cut anything out. What you had to do was go faster. That became very difficult. The things really should have had three or four minutes cut out. You simply could not cut one word out. All we could do was race through them. She forced her tempo on the actors and the director.

JASON: Those shows did have one advantage that a fifteen minute show wouldn't have today. That was the fact that there was never a central commercial, just one at the start and one at the end. The plot flowed a little better without the interruptions that we have now.

BETTY: Except when Irna did her shows. She put two or three of them together, a half hour or forty-five minutes. When we did Guiding Light I think there was a trial scene. The whole business of interweaving the shows together was done with a continuing theme running over three, sometimes four shows filling up a full hour. It was *Guiding Light, Road of Life, Woman in White* and one more that I can't remember. It was known as the Irna Phillips Hour. She had a tremendous amount of control.

JASON: That required quite a bit of coordination, to be able to write three or four shows every day. Several people must have been involved.

BETTY: Irna had ghost writers, sub writers. She had total control over them. I remember Art Greb wrote for Irna. I've forgotten a number of the people who did. Jane wrote all her own. Pauline Hopkins wrote *Midstream.* I played the lead in that.

JASON: Then there were the Hummerts, that we talked about a little earlier. They ran something similar to

	a production line. They would float a rough idea to their staff of writers and they would take it from there.
BETTY:	Was that their method of handling it?
JASON:	That's what they did. They had as many as fifty-five or sixty shows at any given time. They were buying 18% of all available airtime during the late '30s and early '40s which was a lot of radio time.
BETTY:	Just an awful lot.
JASON:	As you said, they were making scads of money.
BETTY:	Hand over fist.
JASON:	You did at least one kid's show that I'm aware of. The one I'm thinking of was an adaptation of a comic strip, *Don Winslowe of the Navy.*
BETTY:	I've forgotten the name of the chap who wrote that. He knew everyone in Chinatown. He took the whole cast of Don Winslowe down to Chinatown for a Chinese banquet. I'd never had such glorious food in my life. That was a fun show.
JASON:	Did you do any other kid's shows? I don't have any others in my notes.
BETTY:	No, that was the only one. A lot of adults liked that one too. It was kind of a good show.
JASON:	One final question, Betty Lou, are you still active in show business today?
BETTY:	I do work for Disney whenever they need me and call me. I'm also working for my husband in our

	own company which is an answering service, mostly for actors. I'm here at the office all the time. I love it.
JASON:	None of the people I've chatted with on this show said they would ever voluntarily retire, which makes show business a very unique field.
BETTY:	Goodness no. Nobody who has ever acted is going to give it up. I think it's because we're always interested. I couldn't think of retiring. Actors just don't retire. Nobody in show business does.

****

When he was in his mid-eighties, Ralph Bellamy told me that he was still always on the alert for that perfect part in that perfect show. He said he did not know exactly what that meant, but he would know when he saw it. That is exactly what Betty Lou Gerson was saying when she said actors never retire. That seems to be true. Not one person in that business that I've ever spoken with, regardless of age, was even considering complete retirement. The door was always left open.

Betty Lou was honored by the Disney Studios in 1996 as a Disney Legend. Her work for them went well beyond her portrayal of Cruella De Vil. She was the voice of the narrator in the original animated *Cinderella* back in 1950 and her last voice movie work, which was also for Disney, was in *Cats Don't Dance* in 1997. She did numerous fill-ins for them through the years, though she was not always credited on screen for her work.

If you could hear rather than just read her words, you would realize that she has maintained the charm and a bit of the speech characteristics of her native Chattanooga, Tennessee and Birmingham, Alabama. At the same time, she had very definite opinions and was not afraid to take on some of the biggest names of her era on radio.

She died as the result of a massive stroke in 1999.

Act V: Scene Three
Keep On Keeping On

We have talked with so many folks who look at retirement as anathema, but here is an example of someone who took it a step further at an advanced age.

Continuing in the genre of serialization I think it would be fair to say that this gentleman was the king of them all. His longest running series has often been misnamed as a soap opera, but you would not want to call it that when speaking with him. He was very offended by such accusations. It was a serial drama. No other title fits it properly so you will not hear me refer to it as soap. He was responsible for two major serials as well as many other shorter running ventures we will discuss.

The man I'm speaking of was Carlton E. Morse. I had the distinct pleasure of interviewing him on July 21, 1986.

****

JASON: Good morning Carlton. We've got a lot of ground to cover, but before we get into your past lane I think we should hear about your present and future lanes. I know there's something going on right now that you're very proud of.

CARLTON: There is indeed. Just to prove to myself that you're never too old to start a new venture I've started a company that's just getting on its feet. I've become a publisher.

JASON: That is exciting, please tell me more.

CARLTON: Well, it's called Seven Stones Press and we've got our first two books now almost ready for release. My idea was to use it as an outlet for my own material, but the first book is not one of mine. It is called *War according to Anna* and was written by Kamilla Chadwick, who was a ten year old child when growing up in the waning days of World War II in East Germany. It's not only an attention holding story, but in spite of her current age, it is written from the perspective of a ten year old. It's a very riveting tale.

JASON: I would love to read it because it would strike very close to home for me. I was about the same age when my family and I managed to escape from Stuttgart where I was born, but that's another story that I won't go into now.

CARLTON: I'll see that you get a copy as soon as it's available.

JASON: I'd really appreciate that. What's the other one?

CARLTON: It's one of my own. As you know, I've always been interested in mystery as many of the shows that I wrote were of that nature. What I'm doing now is writing some of those kinds of adventures. The first one, the one that's almost ready now is called *Killer at the Wheel*. If you liked my old *I Love a Mystery* series you should enjoy this book. I'll make sure you get it as soon as I can. That way I'll know that I have at least one reader.

JASON: I'm sure you won't have to worry about that. I know how well you write. Do you have any others on the drawing board?

CARLTON: Very definitely, I'm working on another one called *A Lavish of Sin* and I have an idea brewing for one that will probably be titled *Stuff the Lady's Hatbox*. I'm also planning to put out in print form some of my scripts from *One Man's Family* and *I Love a Mystery*.

JASON: I don't suppose you're willing to let me in on the plots of those first three?

CARLTON: Of course not. That would spoil the reading.

JASON: I understand, but you can't say I didn't try. I do love a mystery. It sounds like you have your work cut out for you.

CARLTON: Not too bad for an octogenarian, I'd say.

JASON: No, definitely not. Let's go back now to your early days. You didn't start your career writing for radio, did you?

CARLTON: No, no, I spent six years as a journalist for papers all up and down the west coast, Sacramento, San Francisco, Seattle, Vancouver and Portland. Oregon. When my last paper went out of business I had some offers from others, but I'd decided that I'd had enough. I had been writing some radio scripts for some time, but I had never submitted any of them to anyone in the business. When I left my last newspaper job I took a few of those scripts to NBC in San Francisco. To make a long story short, they liked what they read and low and behold, they hired me. What makes it even more interesting is that that was just two weeks before the market crash in 1929.

JASON: If I'm not mistaken, those were mysteries. Wasn't the station KGO?

CARLTON: Right on both counts, however those were not the scripts that were used for my first series after I was hired as a staff writer. That was a series called *House of Myths*. They were based on Greek mythology, but in a modern form. I had to be very careful not to offend any of the listener's concepts of the material. Some thought I went too far with my updating.

JASON: You did some other programming in those early years, mostly mystery and detective formats. All of those early broadcasts were West Coast only.

CARLTON: Yes they were. I did a series called *NBC Mystery Serial* on which I worked with the San Francisco Police Department. They were very helpful. The Chief, William J. Quinn, narrated all of those for me giving them authenticity. They were all based on true stories.

JASON: Then in 1932 you decided to take a different route.

CARLTON: About that time I was getting a little weary of murder and mayhem so I thought I'd try something entirely different. I thought about John Galsworthy's *Forsyte Saga* and I asked myself why something along those lines wouldn't work on radio? I put together four demo scripts using some of my own family experiences for background. I was the eldest of six children so I knew a bit about large families and sibling rivalries. I showed them to the production manager and was stunned by his reaction. He said it looked like I was written out and should probably resign. Well, I couldn't let that pass without a fight. I was angry enough to take my work to the big boss at NBC on the West Coast, Don Gilman. He read them, said he liked them very much and ordered that they be put on the air, much to the disdain

	of the production manager. I can't remember his name right now.
JASON:	What you're talking about, of course, is *One Man's Family*.
CARLTON:	That's right. It started out as a sustaining show on just three West Coast stations on April 29, 1932.
JASON:	And its swan song came twenty-seven and a half years later.
CARLTON:	Yes it did, but there were times when it looked like the end had come long before that last show. It began very well. At first we were only on stations in San Francisco, Los Angeles and Seattle. It wasn't long before other West Coast stations heard it and wanted it. It was very popular out here on the coast, but it remained a sustaining program throughout that first year. Sustaining means that we had no sponsor, as I'm sure you know. NBC was thinking of dropping it at the end of that first year, but the overwhelming fan support in the form of literally tons of mail prevented that move. A very clever sales manager managed to get some potential sponsors to read some of those letters. In January of 1933 we had Wesson Oil as our sponsor.
JASON:	But that's not the sponsor most of us remember.
CARLTON:	No it's not. That is because they only sponsored the West Coast network. In May of '33 we began piping the show to the East Coast, where it again became a sustaining program so Don Gilman set out to find a nationwide backer. He came up with Kentucky Winners Cigarettes. The churches were up in arms about that, thinking that we were ruining people's morals so that didn't last long, only a couple

of months. The end result was that Standard Brands came onboard and stayed with us for many years. Their product, Tender Leaf Tea is probably the one you remember, or Royal Gelatin.

JASON: Right, they were the products advertised on all of the programs I have copies of.

CARLTON: You know, when I think back, it was really interesting the way the family developed through the years. They just kept moving around and growing so that by the time it was over we were hearing from great grandchildren. After all, isn't that typical of most families over a twenty-seven year span?

JASON: You had an interesting way of organizing the whole saga. Instead of naming the episodes by numbers you presented them in book form, Chapter One, Book One, etc.

CARLTON: It was just a random idea at first, but it worked out well so I stayed with it. Each book had many chapters or episodes. By the time it was over there were 136 books and a total of 3256 chapters. I look back and marvel at its longevity. I guess it's still some kind of record for a dramatic series. Some folks like to call it a soap opera, but I won't stand for that.

JASON: That was a whole lot of writing and directing. Surely you must not have done it all yourself?

CARLTON: For quite a few years I did. Later on I had some help from Michael Raffetto whenever I was unavailable and much later Harlan Ware did some.

JASON: I've heard that you had a peculiar way of writing, and I don't mean that to sound negative.

CARLTON: That's all right. I know what you mean. Yes, you might call it peculiar. I could never write if anything distracted me. I would go into a sort of trance and if anyone disturbed me I would have to start all over again. That's why I used to go to my office at five in the morning when no one else was around and write each episode straight through from start to finish. It may sound strange to some, but that was my method. It certainly worked for me.

JASON: We can't knock success. You mentioned Michael Raffetto. It seems like just about every radio actor in Hollywood showed up on *One Man's Family* at one time or another, but Mike was one of four who had real staying power.

CARLTON: Yes, he was with me from '32 until he developed some voice problems in '55. The other three you're talking about stayed with me for almost as long or in one case, for the entire run. Mike was one of the sons, Paul Barbour.

JASON: That one person who played the entire run was J. Anthony Smythe who was Henry Barbour or Father Barbour.

CARLTON: He was, and during that time he never played any other role on any other show.

JASON: The other two were Minetta Ellen, who played Fanny or Mother Barbour until 1955 and Barton Yarborough who was Clifford until his sudden death in '51. You then wrote out his character. I would call that some kind of job security.

CARLTON: Yes, but you know, I never considered any of the people on the show as employees. I was never their boss. We were all just good friends. It was

	like a real family. You can't beat that for working conditions.
JASON:	Just for fun, let's listen in to a portion of one of those many shows. This is from Chapter Nine, Book Seventy-One, and episode called "Father Barbour's Rampage and what became of it." It seems that Father Barbour could be a little crotchety at times.

****

ANNCR:	Father Barbour came back to the Sky Ranch this morning, joining up with Nicky and Claudia and he is not in his most amiable state of mind, if we may indulge in understatement. He went way out on a limb at Sea Cliff when he predicted that Joan's absence overnight indicated that Paul's faith in the girl was sadly misplaced. He made some outrageous accusations, and though he was proved wrong, he's not yet apologized to anybody. Something else has upset him too. He can't find his favorite comb and brush. Now he sits in the farthest corner of the front porch staring off at the purple mountains.
FATHER:	This is a lot of folderol, that's what it is, a lot of newfangled nuisance.
JACK:	Hi Dad.
FATHER:	Who's that?
JACK:	Remember me, your youngest son, Jack? The one with the triplets? Did you have a nice time at Sea Cliff?
FATHER:	Hey Jack, have you seen my comb and brush?
JACK:	Dad, how would I see your comb and brush? I never go in your room.

Act V: Scene Three: Keep On Keeping On

FATHER: Your children do. They all go into my room. They run in and out with no regard for privacy whatever. I unpacked my comb and brush and put them on my little table by the bed. I was going to place them on the bureau. When I came out of the shower there was no comb and brush.

JACK: Are you sure you didn't leave them at Sea Cliff?

FATHER: Jack, I just said I left them on the end table. I'm not entirely devoid of common sense.

JACK: Did I imply that? I didn't even know we were talking about common sense.

FATHER: Well, sometimes people act like I'm not totally responsible. It's a black comb and a black brush with white bristles and my initials are on the back, big white letters. It was the first thing I took out of my bag. I always take the comb and brush out of my bag first and then put them on the bureau. (Door opens and closes) Well, Cliff, what are you all dressed up for might I ask, Clifford?

CLIFF: Oh hi Dad. How do you like the new suit?

FATHER: Hmmm, it's kind of racy looking.

CLIFF: Oh Dad! It's the best suit I've ever had in my life, well, up until 1938. What I wore during those eleven years, I don't know, maybe a barrel.

JACK: Dad's lost his comb and brush, Cliff. He's worried—

FATHER: I don't like that flippant tone, Jack. I don't like it at all.

JACK: It's a swell suit, Cliff. Turn around. Hey, look at those shoulders. Look at that drape.

FATHER: I asked a question and nobody answered. Oh, he's an old man with an allergy. Everybody says so, ignore him. If he asks a question just don't bother to answer it.

JACK: Which question was that, Dad?

FATHER: I asked Cliff where he was going all dressed up, a perfectly civil question. All right, don't answer.

****

JASON: I sure hope he found his dad-burned comb and brush. Such a terrible problem! There was something else that you rarely did, something that would have saved a lot of writing time. Very seldom did you use flashbacks when there was so much history to flash back on.

CARLTON: No, I didn't like that gimmick. On the few occasions when they were used it was because someone in the cast was ill or had some personal problem that kept them away.

JASON: You know, Carlton, by the time *One Man's Family* reached its final bell there were nearly one hundred characters in the scenario. It surely didn't start that way.

CARLTON: In the beginning there were just seven characters. They were Mother and Father Barbour and their five offspring. Paul was the eldest. Jack was the youngest. In between then were Hazel and the twins, Claudia and Clifford. But you know what happens with families, they tend to grow. We ended up with the children's children and then their children. We had husbands, wives and friends of the children and the children's children. It got rather complicated at times. Occasionally I had to refer to the family tree I had made up to keep them straight.

JASON: And yet, you were told that it would never fly when you presented those initial scripts.

CARLTON: Who do you think got the last laugh?

JASON: No doubt about that. Speaking of laughs, I'm sure you must be aware of the spoof Bob Elliott and Ray Goulding did on your show called *One Fella's Family*. Did that bother you?

CARLTON: Quite the contrary, imitation is the finest form of flattery. What they did was great fun. It also proved that at least someone remembered the show.

JASON: You're being too humble. I'm sure there are millions who remember *One Man's Family*. I know I do. We could spend hours talking about *One Man's Family*, but you did much more than that. My own personal favorite was the other long running series you did, which was a return to the mystery/adventure format that you began with in 1929. You know what I'm referring to. It began in 1939. *It was I Love a Mystery.*

CARLTON: The first one aired in January of 1939. In some ways it was similar to *One Man's Family* as far as the layout was concerned. Each story was told with a series of episodes, sometimes as many as twenty. It was like a book with twenty chapters, just like *One Man's Family*. Since the three main characters remained constant throughout, or almost throughout, there was a sort of continuity to it all.

JASON:	The way you set it up you could put them in just about any location in the world for a particular tale. Each of the characters was so well defined that we never had to think twice about who was speaking.
CARLTON:	It was great fun to do, but some of the stories seemed to worry a few parents because they thought their kids might get too involved and thus, traumatized. I have to admit that there were some intense scenes, but my primary target was not the kids, at least not the younger ones. There was never any drinking or sex involved. No one ever even carried a gun.
JASON:	They were all well thought out and sometimes very complicated adventures. On some of them I thought I was listening to a pre-curser of Indiana Jones. When you started the series in '39 you had some of the same actors from *One Man's Family*, which meant they were involved in family life and adventure at the same time.
CARLTON:	Yes, in the beginning I used both Michael Raffetto and Barton Yarborough. I was very comfortable working with them. Mike was Jack Packard, the head of the A-1 Detective Agency. Barton was his side-kick with a Texas drawl, Doc Long. The other principle role was Reggie Yorke, played by Walter Paterson with a British accent.
JASON:	Walter's history was tragic.
CARLTON:	Yes it was. He killed himself in 1942. I didn't have the heart to continue his character with someone else. He was a good friend. I simply wrote Reggie out of the script.
JASON:	You had many other actors involved before it ran its course in 1952. One of them was one of your

favorite people, Mercedes McCambridge.

CARLTON: Mercedes filled in doing a variety of characters in quite a few of the stories.

JASON: We'll talk more about her in a little while, but for now, let me interject a bit from one of my favorites, "Temple of Vampires." She is heard as a young lady named Sunny. Jack, Doc and Reggie are all present. This is from episode five.

****

JACK: What are you talking about, Doc?

DOC: Him, I just saw him, I swear, forty, fifty feet up in the air. He started at that wall over there and floated to this here wall.

SUNNY: It must have been a bird.

JACK: Yeah, a bird.

DOC: I saw it, dogone it!

JACK: Now look, Doc, you can see how silly that sounds on the face of it. Why, it's a good 150 to 200 feet from one wall to another.

DOC: I know that. I still say I saw it.

REGGIE: But nothing could pass that distance through the air without wings.

DOC: If there'd been wings I'd've seen 'em, wouldn't I?

REGGIE: Yes, but if it was as large as a man it would have a tremendous wing span. They'd make a tremendous noise.

DOC: All right, smart guys, have it your way. So I didn't see anything as big as a man float through the air up there.

REGGIE: It was almost certainly deception caused by the light and shadows. You may have thought you did.

DOC: Have it your way. You're all a bunch of dimwit sissies. Anyway, what'll we do next?

JACK: Well, is Hermie around?

SUNNY: Uh uh. He's sitting out on the steps with a hamper of food eating a piece of chocolate.

REGGIE: Jack, this is a genuine ancient temple made out of the ruins of a lost civilization. Maybe we should look around.

JACK: Well, help yourself. What do you want, the forty cent tour?

SUNNY: This place scares me, just looking up at the ceiling. Imagine a civilization centuries ago and intelligent enough to construct this temple.

****

JASON: You know, Carlton, I have many of those shows or at least parts of them. "Temple of Vampires" rates at the top of my list. A couple of others that come close are "Battle of the Century" and "Bury Your Dead, Arizona."

CARTLON: They were all fun to do.

JASON: Once more I'm trapped by the clock. We could spend days on *I Love a Mystery*, but we need to

	move on. In 1944 you did *Adventures by Morse*. It bore a lot of resemblances to *I Love a Mystery*, but the main characters had different names.
CARLTON:	It was somewhat similar to *I Love a Mystery*, but the settings were quite different. I often call it my spooky series because it was mostly about the supernatural. The main man was Captain Friday and his side-kick was Skip Turner. They very much resembled Jack and Doc.
JASON:	There was another series in 1948 that was a direct spin-off from *I Love a Mystery*. It was called *I Love Adventure*.
CARLTON:	That was an interesting concept. As the story line went, Jack, Doc and Reggie had been separated by the war. Jack went into intelligence. Doc joined the Flying Tigers in China as a fighter pilot and Reggie returned to England where he became a member of the RAF. After the war Jack was called to London to work for international peace. The group that asked for his help was called The Twenty-one Old Men of Grammercy Park, which was a very hush-hush organization. Along the way that group was written out and Jack returned to California to reform the A-1 Detective Agency. Soon he was reunited with Reggie, who before long disappeared again from the script. Soon after that Doc showed up.
JASON:	Once more you had Michael Raffetto in the lead role and Barton Yarborough as Doc. Tom Collins did Reggie.
CARLTON:	They couldn't resist doing it. They were a good team.
JASON:	Let's change directions again. In '45 you went with

a somewhat different format with a program titled *His Honor, the Barber.*

CARLTON: That was a little like *One Man's Family.* Barry Fitzgerald was my star playing a small town barber who got elected to the bench and often wanted to go back to cutting hair. He was what I thought to be a typical old Irish philosopher, but the Irish in the audience didn't think so. They wanted to throw rocks at me. It was full of old fashioned platitudes and comments about how old judge Bernard Fitz sometimes thought he was on the wrong side of the law. It only lasted one season.

JASON: Ok, let's return to Mercedes McCambridge. There was a show that you wrote specifically for her. It was called *Family Skeleton.*

CARLTON: Mercedes was the Family Skeleton. She came back to her home town wrapped up in what the people thought was scandal. She was pregnant and couldn't produce her marriage certificate because it had been destroyed. I think you can figure out for yourself how well that went over in 1953. Anyway, she was wonderful in the part. I always enjoyed working with her.

JASON: That's exactly what some of my other guests said about her. Apparently she was a very popular young lady in those days. One last show and then I'll let you go.

CARLTON: Don't worry about me. I've got as much time as you want. I'm enjoying this.

JASON: I appreciate that and I thank you very much for the comment, but this portion of my show only lasts an hour. The show I want to bring up began an eight year run in 1951 and was a true soap opera. It always began with this statement: *Imperious man, look into your heart and dwell on this. Without the woman in my house, what would I do?*

CARLTON: That was *Woman in my House*. I didn't write that. I only produced it. It was interesting, but I can't lay claim to it.

JASON: I think there was plenty that can claim as your own.

****

Carlton E. Morse was a very precise, organized and accurate man. His instant responses to my questions were so complete it was almost like an encyclopedia of his achievements. His recall was almost total. My research into his background was really not needed. He could have done it all without my cues. If this makes it sound like he was stiff and rigid to talk with, that is not at all what I mean to convey. He was a very warm and congenial man. After the tape was turned off we continued our conversation for another full hour and we kept in touch after that until he passed away in 1993 at the age of ninety-two. I still have his many letters to prove it. He made good on his promises to send me copies of his books as they became available. They remain in a special place in my own large library.

He was generally well liked by his co-workers through the years and very loyal to them in return. Mercedes McCambridge said she always thought of him as her mentor. She added, that of all the forms of media, she always thought radio was the best. She was well qualified to make that comparison, having had experience on the stage, on film and on television. Russell Thorson, who worked with Carlton for years on *One Man's Family* and then later on *I Love a Mystery* and *I Love Adventure*, said that it was a fun time that he always enjoyed. Tony Randall, a man who openly quoted as saying that he disliked radio, said that it took extraordinary imagination to write the *I Love a Mystery* shows that he later performed on and that Carlton was also a master of sound effects.

There remains no doubt that Carlton E. Morse was a genius of the written word. He came a long way from his humble beginnings in Jennings, Louisiana. His *I Love a Mystery* series is considered by many as the greatest radio show ever produced.

Act VI:
Comediennes

There were many of them. They could make us laugh until our sides nearly split. Sometimes it was just a throw-away line glibly delivered by a minor character. Sometimes it was the star doing her job very well. The simplest line tossed off at the right moment in the right situation could leave us rolling in the aisles. One of those people who could transform a minor role into a major comedic event was Bea Benaderet, who would have made a great guest on my show, but sadly, she passed away before I had a chance to talk with her. Another one was Veola Vonn. She was mostly a small part, but memorable performer on many, many shows including one with my first featured guest in Act IV. Who could forget Verna Felton as Red Skelton's mother and a variety of other parts she played.

A couple of radio stars of whom we have previously spoken were Judy Canova and Lucille Ball. Yes, Lucy did a great deal of radio work before her television days including *My Favorite Husband* and a radio version of *I Love Lucy*.

None of the above will be in this act, but the three ladies I have chosen could match, line for line, joke for joke, any comedienne in the business. Not one of the three was strictly a comedy performer, but each of them made a name for herself in that genre. I sincerely hope you will enjoy my selections.

Act VI:
Scene One
From Bumstead to Jetson

We begin with a lady who was best known for two major long running characters however they were far from the total of her resume. When she began her career at the tender age of seventeen on Broadway where she became known for her agility. She could do forty cartwheels in less than an hour. It was not too long before Jake Schubert noticed that she had other talents and he cast her in his production of *Good News* at the Winter Garden. There was so much that followed that first experience, but I'll let her tell you all about it.

Her name was Penny Singleton. This conversation took place on July 12, 1987.

****

Jason: She was best known for one particular role, but she did so much more on radio, television and in pictures. I want you to welcome Penny Singleton.

Penny: Thank you, Jason. Actually it was just pictures and radio.

Jason: Oh no, did you forget *The Jetsons*?

Penny: Oh yes, of course. I didn't mean to overlook my favorite cartoon, my favorite character. I was just thinking of the *Blondie* part of it.

JASON: Before we get into *Blondie* let's talk a little about your early career on film. You worked in those before you used the name Penny Singleton. I'm not sure which name to use.

PENNY: What names do you have?

JASON: I have Dorothy McNulty and Marianna McNulty.

PENNY: It was both. Marianna Dorothy McNulty was my birth name.

JASON: Your first movie as I have it was *Love in the Rough*. Is that correct?

PENNY: No, my first one was called *That Good News*, done at Metro Goldwyn Mayer. *Love in the Rough* came after that. My very first film was made out on Long Island. It was done in some kind of a church. Gus Morgan was in it and I've forgotten who else. It was so long ago I've even forgotten the title. I think it was called *Girl of the Night* or something like that.

JASON: There used to be many short subjects, music, news and cartoons. Cartoons are almost lost now. Those we always had with a feature film. You did *After the Thin Man* with William Powell and Myrna Loy.

PENNY: That was after 1935.

JASON: '36, I believe. That would have been maybe the last one you did before you were Penny Singleton.

PENNY: No, I don't think so. That was for Warner Brothers. I did one with Humphrey Bogart. He played a newspaper reporter. That was called *Swing Your Lady*. Humphrey Bogart had his first leading role and I was his leading lady.

JASON: That would have been in 1935?

PENNY: I think so. I'm terrible on dates.

JASON: The ones that most people remember from your list of credits, and I know you did others, but you did over twenty *Blondie* pictures, in fact, twenty-eight of them over a period of fourteen or fifteen years. The first was *Blondie* and the last was *Blondie's Hero*.

PENNY: That's right.

JASON: That amounts to at least two or more a year.

PENNY: It was at least three a year.

JASON: Didn't that get to be a little tiring, playing the same character over and over?

PENNY: Oh no, it was always wonderful because the scripts were always so good. People could relate to the Bumstead family. They were always based on families, things that happen in families. *The Jetsons* is about family life too even though they're an outer space family. It's kind of a sort of a sense of humor that suggests some of the same qualities, very clean. We never had anything raw or anything like that in the *Blondie's* and we never did in *The Jetsons*.

JASON: That's very true. They were good family fare and a lot of fun. The *Blondie* movies must have worked well because, as I understand it, Columbia was in a lot of trouble when the first one was made. That movie grossed about nine million dollars which was quite a bit of money in those days.

PENNY: It was. The thing that happened was that when

Harry Cohn watched the first dailies of *Blondie* he couldn't understand it at all. He thought it was the worst mistake they ever made. They were going bankrupt. They were getting ready to file for bankruptcy. Anyway, we finished the picture and sent out some sneak previews. The walls came apart. The audience loved it. Harry thought that somebody had stacked the cards, so to speak. So he was going to find out for himself. He couldn't believe it. He took a few people from the studio and wouldn't tell anyone where they were going. He had his own sneak preview. The walls came apart and they all loved it. What did Cohn do? They didn't include *Blondie* in the sales figures they sent out from Columbia. They kept *Blondie* out of them. So the distributers could not get *Blondie* unless they took one of the more expensive films that hadn't been doing very well. They could get *Blondie* only if they took one of the other pictures with big stars in them, but were failing at the box office. The first *Blondie* picture was made for something like seventy-five or a hundred thousand dollars.

JASON: So they were taking advantage of the less expensive picture to cover the ones that were costing them a bundle.

PENNY: I don't know if you'd call it taking advantage. They had the opportunity to do it because Harry Cohn, who was the head of the studio, thought so little of *Blondie* that he didn't even include it in the salable items that Columbia had. He just thought it was money down the drain. When he found out he had a gold mine, of course it was something different. The *Blondie* picture saved Columbia from bankruptcy.

| JASON: | As I said that picture grossed over nine million dollars. That was a lot of money then. |

| PENNY: | You can you imagine that ratio today for seventy-five to one hundred million dollars. |

| JASON: | Today you can't make the cheapest movie for that kind of money. |

| PENNY: | I know. It just goes to show how much the business has changed. |

| JASON: | The radio *Blondie* series started at almost the same time as the first movie was released. |

| PENNY: | Yes, very shortly after the first movie. Here's a funny story. I had been to New York and I came back to California. I had heard that they were going to go with Campbell's. So I went into the publicity department and I said, "Well, I'm going to be with Campbell's. I always loved their soup. It's just wonderful." Everybody looked at me and everybody got frantic. Lots of phone calls were made. They were checking it out. I thought we were gong on the air for Campbell's Soups. Instead, we were on for Camel Cigarettes. The hysterical part was I didn't smoke. |

| JASON: | The funniest thing was to listen to is some of the old Camel's commercials and hear that more doctors smoke Camels than any other cigarette and that opera singers love them. |

| PENNY: | Isn't that something? It pays to advertise. |

| JASON: | I spoke with Phil Harris a while back and he said he was terrified when Jack Benny went with Lucky Strikes. He said that thirteen weeks with a cigarette

PENNY: sponsor was usually all you got from them. Then they'd dump you.

PENNY: That certainly didn't hold true in that case. Look how long Jack Benny had them for a sponsor.

JASON: There are always exceptions to any rule, but Camels only stayed with *Blondie* for one season.

PENNY: That's true. We went from cigarettes to soap suds. Our next sponsor was Super Suds.

JASON: "Lots more suds from Super Suds," right? You had the same co-star throughout the radio series. Arthur Lake was the only Dagwood on radio or on film.

PENNY: I never worked with another Dagwood, but he worked with other Blondies. I would not do the television shows because when they were putting them together they were going to use the old radio scripts. We had a lot of wonderful production values in the *Blondie* pictures. I just couldn't see using radio scripts. It was sort of slapsticky. The original *Blondies* had been out for many years. I kind of had a feeling about them and was protective of that feeling. They just didn't want to change. That was the way the television people wanted to do *Blondie*. That was the way they wanted them. So it didn't last. Then they tried to do it all over again. The people they had for those shows were very good. The girls who did the Blondie part were excellent actresses and very pretty, but they just were not acceptable. The public just didn't take to them. I don't know if it was because Arthur and I had done it for so long that they were just more used to us, felt at home with us. Then again, we weren't very fancy. I was never much for the glamour part of it. I always tried to be Blondie so I tried

	to make her a combination of Helen Hayes and Molly Goldberg.
JASON:	That's quite a combination.
PENNY:	But you see, both of those ladies were wonderful people. They still are, you know. Well, I think Molly's gone.
JASON:	Yes she is. You're speaking of Gertrude Berg, of course.
PENNY:	Golly, I used to enjoy her show. I thought she was just adorable. Today I have another love, Angela, Angela Lansbury. Do you enjoy her show?
JASON:	You mean *Murder, She Wrote*? Yes I do.
PENNY:	Of course. I saw her at her Central Park affair and then again at the Tony Awards. I had seen her in *Mame*. I went to the opening night and that was a night to remember. She's a doll. She's absolutely a fantastic, wonderful person, so talented.
JASON:	She seems to get even better as time passes.
PENNY:	Yes she does.
JASON:	There were other Blondies on the later radio shows. You didn't stay with it for the full run. I understand Alice White did it for a time and then Patricia Van Cleave who was Arthur Lake's wife off the mike.
PENNY:	He used to say, "She's my real life Blondie."
JASON:	He also made a statement at one time that his life was a little on the Bumsteady side. That he, in some ways was like the character he played.

PENNY:	He was the only Dagwood. He was born to be Dagwood, a warm, sweet, happy go lucky guy. He was that way in real life. Arthur would help somebody across the street and then turn around and get hit by a car. His whole life was kind of like that.
JASON:	That's Bumsteady.
PENNY:	Of course.
JASON:	Dagwood or Arthur Lake, whichever you want to call him, was Dagwood. He grew up in a show business family in a tent show. His father was a strong man and his mother was a stage actress.
PENNY:	His real name was Silverlake.
JASON:	That is pretty close to his stage name. The other characters on the show were played by quite a few different people. I'm thinking now of the kids. Both of the kids were played at one time or another by Leone Ledoux.
PENNY:	That was on the Radio. She was their voices on radio.
JASON:	Exactly. It's not in any of the books, but I believe Jerry Hausner did some of the crying. He was an expert crier.
PENNY:	I'll tell you somebody else who did it. (She cries)
JASON:	I guess I don't have to ask who you mean, do I?
PENNY:	I did it too, and Jerry Hausner. Jerry was a wonderful person. We always had wonderful, warm, good people. We all worked together whether it was on radio or in films.

JASON: Almost a radio hall of fame. If you read the names in the cast you find Hanley Stafford and Arthur Q. Bryan. Both did Mr. Dithers at one time or another, mostly Hanley.

PENNY: . . . and Agnes Moorehead.

JASON: . . . and Elvia Allman.

PENNY: Oh, Elvia and Aggie, yes, wonderful. I'm so sorry that we don't have radio the way we used to have it. I still believe in radio. Radio was wonderful.

JASON: I think, in some respects, what you're doing now with *The Jetsons*. It is akin to radio because you're working with your voice and a lot of imagination.

PENNY: It is and of course, I do that with Bill Hanna and Joe Barbera. The writers come up with some wonderfully funny scripts. When you think of how many of them we have made now and how we started them back in 1964, can you believe that? I was so excited when I came in because I love Janet Waldo and all the rest of the people, Daws Butler and Don Messick.

JASON: Don't forget Mel Blanc.

PENNY: Mel, of course, Mr. Spacely. Who could ever forget Mel? They were all good people. Bill and Joe decided to make more *Jetsons* and they got the whole cast together. Can you believe it? So we made forty-one new *Jetsons*. Then we made some more. A couple of them were features. *Judy and the Rockers*, that's going to be a killer. Janet is so great in that.

JASON: I'm looking forward to seeing it because we talked about it when I spoke with Janet.

PENNY: It's a fantastic film. She's really something, that girl.

JASON: I think all of the people we've mentioned fall into that down to earth category. A couple more were Frank Nelson and Hal Peary.

PENNY: We all miss Frank Nelson and Hal Peary. Wasn't he *The Great Gildersleeve*?

JASON: He was the first one. He did it for nine years and then Will Waterman did it for an additional nine years when Hal left the show due to some contractual problems. They were good friends.

PENNY: I've often wondered to myself how when somebody creates a part, I'm thinking of *The Great Gildersleeve* right now, when Hal created the part and then someone else took it over, how can people do things like that? Do they have to imitate the original? Did the directors insist that they had to do that? Because, a strange thing, in the theatre you know, when we were growing up in the theatre in musical comedy, if someone was going to be replaced we had to stay with the plot. We had to stay with the director's interpretation. The director is very important and the music and dance numbers and everything remained the same all the time. You were told not to do a carbon copy, to put some of your own warmth and your own expression into it, not to try to do a duplicate.

JASON: In the case of *The Great Gildersleeve* I think they made an exception because Hal and Will had worked together on a lot of shows all the way back to *Tom Mix* in Chicago. They sounded exactly alike. Will told me the script dictated the voice.

PENNY: In the theatre we were always taught to be a little bit different, to be sure you got a little of yourself into it.

JASON: Since you brought up the theatre, I'm a little curious about something. You were in *No, No, Nanette*. I'm wondering if that was the same cast with Evelyn Keyes.

PENNY: No, I replaced Ruby Keeler in New York. I did the show with Patsy Kelly and the original members of the *No, No, Nanette*. The show that you're talking about was the road show, wasn't it?

JASON: Yes, it was. Evelyn played the part that Ruby Keeler played. She told me she hadn't had her dancing shoes on for years at the time. It really terrified her.

PENNY: Evelyn is a good dancer. I hadn't had my dancing shoes on either for years, but in a couple of weeks I was fine. I was running the union out there and I was rehearsing for the show. Then when I was appearing in the show I was still heading over to the union office during the day and doing that business.

JASON: You did quite a bit of work on Broadway. One show that comes to mind is *Hey, Nonny, Nonny*.

PENNY: That was with Frank Morgan and Mitzi Gaynor. It was a summer show. It would have lasted much longer but our star, Frank Morgan got a call from MGM and was told he had to get back there. Our producers said they were trying to find another Frank Morgan. I told them that was impossible.

JASON: No, and they haven't since.

PENNY: I was there for a couple of years. That was when a show could last. There are still some shows that do. Our theatre is gone, as Helen Hayes says, "The world is getting larger, but the theatre seems to be shrinking." She can't understand why. I can't either.

JASON: I think part of the problem is that production costs have soared and it's hard to sustain some shows. Some don't start off on the right foot. By the time they get onto the right track it's too late.

PENNY: I know. The cost of putting a show on now is prohibitive. And also, many of the writers won't come out to do them. If they're going to write a Broadway show it's going to tie them up for a long, long time, possibly a year. There are months of rehearsals, months of getting the costumes and everything else together. They can come out here and write a script and sell it. Then they're in business. It takes so much time and you really can't make the money writing for a show that you can writing for a picture. As a writer I'm not too interested in doing anything for Broadway, for the shows.

JASON: I can think of a good exception to that. I'm thinking of Jerry Lawrence and Bob Lee. They're still doing a lot of Broadway work.

PENNY: Oh well, that's different. They're very talented. They really love the theatre. See, that's an interesting thing. Everybody has loves in their lives. With them it's a ruling relationship. They love their work. I too love the theatre.

JASON: You know, it's a funny thing, when I spoke with Bob and Jerry they both agreed that radio is still their first love.

PENNY: I think so too.

JASON: I don't think I've talked with anyone that ever worked in radio that didn't feel the same way about it.

PENNY: It was instant communication. It was communication where people could feel relaxed. They could listen. They could follow things. I can remember living through *Myrt and Marge*. I just lived through that and *One Man's Family* and all of those shows. They were just simply wonderful. Vaudeville went out and talking pictures came in and then along came radio and knocked out talking pictures. Then along came television and knocked out radio.

JASON: People who did silent films didn't always have the voice for the talkies and yet, they did have the image. Another thing that happened on that same train of thought was that many people who had good voices for radio, when television came into being, they didn't fit what the public wanted to see.

PENNY: You're very bright in your observation. Did you ever see Ethel Merman on stage or Mary Martin? You would never want to see more sparkling, more brilliant and vibrant live talent. Those women were absolutely beautiful on stage, thrill you to death. But Ethel Merman was too much for cameras. She had so much energy. She could sing from here to tomorrow. The camera magnifies and she just didn't come off. Ethel, to me, was superb on the stage. Films never really did too much for Mary Martin either.

JASON: I never did see Ethel on the stage, but I did see Mary Martin in New York so I know what you're saying.

PENNY: And Chita Rivera. Our business is wonderful. There's no business like show business. It's really true.

JASON: Well, Penny, I don't want to keep you on the phone all day although I'd really like to.

PENNY: Don't say that. I'm having fun. I hope everybody listening will enjoy it as much as I am. Can I say something special to them, Jason?

JASON: Of course you can.

PENNY: On behalf of the whole family, Dagwood, Daisy, Baby Dumpling, Alexander, Alvin, Mr. Dithers and of course, Cora Dithers, we send you our love and wish you well and all God's blessings to you and yours. Don't forget it!

****

Penny Singleton was a true lady always thinking about other people over herself. She mentioned her work with the union. It is interesting to note that way, way back in years she was the driving force in leading a strike against Rockefeller Center on behalf of the Rockettes who did not feel they were being treated fairly at the time. Penny was always around for anyone who needed any kind of help, sometimes ignoring her own problems to try to take care of theirs. She never sought any kind of publicity for her efforts on behalf of others, in fact, she shunned it. It was a privilege to have had a chance to talk with her.

Penny died in 2003 at the age of ninety-five.

Act VI:
Scene Two
Seriously Funny

She was a very serious lady who could turn on her funny streak at the drop of a hat. We usually identify her with a role that she played on radio and television that brought her to the top of the comedy genre for several years. She was somewhat unique in that she was born in California and died in California, but in between she made the world her oyster on the stage and on film as well as her radio and TV work. She began her radio career as a high school teacher and in two of her latest pictures she was a school principal.

I am sure I have given her identity away with those little bits of information. If you still have not figured it out I will help. Her chosen name was Eve Arden. On June 15, 1986 we had this discussion twice. I will explain why at the end of this piece.

****

Jason: Today we have the pleasure of hearing from a true gentlewoman of the performing arts, Eve Arden. Although she had many credits on film, radio and television, I believe her first love is still the stage. Isn't that right, Eve?

Eve: That's very true, Jason. I love working with a live audience where every word and every action can be scrutinized by them. In the theatre you can't depend on your last performance because every audience is very different from the last or the next. It keeps you on your toes. You can't depend on reviews even if they're very good. In a sense each night is like opening night which means you can't depend on anything except the moment you're in. It's great fun when it works.

JASON: Then I must assume you've had a lot of what you call great fun. You've worked on stage all over the country and mostly to good words from the critics. Even though you were California born, it seems to me that your first notable stage performances were in the *Ziegfeld Follies* at the Winter Garden in New York, as a featured part of the show, I must add. How did that come about?

EVE: That's all true. I was born in Mill Valley, a little town north of San Francisco. I dropped out of high school and joined a stock company when I was sixteen and things began to happen. I did my first movie when I was nineteen and sometime later I was noticed by Jacob Schubert who was directing the Ziegfeld reviews in New York. I'm over simplifying, but in '34, he made me a featured player in the Follies. It was wonderful working with Fanny Bryce and Buddy Ebsen and the rest. In '36 I also got to work with Bob Hope and Judy Canova. I learned a lot from all of them.

JASON: The first movie you did was *Song of Love*. You were still using your birth name at that time.

EVE: Yes I was. That's a story I've told more times than I can count, but here I go again. As you obviously know, Jason, I was born Eunice Quedens. Along the way, I was told that that name was too long to fit on most marquees. Without a lot of thought I noticed a vial of Evening in Paris perfume and some Elizabeth Arden cosmetics on my dressing room table so I simply took a part of each name and I became Eve Arden, so from that day on that has been my name. It's certainly easier to say, don't you think?

JASON: Without a doubt, Eunice Quedens doesn't flow too well. I'm almost sorry I brought it up.

EVE: Oh, that's OK, it's really no secret.

JASON: I notice on your list of credits that you were pretty active on the movie scene during the time you spent with the *Follies*.

EVE: I was a bit of a cross-country commuter in those days. I was also doing other stage work at the time. I was a very busy young lady.

JASON: You did a lot of theatre through the years including, much later, the title roles in *Hello Dolly* and *Auntie Mame*. *Auntie Mame* and *Mame* were both written by Jerry Lawrence and Bob Lee.

EVE: I did have the pleasure of working with Jerry and Bob. They were marvelous guys. As you said, those two plays came much later, in the '60s.

JASON: Before which you did many others. Two that come to mind are Neil Simon's *Barefoot in the Park* and Leonard Bernstein's *Wonderful Town*.

EVE: There were so many others as well.

JASON: Along the way you appeared in many movies. You even got an Oscar nomination for your work in *Mildred Pierce*, which incidentally, is my wife's all-time favorite picture.

EVE: Yes I did, but to this day I don't know why. I didn't think my work in that one was so exceptional.

JASON: Someone must have thought so.

EVE: I guess they did and I'm grateful.

JASON: We'll come back to your movie work later, but it's inevitable that we talk about *Our Miss Brooks*, a show that made it to the top on both radio and television. For a long time it was on both. On radio it out lasted the television version.

EVE: Of course, that's the one most people remember me for.

JASON: I must tell you, *Our Miss Brooks* was also my wife's favorite radio show. We have many of them in our collection. She still breaks up when I play one of them.

EVE: It sounds like I should have more fans like your wife. Thank her for me. We had fun making them.

JASON: It was a show that shot to the top of the ratings in very short order and then took a dip when the time slot was changed.

EVE: It's so important to be on with the right show preceding it. It gets people in the habit of not changing the dial unless they hear something they don't like. I don't know why they changed our time and day, but the results were not good.

JASON: I understand that you were not the first choice to play Connie Brooks.

EVE: They looked first to Shirley Booth, but she refused for some interesting reasons. Then they thought of Lucille Ball however she was, at the time, too wrapped up in her own radio show *My Favorite Husband*.

	Whatever their reasons for refusing the role, I thank my lucky stars that they did.
JASON:	Is it true that you gave your character her name?
EVE:	Yes it is. Connie Brooks came from my daughter Connie and my husband Brooks West.
JASON:	I always wondered about that, especially the Brooks part of it.
EVE:	Well, that's the story, Jason.
JASON:	Let's talk about some of the other people on the show. One of my favorites was Margaret Davis, your landlady.
EVE:	Oh, Jane Morgan, you know, she was exactly the same person off the air, so unassuming and perhaps a bit flighty, but so much fun to work with. She used to do some of the same things in real life that she did on the show. She was just a delight.
JASON:	I think we should listen in on Connie Brooks and Mrs. Davis from an episode called "School Garden." As was often the case, Mrs. Davis had a surprise breakfast treat for Connie. We will also hear from Walter Denton as played by Richard Crenna.

****

CONNIE:	As I went into the dinette for a quick cup of coffee my landlady had a little surprise.
DAVIS:	Connie, instead of bacon and eggs this morning, I fixed you something rare and exotic. How does it look, dear?

CONNIE: Indigestible, oh, I'm sorry, Mrs. Davis. That was unkind of me. You tell me what that stuff is and I'll eat it.

DAVIS: Oh, it's only some arrowroot, papaya, lucuma and pola.

CONNIE: I still say, tell me what it is and I'll eat it.

DAVIS: These are Hawaiian fruits and vegetables. My neighbor, Mrs. Anderson, is vacationing in Honolulu. She sent me a whole crate full of this stuff.

CONNIE: Mrs. Davis, I'm not really very hungry this morning.

DAVIS: Oh dear, I had a feeling you wouldn't go for this Hawaiian mess, but Connie, if you try it you might get used to it.

CONNIE: Well actually, you won't even need this stuff, Mrs. Davis. In another few days I'm going to treat you to a real fresh batch of home grown vegetables right out of the school garden that I planned.

DAVIS: Oh that's right the inter-school gardening contest is in a few weeks, isn't it? But how do you know the vegetables will come up on time?

CONNIE: Oh, they'll come up even if Mr. Conklin has to plant me underneath to push them up. He's really determined to beat out Jason Brill for the trophy this year particularly since Clay's principal won the award last year. You never saw such vegetable gardens, radishes, celery, tomatoes and spinach.

DAVIS: But what did Mr. Conklin's garden produce?

CONNIE: A half-acre of nice blooming jasmine. He bought

	the wrong seeds. He's warned me that if I fail him in this project I won't have an evening to myself for the rest of the semester.
DAVIS:	Connie, that isn't fair. I'm sure he hasn't been that strict with the rest of his faculty.
CONNIE:	Well, perhaps he doesn't have to be. So far Mr. Boynton has done a good job of handling the cafeteria. Miss Miller's tossed out most of the school rubbish.
DAVIS:	What about Miss Enright's project?
CONNIE:	That one really confuses me. She chose as her project the care and feeding of Catherine, the school goat and mascot.
DAVIS:	Maybe Miss Enright likes goats, Connie.
CONNIE:	Maybe so, she's certainly been trying to get mine for years. (*phone rings*) I'll get it, Mrs. Davis. Hello?
WALTER:	Miss Brooks, Walter, I have terrible news for you Miss Brooks, awful news. Disaster has finally struck.
CONNIE:	What is it, Walter? What happened? You're not hurt, are you?
WALTER:	Oh, nothing like that. This is worse, much, much worse. Oh, this is terrible, simply awful. I just went back to the school garden and there isn't any.
CONNIE:	No school garden? Not a thing? Walter, you don't mean it's completely barren?
WALTER:	You just go over there, Miss Brooks. You've got Death Valley.

****

Eve: If you know that episode you know that all of Mrs. Davis' Hawaiian fruits and vegetables came in handy before it was over. They replaced the peas and carrots that had been eaten by Catherine, the school goat.

Jason: Much to the chagrin of the school principal, Osgood Conklin. That was Gale Gordon, of course.

Eve: He was always upset with my shenanigans. Gale was a very busy character actor. He did a little of everything.

Jason: He still does. I talked with him not too long ago. He was in Vancouver doing a very physically demanding play, pretty good for a man over eighty.

Eve: Yes, he never really slowed down. I don't see him much anymore which is a shame.

Jason: Another man who did most of the radio versions of *Our Miss Brooks* was Jeff Chandler. His death came much too soon due to some horrendous medical malpractice. He was only forty-two at the time. He went in for what should have been routine disc surgery, but the surgeon nicked an artery before sewing him up. After a couple of desperate attempts to correct the problem he was gone.

Eve: That was terrible and should never have happened. He got fifty-five pints of blood during the first attempt to save him and an additional twenty during the second one. He was a great guy, very laid back and very comfortable to work with.

JASON:	As you said, it was a dreadful waste of talent. Nothing but good things were ahead for him. I understand the only reason he left your show in its TV years was because he was so busy doing pictures.
EVE:	He was the only member of the radio cast who didn't carry over into the television series. He was just too occupied elsewhere. Bob Rockwell took over the part of Mr. Boynton when Jeff left the show.
JASON:	Here's a short segment from another episode on radio called "Boynton's land deal." Connie was obviously contemplating something else when he urgently contacted her on the phone.

****

BOYNTON:	Miss Brooks, in all the time we've known each other we've never shared in one big venture together.
CONNIE:	Are you forgetting your gasoline bill?
BOYNTON:	No, I'm serious, Miss Brooks. I'm not much of a boy for these kind of speeches, but I feel the time has come for me to take a step that might well be the turning point in my life.
CONNIE:	Why, Mr. Boynton!
BOYNTON:	Miss Brooks, I've got a proposal to make to you.
CONNIE:	I do! I do! I mean, go ahead Mr. Boynton.
BOYNTON:	What I'm suggesting is a partnership founded on mutual regard and integrity and a simple hand shake.
CONNIE:	My hand's shaking already.

BOYNTON: Actually, I'd like to keep this proposition a secret until we work out all the details.

CONNIE: Naturally! Naturally!

BOYNTON: I don't like to talk about a thing like this on the phone. Would it be possible for you to have lunch with me today?

CONNIE: Possible? It's positively probable. What time and where, Mr. Boynton?

BOYNTON: Well, you mentioned a pot roast I believe.

CONNIE: Of course, we'll have lunch right here. How about twelve o'clock?

BOYNTON: I'll be there, Miss Brooks. Somehow I have a feeling this might lead to pretty big things.

CONNIE: Well, goodbye, Mr. Boynton—dear.

BOYNTON: Goodbye Miss Brooks—likewise.

****

JASON: But when he came over to explain himself Connie's eternal bubble burst yet another time.

****

BOYNTON: Hi, I hope I haven't kept you waiting, Miss Brooks.

CONNIE: It's only been four years. Come on in, Mr. Boynton.

DAVIS: Hello, Mr. Boynton.

BOYNTON: Hello Mrs. Davis. How are you?

ACT VI: SCENE TWO: SERIOUSLY FUNNY | 317

DAVIS: Oh, I can't complain. How's the weather out today?

BOYNTON: I should say the temperature's about sixty-eight with the relative humidity about twenty. However, barometric pressure indicates a warm front moving in from the southeast which would elevate the thermometer considerably.

CONNIE: Roger! Wilco! Over and out!

DAVIS: I'd like to stay and chat with you, Mr. Boynton, but I've got to rush back into my room.

BOYNTON: What's your hurry, Mrs. Davis?

DAVIS: It's the only way I can think of to make myself scarce. Now, you be a good boy, Mr. Boynton. Connie, if you need me just yell.

CONNIE: I should live so long. See you later Mrs. Davis.

BOYNTON: Miss Brooks, before we sit down to lunch I'd like to clarify some of the remarks I made to you on the telephone. You see, I got the feeling at times that you didn't quite comprehend the nature of this deal.

CONNIE: Deal?

BOYNTON: Yes, it's a real estate deal. My Uncle Harry over in Florence has given me the opportunity to pick up the option on a couple of choice lots. I'm letting you in on the ground floor, Miss Brooks.

CONNIE: I couldn't feel any lower if you let me in, in the basement. What am I supposed to do with a couple of lots?

BOYNTON: They're not just any lots, Miss Brooks. They're a wonderful buy. My uncle said they should triple in value in a couple of months. He ought to know. He's Justice of the Peace in Florence and knows everybody in town.

CONNIE: Your uncle is Justice of the Peace?

BOYNTON: He has been for several years.

CONNIE: It's a good thing he doesn't depend on you to throw business his way. How come you never mentioned him before?

BOYNTON: Oh, I don't know. I haven't thought of it. He's always been after me to get married and settle down—cheerful old codger.

CONNIE: Be careful, Mr. Boynton, you're speaking of the uncle I love.

****

EVE: As you can see, I never got my man. He was too elusive or just unaware of my charms. He was always too wrapped up in his pet frog to notice me.

JASON: That was his loss. Is it true that when the television version began the producers wanted to replace Dick Crenna in the role of Walter Denton?

EVE: Yes it is. They said Dick was too old for that part when he could be seen. I told them that while that may be so, he still looked much younger than he was. We went around and around, but in the end he stayed with us and did very well as Walter. I couldn't picture anyone else doing it. We had the entire cast from the radio show on the television version with the exception of Jeff. That included

Gloria McMillan as Harriet Conklin, Walter's love interest and Leonard Smith as Stretch Snodgrass, the not too bright athlete.

JASON: Both shows were very well received. Later you co-starred on another television series with Kay Ballard called *The Mothers in Law*. It ran for a couple of seasons and also got good reviews.

EVE: That was produced by Desi Arnaz. It did very well while it lasted.

JASON: Before I let you go I want to bring up just three more of your many movie appearances. One was *Anatomy of a Murder* with Jimmy Stewart, which also featured your husband for many years, Brooks West. You worked a lot with Brooks through the years.

EVE: We worked together as much as we could, both on stage and in several movies. Brooks was more than a husband and a father to our kids. He was my protector and in many ways, my hero. I still miss him so much.

JASON: I'm quite sure you do. I know that he passed away in 1984. That's not so long ago. The second movie I want to bring up was made in '78. That one found you on familiar ground. I'm sure you know which one I'm referring to.

EVE: I think I do. It was a big promotion for me in the educational system. I was the always put upon principal at another high school. That was with John Travolta and Olivia Newton-John. It was *Grease*. I was sort of Osgood Conklin revisited.

JASON: Right. The last one I want to bring up was one that didn't get great reviews. It featured Chevy Chase, Carrie Fisher, Billy Barty and many of the little people in Hollywood.

EVE: That would be *Under the Rainbow*, a story that was very loosely about the making of *The Wizard of Oz*. You're right, the critics panned it, but it had some bright spots. I was the owner of a small dog, or I should say, a series of them because terrible accidents kept happening to the poor canines. I wasn't supposed to know that so they had to keep coming up with acceptable look alikes. It was a sad, but funny concept.

JASON: Well, Eve, by my count you appeared in sixty-three movies and of course you did innumerable stage plays to go along with your radio and television work. You said that Gale Gordon has been busy. I think you may have surpassed him.

****

I promised to explain why I talked with Eve twice in the same day. It was a strange story, but bears retelling. When I did interviews I would start the tape recorder in the control room of the radio station I was working for and then go around to the studio where my headphones and microphone served as my telephone connection. When I finished my first conversation with her I went back to the control room to get the tape, but what I didn't and couldn't know was that during our talk we had had a nearby lightning strike that had caused a brief glitch in our power. We had an emergency back-up system, but it wasn't instantaneous. The storm had shut down the recorder near the middle of our chat. I called her back to tell her what had happened. Her response was simply, "Let's do it again." This is just another way of proving what a nice person she was.

Eve Arden left us in 1990 at what I now consider a young age. She was just eighty-two. In show business years that is still young.

ACT VI:
SCENE THREE
MCGEE'S NEIGHBOR

Most everyone has a friend or neighbor who becomes closer than all of the others they encounter. Radio and television often made those connections just as it happens in real life. Most of the main characters always seemed to have a particularly amiable associate who showed up on nearly every episode. Chester Riley had Gillis. Phil Harris had Frankie Remley. Lucy had Ethel. Ralph Kramden had Ed Norton. And so it goes. Almost every show had a connection to someone like that. Fibber McGee was no exception to this rule. He had several of these sorts of characters on his show. One of them was a young lady named Alice Darling who rented a room in the McGee household. She could never quite get her words right. Everything she said became a double entendre.

I spoke with the lady who played that role and many others on February 20, 1987. Her name was Shirley Mitchell.

****

JASON: Shirley, before we get into anything specific about your radio and television career, why don't you bring us up to date on how it all began.

SHIRLEY: I actually got into radio in Toledo, where I was born, Toledo, Ohio. I started in actor contests when I was like six or seven or eight. I can honestly say I've been doing radio nearly all my life without any formal training whatsoever. There was a man in Toledo who really helped me. At the time I was a very young child. Jules Blair in Toledo had one of those Saturday morning shows. He had little amateur contests and I went on one when I was eight. I did imitations of Katherine Hepburn and Greta Garbo and a few more. I won and I became a regular on that show. I finished grammar school, but during the time I was in high school, when I was thirteen, I went to Detroit to audition for *The Lone Ranger.* I took the bus, which was quite a trip for me in those days, alone. I got a part on *The Lone Ranger.* That was the first professional job I'd ever done. I'll never forget, I got three dollars and fifty cents and I think I kept that check for years. I was so proud of that show. Then I went off to Chicago to try to break into radio. Finally, after a few months I got an audition with a man whose name was Joe Ainley, who was doing two shows, *Woman in White*, which was a soap opera, and *First Nighter* with Les Tremayne and Barbara Luddy, which everybody knew about. My first big job came when I was seventeen and a half. I played, of all things, a southern woman on *First Nighter.* That really started me. I proceeded to work in Chicago. Then *The Ransom Sherman Show* was replacing *Fibber McGee and Molly* for the summer in Chicago. I can't quite remember how it happened, but I got an audition with them and they liked my comedy timing. I did that show for six weeks in Chicago. Then Ransom was coming back here to the west coast. I was so desperate to come out here that I lied to my mother. I told her they'd given me a regular job, which of course, they had not. I got myself a round-trip ticket on the Scout in coach. I sat up for four nights. It cost $75, that ticket. I met a sweet lady on the train who let me spend my first night in California at her house. Talk about courage! I could not have done it if I was any older or smarter. I was just young and dumb and I figured

ACT VI: SCENE THREE: MCGEE'S NEIGHBOR

it would all work out. Strangely enough it did. That was really the beginning of it. I came to California when I was eighteen. I've been here ever since.

JASON: You had to have nerves, but it seems to have worked out for you.

SHIRLEY: I know. At one point I was doing *The Jack Carson Show, The Bob Crosby Old Gold Show, The Great Gildersleeve, Fibber McGee and Molly,* the *Rudy Vallée Show,* a soap opera called *Woman in My House, The Phil Harris/Alice Faye Show, The Red Skelton Show,* where I played Freddie Freeloader's wife, another one with Ransom Sherman and another one called *Best of the Week.* Then I would do all the dramatic shows. They had a thing for many of us. We would run from CBS to NBC and maybe have five minutes. So they would have special ushers at the side doors, one to let us out and one to let us in. We would rush into the control room, pick up our script and go right on the air without a rehearsal, which was incredible. We might have rehearsed in the morning, but we hadn't done the dress. There were many times when I did six shows in a day because we then had to do a repeat for the east coast. It was really hectic. It was the most exciting time in any of our lives. We discuss it now because there's TV and how mundane it has become. You meet people and then you leave. We were all family. It was just the most exciting, wonderful time, certainly in my life. I'm sure many of the other performers would say the same thing.

JASON: Most of my guests have said precisely that. You mentioned someone whose name comes up quite often, but people in general don't really remember him. He was always appreciated by other people in the business. Not as much by audiences. He did fill-ins for *Fibber McGee* nearly every summer. He was Ransom Sherman.

SHIRLEY: One of the funniest guys I've ever known. I met him, Jason, because when I first just came to Chicago I was living at the YWCA. There were a lot of days when I didn't have anything to do so I would come down to the studio. He was doing a show called *Club Matinee*, which I'm sure you've heard of, long before Gary Moore did that show. Don McNeill would do *The Breakfast Club.* I would go down and watch *Club Matinee* and just admire this master of comedy and timing. It got so that he knew I was there because of my laugh. I have a very raucous laugh. I would just go crazy. I learned so much watching him. What you said is true. I don't understand why he never really caught on. Maybe for that time his humor was a little too sophisticated. He was just before his time, a very unrecognized, terrific performer. God knows, he was good to me. That was when I just got started.

JASON: You also mentioned doing a southern belle. You did a lot of southern belles.

SHIRLEY: Yes I did. That was my forté I guess, and coming from Toledo, it was really ironic. As it turned out later on I married a southern man. When I went to Virginia I didn't know who was putting who on. My accent was really very legitimate. Sometimes I thought the southerners were less southern than the way I was playing them. I loved Leila from *The Great Gildersleeve.* She was my favorite character. As I told you, my first real national show was *First Nighter* on which I did a southern. Then when I came out here after Ransom Sherman went off in Chicago they knew I could do southern. I think I may have done it once on Ransom's show. I did it for Cecil Underwood who produced that show. They called me to do a one shot. I was on *Gildersleeve* before I did *Fibber*. I did the one shot and they said, "Let's write her in again." Sam Moore and John Whedon were the writers and they were delicious, every word they put in everybody's mouth. They were like Don Quinn with *Fibber*. They could do no wrong. They finally offered me a contract to be on the show which was the most exciting thing that possibly could have happened to me. I loved the character. I loved the show. Hal Peary was wonderful to work with. We had a terrific cast. Lurene Tuttle, who passed away recently, was on it. So was Bea Benaderet who's also gone. It's really so sad. But it was terrific.

JASON: And a lot of your competitors for the Gildersleeve's heart were people we all remember well. Cathy Lewis and Una Merkel were both there.

SHIRLEY: Una replaced me when I got married.

JASON: She was your cousin, Leila's cousin.

SHIRLEY: She was her cousin, right. Curiously enough, when I started doing southern it was because I used to watch Una Merkel in films when I was a little kid and got that accent down pat. She was sensational. That talk was exactly how she did it. I imitated her. To think that after I left she replaced me, wasn't that something? When I came back Una and I were very good friends so I once told her that story. She thought if was great.

JASON: We'll come back to *The Great Gildersleeve* in a while. A little later on you did yet another southern belle type working as Janet Waldo's roommate on *Young Love*.

Shirley: Yep, on CBS, written by Janet's husband Robert E. Lee and his partner Jerome Lawrence. Bob and Jerry are well known playwrights. They wrote *Inherit the Wind* and *The Caine Mutiny Court Martial.*

Jason: They also did *Mame* for Broadway, and *Auntie Mame.*

Shirley: Yes they did. Mame just happens to be the most colossal success there ever was. Another one who went on to acquire a lot of fame and whom I see all the time since we've remained good friends, is Dick Crenna, who played Marjorie's boyfriend and eventually her husband on *Gildersleeve.*

Jason: All the regulars were there, Gale Gordon, Hal March, Herb Butterfield and even Jerry Hausner.

Shirley: That's right. I saw Jerry just this week. We were on a commercial interview together. He's fabulous, still working. He just appeared in a wonderful TV movie with Kirk Douglas.

Jason: I remember a story John Dehner told me about Jerry, which leads me to think he's a very funny man.

Shirley: He is, he's hysterical.

Jason: The story has to do with a recent series that many of you worked on. I think it was *The Sears Radio Theatre.* Anyway, when Jerry came in a good many of the old radio gang were sitting around discussing a script, John Dehner, Bill Conrad, Vincent Price, Elliott Lewis and a couple of others. Jerry walked in and gasped, "My God! This is like looking into an open grave!" It had been a long time since the last time they had all been together.

SHIRLEY: I heard another one this week. I saw Parley Baer at an interview and I said, "Oh, Parl, it's terrible. Some of our dearest friends are dropping. My God, I guess we've reached that age and I don't want to think about it." Herb Vigran had just died. He was a good friend and a wonderful actor. Parley said, "Well, that's like the story of the actor who gets up in the morning, looks at the obituary column and if he doesn't see his name he shaves and has breakfast."

JASON: Let's talk about *Fibber McGee and Molly*. You did that one for several years. You played a young lady who could never get her words out separately. She always ran them together. She was Alice Darling. She never could really finish a sentence.

SHIRLEY: No she couldn't. It was a good gimmick, but not always easy to read.

JASON: You actually met some people on that show that you worked with on other shows. One was Bill Thompson.

SHIRLEY: And Arthur Q. Bryan, wonderful character actor.

JASON: He was the first Elmer Fudd, Arthur Q.

SHIRLEY: Was he?

JASON: He did it until he passed away. Then Mel Blanc took over the voice of Elmer.

SHIRLEY: I didn't know that. I thought Mel had always done it. Incidentally, Mel did a lot of the *Fibbers* and a lot of *Gildersleeves*. Mel did a lot of everything. He was also a very good actor along with the animal noises he made. He's incredible. He just goes on and on. Arthur was a darling. Now you made me think of Earl Ross who did Judge Hooker and Gale Gordon who's now living in Santa Barbara. He just came back to do a new *Lucy* series, which didn't go. He hasn't changed. He's exactly the same. Not too long ago they gave Jim Jordan his star on Hollywood Boulevard. He had not had a star. Can you imagine, a man with his talent, actually the biggest star on radio at one point, he and Marian. So Robert Amundsen and the Amundsen Foundation, located where the old NBC studio used to be, decided to sponsor Jim and put his star on Vine Street where the NBC artists entrance was. We were all there for the occasion. Jim was then eighty-nine. I loved Jim Jordan. He's a very special person in my life. You know, I've never told this story very much, but on one of the Tuesdays when we were doing *Fibber* my father was going to have surgery in Toledo. I think that was on a Monday. On Tuesday we had rehearsed in the morning. I came home and changed my clothes. I was getting ready to go back to the studio, but I'd come home to see how my dad was doing. I called home and I heard my mother crying so I knew what had happened. Someone else picked up the phone and I asked, "What happened?" They said they couldn't talk to me right then. I said, "My dad died, didn't he?" They were so shook up they just hung up. They called me back. My brother was there and he said, "Yes, it's true." I said, "Okay, Marv, I'll come right home." In those days it was difficult to get a plane because it was all priority due to the war. In any event, I called the guy I was dating, Paul Weston, the musician, who since has married Jo Stafford. I said, "Paul, my dad just died and I've got to go back." He was working on the *Johnny Mercer Show* at the time. He said, "Let me run in and tell Cecil Underwood," who produced *Fibber McGee* at that time. He said, "You can't do the show." I said,

"Yes, I can." So Cecil went in and told everyone on *Fibber* and also told them I was having trouble getting a plane out. When I got back to NBC they said, "Look, with what you just went through we don't want you to do the show." I said, "No, I know my father. He would never forgive me if I didn't do the show. I must." Jim and Marian came in and hugged and kissed me. Harlow Wilcox and Don Quinn were there. I'll never forget. They were so supportive. They had arranged for me to get a plane right after the show that evening. We got to a certain part of the script and Jim came into the dressing room with me alone. He said, "Listen, Shirley, there's a last line in the show and I don't know if you should do it." My last line, and I'll never forget it Jason as long as I live, that line was "Good night, pop. Good hunting to you." When I did it everybody just broke up. I flew out of there. They got me to the airport and I got on a plane, but I just want you to know what those Jordans were like. They were my family. I couldn't possibly have let them down. They kept saying to take my time about getting back. They were the most loving people and Jim still is. He comes to the Pacific Pioneer luncheons and every now and then he comes up with the driest wit. He's just as young up in his head as he ever was, incredible, incredible! I've never told that story very much and yet, I'll never forget it. I'll never forget the love that I felt emanating from all those people. I got a call from Pacific Pioneer Broadcasters about five months ago. They said, "Shirley, we're going to take out a full page ad in *Variety*. Will you join us?" I said, "My God, of course." It was wishing Jim a happy birthday. It was his ninetieth, right? He's going to be ninety-one, I think. The incredible thing about him is that he's just as facile now as he ever was. Physically he's not up to a lot of things. He gets tired. You can certainly understand that, but he still comes around to those luncheons and sits on the dais. I hope I'm like that at ninety is all I can say.

JASON: Let's go back to *The Great Gildersleeve.* You worked with Hal Peary, but later you also worked with Will Waterman.

SHIRLEY: I went back on when Willard replaced Hal. Then it went off for a little while. Then it came back on, on NBC. We were in a little studio instead of the large one we had had and with a very small audience. That was after I had had my kids so that would have been maybe twenty-five years ago, still a long time. I was on until the very end. They just couldn't keep it going. The sponsors were switching rapidly over to TV.

JASON: There's an interesting story about your Leila Ransom character. At one time in the series Gildy was engaged to both Leila and Eve Goodwin, played by Bea Benaderet. You got him as far as the altar, but a ladies club picketed the studio, which is very funny. Talk about free publicity!

SHIRLEY: They didn't want him to get married. They said he'd lose all his charm. I honestly think the writers had something to do with it. The whole thing was that you could never get him up to the altar. No way. Hal was highly under rated, I think. I don't know what people think of him now, but, boy, his timing was impeccable. You know, he really sang beautifully. Remember how he used to sing "Speak to me of Love" to Leila?

JASON: Will Waterman told me that was a problem for him because he couldn't sing as well as Hal.

SHIRLEY: Right. Did Will tell you that we were invited back to be honored by a radio archives group in October of this year? We were awarded a very special trophy. Both of us got a standing ovation. The people in New York had also rounded up Louise Erickson who was the original Marjorie, if you can believe. She replaced Mary Lee Robb, or was it the other way around, I can't remember. No, the original Marjorie was Lurene Tuttle and then Louise took over. Anyway, they found Louise. They found Will Waterman and they found me. Ken Roberts did one of the parts. Ed Herlihy did Judge Hooker. It was a very special night. It made me feel so terrific. They had me read one of the original scripts. So when it came time for Will to sing "Speak to me of Love" I wasn't prepared. I hadn't gotten there the day before for the rehearsal because I had to work here on that day. I flew in on Saturday morning and the presentation was Saturday evening, but I'm accustomed to not rehearsing. Those scripts are like the back of my hand, so is the character. After I got dressed I met Will downstairs. I said, "Okay, what are the cuts?" He said, "Well, one of the definite cuts is that I'm only going to pretend to sing one line of 'Speak to me of Love.' Come in right over it." I said, "That's right, Will, you've got a thing about singing." He said, "Yeah, I can't sing." But I thought he carried it off rather well.

JASON: He surprised me when he told me that. Sometimes he had to do it. I've got some episodes with him singing.

SHIRLEY: I think he was more fearful of doing it than anything else.

JASON: It was an interesting transition when Will came in for Hal, who left the show to do *Honest Harold*, but that's another story. You could hardly tell, even if you listened to them side-by-side. They were that similar.

SHIRLEY: You're right. Unless you know the date of the broadcast you can't know which is which. You see, Jason, that's why NBC had that thing over Hal's head. Every time he would demand something they didn't think was right they'd say, "There's always Will Waterman waiting in the wings." The two voices were incredibly so similar that it was really difficult to tell them apart on the air, however, as actors they were quite different, which is interesting.

JASON: They were good friends. That made it a little hard for Willard.

SHIRLEY: Yes they were. Hal never resented him, but Will always worried about it. He always worried about taking over the show, but he had no alternative. He had his career as well.

JASON: They go all the way back to working together on *Tom Mix* in Chicago.

SHIRLEY: I didn't know that.

JASON: They both did parts on that show. There was another guy on *Gildersleeve* who has since left us. He was on with Phil Harris and many other shows. He did a weekly bit with W.C. Fields on *Your Hit Parade*. They used to do inserts between the songs. That person was Walter Tetley.

SHIRLEY: Walter was divine. Hal always kidded him about his age. He'd say, "Come on, Walter let's get the truth out of you. You're really fifty, right?" You know, he was doing this thirteen year old kid and

	he would never say, but boy, what an actor that Walter Tetley was.
JASON:	I remember some stories of him doing some strange things like setting the studio clocks ahead. The other actors knew about it but the director didn't. He thought they were on the air while the cast was saying all kinds of things that were taboo. It was panic city.
SHIRLEY:	I've never seen him do that, but I've seen him at rehearsals doing all sorts of things. It was a gas. He would light someone's script on fire which was not a very funny thing. He was quite a prankster. He really was a good guy.
JASON:	You mentioned Dick Crenna who played Bronco and also Gale Gordon.
SHIRLEY:	You know, I can't remember what role Gale played.
JASON:	He was Ransom Bullard, an across the street neighbor.
SHIRLEY:	Oh yes, yes. That was at the same time he was doing Mayor LaTrivia on *Fibber*.
JASON:	Among other things.
SHIRLEY:	We didn't mention Dick LeGrand who played Peavey, one of the most lovable characters of all time. No matter what Gildy would say Peavey would say, "Well, I wouldn't say that." It got so that the writers would occasionally put in a kind of story about Peavey having a little crush on Leila. It was such fun because he was such a shy man himself.
JASON:	He really was like the character he portrayed, wasn't he?

Shirley: He WAS the character.

Jason: And so was Earl Ross.

Shirley: Earl Ross was Hooker to the T. He was a big overpowering, blustery guy. He was exactly the same in rehearsal. He always carried a bunch of coins in his pocket. He'd drive me crazy playing with them. But Dick LeGrand was like a little mouse. He would come in and rarely open his mouth. Then he'd go off and we wouldn't see him again until the next week. It was marvelous. He WAS Peavey. The guys knew it. That's why they'd write Peavey in. He had come on to do one shot. They saw this delightful little guy and they thought, "Oh my God, we can make use of that character." So they kept Peavey in. They very often did that. They wrote the character for the actor.

Jason: He was the kind of person who always ate vanilla ice cream.

Shirley: And never changed, never diversified. You're right, absolutely.

Jason: Getting back to Hal Peary, the *Gildersleeve* character he did came right out of *Fibber McGee and Molly*. He was McGee's neighbor up until '41, long before he was the Water Commissioner.

Shirley: I didn't know much about *Fibber* at that time. I was in school waiting to be an actress. I would listen to stuff like *Myrt and Marge* and all the soap operas that little girls listened to. But I know, after having worked with him for so long, that Hal started with Jim and Marian in Chicago. He came out to the west coast with them. As a matter of fact, *Gildersleeve* was a spin-off and started as a summer substitute for something else. They didn't even know if it was going to stay on the air. It caught on and became one of the hottest comedy shows ever. It was a sweet show, brilliantly written. The two men who wrote it were incredible.

JASON: It held on for eighteen years, nine with Hal and nine with Will.

SHIRLEY: Can you think of any TV show that held on for eighteen years?

JASON: No, but things were a little different then than they are now, as you well know. A lot of shows that were mediocre at best hung on for several years. It's all about money now. Believe me, I'm not knocking *Gildersleeve*. That was a great show.

SHIRLEY: It also went to the small screen.

JASON: And it only lasted a few months. The problem was that they changed writers and the whole basic concept went out the window. Will said they tried to make Gildy a skirt chaser, which he never was on radio. It didn't work at all.

SHIRLEY: But on the other hand, *Life of Riley* went from radio to television and was very successful. I think one of the reasons, Jason, was that Bill Bendix looked exactly like what we always thought Chester Riley would look like.

JASON: A funny thing there is that when *Riley* went to television Jackie Gleason played the lead for the first couple of weeks.

SHIRLEY: He did?

Jason: Yes, the first two or three weeks. I'm not sure exactly how long, but then Bill Bendix took over the role again. You were also on that show.

Shirley: Yes, I later went to TV with it. That was fun. I did another southern on it. John Brown was Digger O'Dell.

Jason: And he was Gillis, the neighbor on radio. You played Mrs. Gillis.

Shirley: Right, isn't that crazy?

Jason: John Brown was another example of a great character actor. He popped up all over the dial.

Shirley: He was a wonderful actor. Unfortunately he was involved in the McCarthy thing and work became very difficult for him to find.

Jason: Yes, as so many innocent people found out.

Shirley: Minerva Pious was another one. It just did her in for a long time. I think that's why John Brown died. He had a heart attack and that was it.

Jason: And the people from *Counterattack* and *Red Channels* were also much to blame, going on little bits of information that had no true value.

Shirley: None. I mean, the things that they would think up had no value. They would print them and then the sponsors and the networks wouldn't hire you if your name was even mentioned in any of those rags. They were totally black listed.

Jason: It's a subject that makes me furious. So many good people were at least temporarily ruined by that whole

|SHIRLEY:| pile of hog wash. Let's go on to some more pleasant things. There were other shows you did that people may not remember as well. Joan Davis was quite a comedienne and Bill Goodwin, who began as an announcer. You did both of their shows.

SHIRLEY: I did do them both. I was Bill Goodwin's girl friend on his. He played a newspaper reporter. He was a darling man and a fine actor. He was an announcer, but he always wanted to be an actor. He continued on TV until he died. We would very often be on the same shows together, like *The Danny Thomas Show* or *The Joey Bishop Show*. Bill never made it big and I still don't know why. He was so talented.

JASON: Did you ever sing when you were on the *Kay Kyser Show*?

SHIRLEY: No, but I sang on the *Old Gold Show* with Les Tremayne, *The Old Gold-Bob Crosby Show* It was on, on Sundays. We did that a lot. We were like Master and Mistress of Ceremonies. We did that for a whole season. We sang almost every week. We would do parodies and male-female duets. It was really great fun. On *Kay Kyser* I mostly acted. I never sang on that. I'm really not a singer, but if I have to I can. We keep hoping maybe radio will come back. I seriously doubt it. It was certainly a wonderful time for all of us.

****

We did not talk much about Shirley Mitchell's television days, but she was a big part of that industry for a long time. You could have seen her playing friends, neighbors and relatives on many shows. She did *Bachelor Father, Petticoat Junction, The Real McCoys, Please Don't Eat the Daisies* and innumerable others. She is still with us as I write this and is still doing some voice-overs for national commercials*. She did *I Love Lucy*. She did *Beverly Hillbillies*. She did *Green Acres*. She was always around when a camera or a microphone was present. She is one of those people we all know, but cannot always recognize by name, the backbone of our industry.

---

*This piece was written a couple of years ago. Unfortunately, Shirley passed away in November of 2014 at the age of 94.

Act VII:
Tecs

They were known by many names. They were called gumshoes, shamuses, shadows, private dicks, sleuths, PIs and also tecs or detectives. They ran rampant on the radio airwaves in many different forms and identities. There were all sorts of detectives, official and otherwise. I will further discuss that subject a little later in the encore, but for now, we will just consider the people who played three of them. They were characters based on the books of S. S. Van Dine, Dashiell Hammett and Leslie Charteris. By using this as a way to group these three gentlemen, in no way do I mean to implicate that it was the sum total of their careers. Playing detectives was merely a small fragment of the work that each of them did.

Radio was no different than any other form of media when it came to dominance of any one type of genre. On television we had an era of westerns, a period when medical shows took over and so on. Radio detectives ruled the roost for several years, some very good and others that did not compare to the artistry of the good ones. As I have previously stated, not all of the old radio shows were great; in fact, some of them just could not cut the mustard. What we will present here are three of the better ones.

ACT VII:
SCENE ONE
PHILO VANCE

Here we have a man who played that always clever detective for a brief period. Due to the fact that he was better known for much of his other work we didn't spend much time during our discussion on that subject, but it is a way to get him into this act. As a native New Yorker, born in Manhattan, he spent most of his career working there and eventually he died there. He is buried in Brooklyn. He played many diverse roles on-the-air as well as doing a great many animated cartoon voices and movie narrations.

He was Jackson Beck. On September 16, 1987 he had this to say.

****

JASON: My guest is a man with extensive credits in all forms of media who has often been called "The Voice." I'm not sure where that came from. Would you care to elaborate, Jackson?

JACKSON: No, it's just that some people starting calling me "The Voice" and it's kind of taken over. I had nothing to do with it. Sometimes I'm a little embarrassed by it, but so be it. If that's the way people think of me I'm flattered.

JASON: Just from hearing you I guess I can understand the moniker. I'm a little curious as to where your network radio career began.

JACKSON: Let me preface this. I worked around in radio until I really learned my business on a lot of small stations. There were twenty odd stations in New York at the time and I guess I worked at every one of them at one time or another. The first network show I finally auditioned for was *Death Valley Days* on NBC. In those days radio was very glamorous. We did the shows in front of a studio audience. The men were all dressed in black tie and formal wear for the ladies. I finally got myself a job as a cowpoke or something on *Death Valley Days*, in the middle of which, I must admit, I dropped the script. Someone knocked it out of my hand so I just ad-libbed, a complete no-no in those days, until somebody shoved another script in front of my face and picked up the one I dropped. I just went on, you know, no dead air was permissible. In those days you put in a couple of days of rehearsal while they polished the script and rewrote it or whatever. That was my introduction to network radio, but I had had a couple of years of experience on all the small stations, something that is unobtainable these days. Most of the small stations are on cart. There's no radio drama anyway. You learned the business the hard way by starting in the boondocks and worked your way up, like a minor leaguer.

JASON: So many of the small stations in small markets these days don't even have any on-air people. They just take satellite feeds from other remote places.

JACKSON: That's what I meant by cartridges and as you said, satellite feeds. There's nobody there but an engineer. Sometimes even they are part timers. They put the stuff in a machine or tune in on a satellite to take their feed from somewhere else. It's a great deal different. In those days we had a large cast and twenty-four people in the control room including the clients, representatives of the agency, representatives of the network and of course the technical people, the engineers and so on. They're all gone now.

JASON: Even this type of phone interview is getting outdated because so many are done via satellite up-link so that it sounds like you're in the same room.

JACKSON: I've done commercials on up-links. I recorded my part in New York while the bulk of the commercial was really being done in California. That way they'd get first generation reproduction. Why they can't do it by taping it in New York and shipping it to California I don't know. I don't know, but that's their choice. Marvelous! Sometimes the bird goes down so we have to wait until it gets fixed. It's a strange racket these days. I'm not sure I like it. Even if you do a dramatic spot you never see the other folks on it. You do your little piece, take a pause and go on from there. Most of the time, there's no interplay between yourself and anyone one else. You often don't even know who else is on it. It's very strange and I find it dissatisfying. I'll tell you, I go into the super market and there's a little lady imprisoned in the cash register who announces all the prices. I'm afraid some day they may get around to doing that with actors and announcers.

JASON: There is a gentleman I talked with about a year ago. He worked in the very early days of radio, a real pioneer. He said you were his number one boy. I'm referring to Bill Robson.

JACKSON: Oh God, you're talking about the master.

JASON: We talked about *Man Behind the Gun*.

JACKSON: Best show I ever did. Best director I ever worked for and the most enjoyable time of my life. That's not just in retrospect. The actual experience was unbelievable and probably the greatest thing I ever did in my life. After that it was pretty much all downhill and that was long, long ago. He was the best. No doubt about it. If you can imagine a studio with a full orchestra of about thirty pieces with Van Cleave conducting and writing the music too, and seventeen sound tables, a cast of people who were all at the top of the profession, people who later went on to do other great things. Frank Lovejoy. Myron McCormick, Larry Haines, Mandy Kramer, Bill Quinn—the list goes on and on. They were the best people in the business. The shows were magnificent. That was really one of the highlights of my career. It was an absolutely stupendous experience. I'll never forget it. I saw Bill about two years ago. He looks the same and he's well on in years. So am I, for that matter. I still feel like a kid in front of him, ready to learn something.

JASON: Of all of the things that he had done, the two that he selected as being the most important in his own mind were *Man Behind the Gun* and *Fall of the City* which came much earlier.

JACKSON: He was marvelous to work with and in complete command at all times. He was something else, believe me. I guess that was really a milestone in my career. The fact that I even got the job in the first place was remarkable, I thought, because there were a lot of talented people around. He picked me. I'd been working and I was fairly well established, but this really cemented my position in the business.

JASON: One of the other people he auditioned for narrator on *Man Behind the Gun* was Burgess Meredith, who didn't get the job.

| JACKSON: | Burgess had a lot different voice than mine, much softer. That was a job that called for a tough regular guy kind of thing. My voice is a lot deeper than Burgess Meredith. I sounded like a doughboy or a serviceman. I could handle the vernacular without sounding like I was putting it on. I've got this gravely kind of voice so it sounded pretty real. |

| JASON: | The approach was very similar to Norman Corwin's *On a Note of Triumph* or *14 August*. |

| JACKSON: | That was another good guy. He was great too. At that time CBS had marvelous people. Along with Robson and Corwin they had Brewster Morgan and Irving Reis and a few other people, all of whom were absolutely marvelous, talented, wonderful people who could write and direct and who understood actors. If I've left anybody out I'm sorry. There was really a core group over there of people with intellect and imagination and talent, people who knew what they were doing and did it well. That's why CBS was pre-eminent. They did wondrous things. They weren't afraid to experiment. Nothing was spared when it came to production values. It really was a marvelous place to work and a wonderful group to be with. |

| JASON: | Another thing that was apparent then, but would never happen now was that the writers and producers and directors were given free rein. A lot of the material would be on the air before anyone at the top had even read it. |

| JACKSON: | That's why CBS was the classiest network. I wish they'd get back to it. We've got book keepers and number crunchers running this racket now and it's pretty sad. The whole business has deteriorated artistically. And of course, that particular forum |

will never come back and that's economics. You can only take so many commercials during a show without destroying it. You put a disc jockey on and in an hour he gets in thirty commercials with a minute and a half or two minutes of music in between. The economics killed us. Good shows cost a lot. Disc jockeys don't. You can get much more commercial time in than you can with a drama. It's a different kind of society we live in. The day of the hero is gone. That's really what it was then. When you named the heroine Mary Noble you knew what you were getting. Mr. Blackstone was always the villain. You know, it was white hats and black hats. People don't accept that anymore. They want something else.

JASON: Speaking of heroes, I think we should bring up some of the shows you were on. You played Cisco Kid and you did the narration for another hero known as Superman. You also did Tom Corbett and Mark Trail, heroes from different times.

JACKSON: Yeah, those were all heroes of one kind or another. You don't find any heroic figures anymore. There are a lot of detectives, a lot of cops, but even they have been brought down from the heroic. They're just regular Joes. The old standards are out of date. There are new standards in now. That's life. Maybe in fifteen or twenty years it will all change back, but who knows?

JASON: If you look at some of the current detective shows and just compare some of the acting—I don't know if I even want to get into this.

JACKSON: There's very little that's heroic about any of them.

JASON: I'm thinking about garbage like *Miami Vice* as

	compared to your *Philo Vance*. You did that from '48 until '50.
JACKSON:	The scripts were so damned different. I like to watch *Murder She Wrote*. It's a radio show with pictures because those plots are basic, elementary and as transparent as hell. It caught on because of the absolute simplicity of the plot line and the cleverness of the protagonist. It's really radio with pictures. It's amazing that it has hung on. It shows that the basic story, even though you know it's going to come out the way it's going to come out, it's very well done. I'm not criticizing that, but actually there are very few unusual plots. *Miami Vice*, I think I've tried to watch it four or five times. I can't stand that show. It's terrible. *Murder She Wrote* is good because it's basic, it's simple. Everything's going to come out right in the end. The body is the only dead one.
JASON:	Another great thing about *Murder She Wrote* is that they use all the old pros. They don't use many young actors.
JACKSON:	That's what carries it. They've got excellent people. It's a very well done show. I watch it all the time. I hate to miss one. It's very simple and elemental. If I sound like, well, the good old days were so much better, they were. Most of the people around now don't know what the good old days were like. They never had the opportunity.
JASON:	You worked with another fine director who wasn't among the names we've already mentioned. I'm talking about Jock MacGregor.
JACKSON:	We did *Cisco* and *Brownstone Theatre* and a couple of others. I was very fond of Jock.

JASON: *Brownstone* was in many ways similar to *First Nighter*, the way they presented the stories.

JACKSON: Not exactly because on *Brownstone* Gert Warner and I did the steady leads. We would have a theatre guest star in every week. Clayton Hamilton was the owner of the show and the producer. He was also a theatre critic and he'd come on and say a few words too. He'd been in the theatre for many years. I was in my thirties and he must have been over sixty. We would have these guest stars in, mostly leading ladies. I did another show like that called *Stonewall Scott*, which was a summer replacement for *Camel Caravan*. I was a detective sort of guy and I always had a leading woman. That was just me and whoever happened to be available from the theatre. There was June Havoc and a lot of other people of her caliber. She killed me one night because we rehearsed up until dinner and then broke to eat. She came back and she had garlic. I don't know where she'd been. We were working the same side of a microphone. We were very close together. She was blowing garlic in my face all through the show. I thought I'd die. I like garlic, but I don't like the smell of it on other people. I don't know if it was her sense of humor or she was just trying to upset me or whatever the hell it was. It was a disaster until the end of the show because she kept breathing garlic in my face. I thought I was going to choke to death.

JASON: You just brought up a couple of things that people may not remember or realize. The first one is summer replacements, something that no longer exists.

JACKSON: No, now they just repeat and repeat. As you probably know, a season is now only thirteen weeks, just thirteen new shows each year.

JASON: Exactly, there were some big names that got started on a summer replacement.

JACKSON: But at that time, if a summer show was a success, chances were that it would be kept on as a regular member of the schedule.

JASON: In other words it was sort of an audition ground for many not yet known actors.

JACKSON: And for the shows themselves. They didn't make too many pilots at that time.

JASON: The other thing you mentioned was two people working on one mike. There were often a lot of people moving in and out on one mike. Even with a large cast there might have been no more than two of them.

JACKSON: They generally kept the leads separate. If I was the lead and I was working with somebody we'd be on one mike together. There'd be another mike for the other characters. Sometimes, in rare instances like *March of Time* there would be more that two. That was a large cast so they would extend themselves and set up three. We'd work in groups. Those were the technical advantages you had when you worked a big show like that.

JASON: What I'm getting at is that there was a lot of traffic moving around in the studios, but we very seldom could hear it. The mikes weren't quite as sensitive as they are now, but they were pretty good.

JACKSON: They were good, but they were separated very well and staged very well. Quite often we were working to live audiences. The mikes would be turned on and off to avoid some of the traffic noises as we moved around. Once the traffic was directed you'd change mikes from time to time because you were in different sequences. You'd work in groups. There never was too much crowding if they could help it. Sometimes, because of those mikes you'd lose lines and also because of those mikes you'd hear extraneous noise so we were pretty careful. We were pretty much choreographed in the way we moved from place to place.

JASON: Occasionally we would hear something out of place on some broadcasts.

JACKSON: But you never knew for sure if it was noise or just static. It was sensitive in the studio, but for the listener it didn't always come across. When it did it was a disaster, but it was so momentary people tended to forget it anyway because they were concentrating on what they were hearing.

JASON: You did a couple of other detective type shows. I'm thinking of *Casey, Crime Photographer* and another one where you followed Gale Gordon and Elliott Lewis, *The Casebook of Gregory Hood*.

JACKSON: I wasn't the lead on Hood. I just happened to be on it. What was the first one you said?

JASON: *Casey, Crime Photographer.*

JACKSON: That starred the great Staats Cotsworth and Matt Crowley.

JASON: Didn't you play Captain Logan?

JACKSON: I wound up playing Logan. I think Matt might have done it before me.

JASON: Some of the ladies on the show were Betty Furness and Leslie Woods and Jan Miner.

JACKSON: All marvelous actresses. People were awfully good in those days, they really were. I not saying that because I knew them or trying to make it better than it really was. Those were excellent people. Jan was marvelous. Leslie was fantastic. Betty was just great.

JASON: The versatility was always there. Matt Crowley was also *Jungle Jim* and *Mark Trail*.

JACKSON: He WAS *Mark Trail*. We had a marvelous time. He was a very good friend of mine. I not only narrated that, I also played Johnny Malotte, the French guide. So I'd go from one character into another, which we all did. We all doubled. Matt didn't. He was the hero. But the rest of us all played more than one part. Sometimes you wound up on a show where you played all of the characters. I used to do a show with Gil Mack. We did a half hour show. We did a couple of them. One was called *Author, Author* on which we did all the characters between the two of us. Another one was called *Twenty Years Ago and a Day* which was a local WOR show. It was a sort of pseudo *March of Time*. Ted Hewlett was the narrator and Gil and I played all the parts. I did a thing called *Brady Kaye* on which I announced and narrated and played all the parts, including women, if you can picture that. I was constantly fading on and off to indicate entrances and exits and so on as a different character. I did about four of five different parts in fifteen minutes. It was a good workout.

JASON: Probably the last radio shows you did were on *CBS Mystery Theatre* not long ago.

JACKSON: There was one after that, a series of them that Bristol-Meyers tried to put on. A series of fifteen minute shows that Peg Lynch did, *Ethel and Albert*. Then we surrounded that with two or three other shows. I thought we were doing rather well, but Bristol-Meyers pulled out too soon. I tried to rally round all the people I knew in radio, the golden age groups. I got an awful lot of mail. I got about 5000 letters sent in to Bristol-Meyers to please keep the things on. There was some kind of a political furor inside Young and Rubicam and they cancelled it. That was really the last gasp. Maybe six or eight years ago they did that. People have tried to revive it from time to time. I've been on some of the attempts. There isn't anyone around who knows how to write it anymore. You just can't get writers. Writers are so expensive these days. They've got to get four figures for a script. I don't think that's wrong. I think they deserve it. It's hard to hold down the expense of doing it when you're not sure you're going to pick up an audience. I thought we were doing quite well with the hour divided into four fifteen minute shows. We began to get ratings and then Bristol-Meyers pulled out.

JASON: Something you were talking about and it's something that still exists, is doubling characters. I'm talking about cartoons because it still happens there. You did quite a lot of voice work for animated characters and you still do.

JACKSON: Right now the only cartoon thing I have on is *G. I. Joe* and Marvel Comics stuff that goes on because I also do commercials for *G. I. Joe* toys. Those are the only things I have on now that are animated. I used to do a lot of animation. There's none of it here in New York. There's no animation production to speak of as far as cartoons are concerned.

I wild track my narrations so it's not necessary that I go to California to do them. That's where all the cartoon action is. I did some cartoon shows here years ago, *Rocky and His Friends*, I did some characters on those, and then I had a thing called *King Leonardo.* I played about three parts on that. I played the king. I played the magician, a Merlin kind of character, and a couple of other things. Then of course, I did all those *Popeye* and *Little Lulu* things where I always did trick voices. I don't do much of that anymore. Most of what I do is confined to commercials. Once in a while I do a character commercial, but not very often.

JASON: You still work quite often with Arnold Stang.

JACKSON: Yeah, a couple of weeks ago, as a matter of fact. Arnold's a good boy. It's nice to work with him because he's a pro and he knows what he's doing. You work very easily with people like that because you know each other's timing. You know each other's little foibles and idiosyncrasies. You know what to expect all the time so it's easy to work together. That's one thing that radio had that television doesn't have. Today I work alone. Everybody works alone. In those days there were always five or six or a dozen people around to do a show. You made friends and you kept up with them and all that sort of thing. That doesn't happen anymore. You miss people. The whole thing is so mechanical. It's really frightening. It's no fun anymore. You never meet any people. I, for one, do not like it.

****

Those comments were made by Jackson Beck way back in 1987, but what he said has become an international tragedy. People in general no longer know how to communicate with each other one on one.

It has become a sad normal procedure to use Email or Text Messaging instead of picking up a phone or making an effort to meet, even though the other person may only be a short distance away. I, like Jackson, find it all very distasteful and depressing.

Jackson did many background voices on the big screen, most notably working with Woody Allen in both *Take the Money and Run* and *Radio Days*. He continued to use his distinctive voice to do commercials almost to his dying day in 2004. He was another one of those people who might make you say, "I know that voice, but what's his name?"

Act VII:
Scene Two
Sam Spade

He was truly a man's man. From the tip of his toes to the top of his head he was the character he played on the air, Sam Spade. Yet, it was only due to a lucky set of circumstances that he landed the role in the first place and some devious government interaction that took it from him, along with a skittish production team. As you read on you will discover what I mean by all of this.

He later became better recognized for all of his work on television and in pictures.

We conversed on September 23, 1986. You know him as Howard Duff.

****

JASON: Howard, you were born in Bremerton, Washington, across Puget Sound from Seattle?

HOWARD: Correct, only I might add that at that time it was not Bremerton. It was Charleston. Charleston was right next to Bremerton which later swallowed it up. When I was born my father was mayor of Charleston.

JASON: I understand your first ambition was the same as John Dehner's original plan. You wanted to be a cartoonist. How did that change?

HOWARD: I used to enjoy drawing and I was fascinated by caricatures. Those were quite popular when I was a kid. I used to copy them out of the papers and I began to think that maybe that was what I wanted to do. I never did it, not really. I got involved in acting when I was in high school, Roosevelt High School. I had a very supportive drama teacher. They called it oral expression at that time, if you can believe that. That's how I got the acting bug. I was looking for an easy course to take so that's the one I picked. I found out I kind of liked that stuff so that's where I began. I've never had any regrets.

JASON: As far as your professional life was concerned, wasn't your first work of any kind in the theatre?

HOWARD: Yeah. We had a very fine community theatre called the Seattle Repertory Playhouse, not to be confused with the Seattle Repertory Theatre, which they now have. I just kind of went from high school to that. They accepted me. It was like a university to me because I had never done any classics. I did Chekhov, not knowing what the hell I was doing and a few other things, Shakespeare, Noel Coward. We did pretty good stuff. I was with them for about five years. I was also a radio announcer. Anyway, that's how I started, in high school. I had a teacher who encouraged me. That's what precipitated me into the business. At the repertory theatre is where I really got my teeth. We had a director who believed that the only way to do it was to do it. She figured we should know how to act before we got there. Unfortunately, that wasn't always true. It was a kind of sink or swim kind of school of acting. We learned and survived by trying.

JASON: Which is the very nature of the theatre.

HOWARD: Yeah. Anyway, it was valuable at the time.

JASON: It wasn't too much later that you were involved with AFR.

HOWARD: Armed Forces Radio. That was after I'd gone down from Seattle to Los Angeles. It was about 1937 when I did that. I did a series called *The Phantom Pilot*, which you won't have in your notes. It was a local show. I did that for about two and a half years. Then I did free lance radio until I went into the army in 1941, March 31, 1941. I was in the army for about five years. During that time I was in the infantry. I was in special services and finally I was transferred to the Armed Forces Radio Service when they formed it. That's where I finished up my hitch. I was a correspondent on Saipan when the war ended. Then I resumed my career and got lucky to land the lead on *The Adventures of Sam Spade*. I got into pictures after that.

JASON: Armed Forces Radio is something we should talk about because that is the agency that is mostly responsible for us to be able to access a lot of the old shows.

HOWARD: One of the duties I had with them was to take those popular shows off the air and reproduce them. We had obvious specifications we had to follow. One of my jobs was to do that, to reproduce the shows we'd taken off the air. Just think of all the shows that were on at that time. That was what we were doing. We'd take out all the commercials, of course, and anything that might be considered intelligence, a violation of secrecy. I think we called that the Rebroadcast Department as I remember. Elliott Lewis and I started that thing and a few other people like Alan Hewitt. It was a good thing to do. I finished up in Saipan and Iwo Jima.

JASON: There are so many of those shows we wouldn't have without that service.

HOWARD: Yeah, I guess so.

JASON: Because there was no thought that they would have any future value. A lot of them were broadcast once and everybody said, "That's it. It was good, but it won't come again."

HOWARD: Yeah. We should probably take a bow for that one.

JASON: I'm just speaking in general of everything before that time. There weren't many copies of anything kept. In fact, I can think of times as recently as the late 60s when I went to WGN in Chicago and WMAQ. They were throwing out old programming that they thought would never be of value to anyone, but there are a lot of people who still want to hear them again, or in some cases, for the first time.

HOWARD: I have a feeling that there are no copies of *Sam Spade* around that I'm aware of. I know some people have them, but I don't think the networks have copies. We didn't really record until the last two years. We used to do everything live. You probably don't remember.

JASON: Oh, sure I do.

HOWARD: We did a show for the east and a couple of hours later we did it again for the west coast. We finally got so that we could record for the west coast. Usually the west coast got the recording. That was only in the last two years.

JASON: That's very interesting because I have several shows from 1948. That must have been about the time

	you started recording. Let's talk about some of your other shows. We'll come back to *Sam Spade* a little later because that was probably the biggest success of you radio days. I have in my records a show that I don't remember at all, a soap opera called *Dear John*.
HOWARD:	Yeah. That was from Irene Rich, sort of a late night soap opera as I remember. That was before World War Deuce. I don't know how long it lasted. I was on that show. The character I used to play was a sort of Jimmy Stewart type, which I could do at that time. I've forgotten how to do it now. I think Jimmy's forgotten how to do it. That was a show I did in conjunction with many others at that time. *Screen Guild Theatre* was one I always did the billboard for.
JASON:	The big radio show for you was *The Adventures of Sam Spade*. That started as a summer replacement, right?
HOWARD:	It might have. My memory isn't that good. It could have been. We all had pretty high hopes for it. We thought we were going on. We weren't a big smash right at the beginning as I remember. In those days you could stay on a little bit even if you weren't a big smash. I think after the first year we were pretty solid.
JASON:	It's very interesting how you got the role in the first place.
HOWARD:	That's true. It was just a case of being in the right place at the right time. Lloyd Nolan was their first choice to play Sam, but as it turned out he wasn't going to be available. There were a bunch of the regular bunch of us sitting there waiting to audition

for other parts on the show. As it happened they were having some legal problem of some sort so we waited and waited, not knowing about the Nolan situation. Finally Bill Spier, the producer and director got tired of waiting so he had each of us read a couple of lines that Sam was to say. In very short order Bill decided I was his man. It was the sort of break we all dream about. In a lot of ways I'm a little like Sam.

JASON: It was a pretty nice character to work with. Dashiell Hammett wrote *The Maltese Falcon*. The film based on his book came out in '41 starring Humphrey Bogart. As we know it was John Huston who wrote the treatment for the screen, not Hammett. It wasn't many years before the radio series began in 1946.

HOWARD: '46, right. When it began I think they wanted me to sound like Bogie. I somehow or other worked out of that and tried to make it sound like somebody I could deal with on my own turf more than I could slavishly do a Bogart imitation. Bill Spier allowed me to go my own way and I did. Anyone who heard the show would know I certainly wasn't doing a Bogart.

JASON: I know that the writers for *Sam Spade* were Bob Tallman and Jason James and then later, Bob Dowd. Did Hammett do any consultation on it at all?

HOWARD: Let me tell you something that actually happened where Dashiell Hammett is concerned. I was at a big Christmas party that a guy named S. P. Eagle, (Sam Spiegel), used to throw and there was Lillian Hellman. I met her and in my boyish enthusiasm I told her I was doing Sam Spade at the time. I said, "Miss Hellman, can you tell me what Dashiell Hammett thinks of the show?" She looked at me

	and she said, "I don't believe he's ever heard the show." That was that. I doubt if Hammett ever had anything to do with the show at all.
JASON:	So he probably didn't have anything to do with any of the other derivations that were based on his work.
HOWARD:	I think at that time he was pretty much a recluse and of course, later I was taken off the show because of my involvement with *Red Channels* and his involvement with the Un-American Activities Committee.
JASON:	When you were mentioned in *Red Channels,* nearly everybody in Hollywood who was either a writer, producer, director or had anything to do with the University of California was on that list.
HOWARD:	I don't know about that. There were a few people who were not on it. I can remember joking with other people saying, "Look at this, so and so has more credits than I have here." It turned out to destroy that show as it did with many others. I had a little trouble getting on the air after that for a couple of years and Hammett went to jail. That was the unfortunate ending of a pretty popular show.
JASON:	It was automatic guilt by association. I had Bill Robson on this show a few weeks ago and he told me what terrible effects this undocumented information had on him. He actually tried writing under a combination of his son's names, but even that didn't last long.
HOWARD:	I wasn't aware that Bill was listed, but I guess he was. It was a sad time for a lot of people.
JASON:	And so uncalled for.

HOWARD: I think so. Most of the people who were in *Red Channels,* including me, were by no means communists, nor did *Red Channels* say we were. They implied that we were communist sympathizers. Implication was all it took. Actually, what they were after were liberals. I suppose I could have been classified as a liberal and I still am, and proud of it.

JASON: I don't think many people looking at that list today would think very much of it, but at the time it had disastrous effects for so many.

HOWARD: You were around at that time. I'm sure you remember the McCarthyism going on. *Red Channels* had nothing to do with McCarthy, but it was part of the whole climate that most of us so-called liberals didn't perceive.

JASON: *Red Channels* was simply an offshoot of the feelings of some at that time.

HOWARD: Well, it was something that I was never ready for. I couldn't believe it until it happened. I just hope that sort of thing doesn't happen again.

JASON: Unfortunately, things seem to have a way of repeating themselves.

HOWARD: And of course, the climate these days is even more conservative than it was then.

JASON: Let's get back to *Sam Spade* and some of the other people who appeared on it with you. Lurene Tuttle was your co-star playing Effie.

HOWARD: She played my secretary, Effie Perrine. A lot of other people were on that show that I'm sure you remember. There was John McIntire, his wife

ACT VII: SCENE TWO: SAM SPADE

Jeanette Nolan, Elliott Reid, Hal March—

JASON: June Havoc at one time.

HOWARD: Absolutely. She was married to Bill Spier at the time. And Cathy Lewis and Han Conried—

JASON: Hans was on everything.

HOWARD: We had the best of the radio actors of the time. Everybody wanted to work the show. It was a lot of fun. It was a good show.

JASON: I have quite a few of those shows in my collection. There were some things that were common to all of them. For instance, your license number was always stated.

HOWARD: Yeah, 137596.

JASON: And the shows always ended about the same way.

HOWARD: More or less. It started with the phone ringing and Effie answering with *Sam Spade Detective Agency.* I'd say I'd be right down to dictate my report on the "So and So Caper."

JASON: Just for the fun of it, here is a typical opening of one of those shows.

****

EFFIE: Sam Spade Detective Agency.

SAM: Hello sweetheart, it' only me.

EFFIE: Oh Sam, why so modest?

SAM:	Women, Effie! Age cannot weather or custom stale their infinite variety. Against their incalculable wiles mere man is but a leaf in the wind.
EFFIE:	Oh, Sam, who was she and how windy was it?
SAM:	Cyclonic, Effie. We had to close every window in the house. If you will just contain your natural feminine curiosity for a few moments, I'll be right down to dictate my report on "The Bow Window Caper."

****

JASON:	A little later, in came Sam.

****

EFFIE:	You look sober as an owl, Sam.
SAM:	Wise as an owl, sober as a judge.
EFFIE:	Oh. When you talked on the phone I thought you'd drowned the shamrock, kissed the black Betty, sliced the main brace, made a death bargain or in a word, gone to give a Chinaman a music lesson.
SAM:	Effie, I wish you'd spend more time with *Harpers Bazaar* while I'm gone and less with the Thesaurus of Slang. I didn't know I could say that. Are you sober?
EFFIE:	Well, I've been riding the choo-choo, drinking Adams Whales and if you don't believe me, ask me to walk the chalk.
SAM:	Okay—Arms akimbo—eyes glazed, now then, the tip of your forefinger to the tip of the nose.

EFFIE:	Oh, Sam, I'm so dizzy.
SAM:	Dizzy Gillespie?
EFFIE:	Oh, Sam.
SAM:	Exactly. Are you not sewn up, shagged, shellacked, shunken, stuccoed, stiffo or just plain crazy?
EFFIE:	Well, you know that, Sam.
SAM:	Sitting posture, limbs cruciform.
EFFIE:	What?
SAM:	Cheesecake style.
EFFIE:	Oh, Sam.
SAM:	That's it now. Just a little higher. Now I'll try to put the pageant on top of the fools cap and proceed. Date—August first, 1948. To Mrs. Netta Martini, 1000 Marina Boulevard, San Francisco, from Samuel Spade, license number 137596. Subject—"The Bow Window Caper."

****

JASON:	Something that I find interesting from a personal standpoint and that I didn't think about until I started talking with you, Howard, is that I always use "Goodnight Sweetheart" as the closing music for my shows. I always have. I always open with "Sentimental Journey" and close with "Goodnight Sweetheart." That was also your sign-off for *Sam Spade*.
HOWARD:	Of course it was. I did one of the eulogies for

Lurene a couple of months ago and that's the way I ended it. It was too much for me. Yeah, "Goodnight Sweetheart," everybody always remembered that.

JASON: It's a song that brings back memories for almost anybody over forty.

HOWARD: Yeah, yeah, and I remember I whistled a lot of "I'm Looking Over a Four Leaf Clover" whenever I was on the way, under sound effects or climbing stairs or whatever, anything to fill the silence.

JASON: It was one of the best shows of its type, at least I thought so.

HOWARD: We thought so too.

JASON: You did some detecting work on television as well. You're locale always seemed to be either Los Angeles or San Francisco. It was always California. I'm thinking of *Felony Squad* for one.

HOWARD: We never identified the city, but anybody who knew Los Angeles knew that's where we were. I did that for about three and a half years. It was all right. I enjoyed doing it. One of the really sad things was that *Spade* never went on to television. It would have been marvelous on television. I see no reason why it wouldn't have been. The only reason I can think of is that nobody did it because it was in litigation at the time. People were arguing about who had the rights to it. As a matter of fact, I don't know why it couldn't be done now.

JASON: That's a good point.

HOWARD: Surely not with me, but with somebody.

JASON: I don't know. I've seen you on television recently. You don't look much older than you did then. Nothing is beyond the ability of cameras and makeup.

HOWARD: I think I'm still perfectly capable of acting it, but I just don't look that young, nor should I.

JASON: Listening to you, I don't think that baritone voice has changed much.

HOWARD: I think I've gotten a little raspier. My wife just played one of the tapes somebody sent us a while ago. I think it was called "The Floppsey, Moppsey, Cottontail Caper." We had some strange capers sometimes. My voice sounds just about the same.

JASON: So, let's get a movement going. Do you remember working on the *Batman* television show?

HOWARD: Yeah, I did that with my ex-wife.

JASON: Ida Lupino.

HOWARD: I don't remember what the hell I was. I played some wild character.

JASON: Ida played Kabella. You were her assistant. That was a show that attracted a lot of big names, people like Burgess Meredith, Joan Crawford and even Otto Preminger was on it. You can just go down the list. Everybody seemed to want a shot at it. It was really high-camp at the time.

HOWARD: It was very campy and a lot of fun, so why not do it, but I can't honestly say I remember much about it.

JASON: What about a show called *Dante*? You worked out of a place called "Dante's Inferno."

HOWARD: That was based on a show that Dick Powell used to do for Four Star. He played this gambler. Every once in a while they'd bring out one of those episodes when it came to his turn. So we said why don't we try this and make him a restauranteur rather than a gambler. An ex-gambler is actually what we made him. We thought we had a hit going there when we got on the air with it. NBC was sending us bouquets after every show and the next thing you know they wanted to cancel. We were up against Andy Griffith. He had the big success of the season. We got pretty well murdered in the ratings. We just lasted about twenty-six shows, one season. They wanted to take it off before that.

JASON: I remember it well.

HOWARD: I thought it was pretty good. It wasn't great or anything, but I thought it deserved a better fate.

JASON: I thought it was pretty good too. The problem with television is the cost of putting anything on. The ratings are so important. It's the same in the business today. Some shows that really should have a chance never get one because of where they're slotted on the schedule.

HOWARD: Right. It depends on who's your lead in. It's a crap shoot. Let's face it. As you say, the shows are so expensive to produce these days they don't want to even start with them unless they think they've got a chance.

JASON: When you say a crap shoot you also have to consider how fickle the public can be. You don't know what they're going to like from one year to the next.

HOWARD: But you've got to give a show a chance to find an audience. They don't give a show a real chance anymore, I don't think. Of course there are some obvious hits like *The Cosby Show* or *Golden Girls*, etc.

JASON: Bill Cosby is never a gamble.

HOWARD: No, Cosby is not much of a gamble. Anyway, I thought the last series I was heavily involved in, *Flamingo Road* deserved a better chance. It certainly was as good as or better than *Dallas* or *Dynasty* or *Falcon Crest*.

JASON: The problem with any of those shows is that they've fallen into a kind of pattern. People either like them or they don't. They'll watch all of them or they'll watch none of them.

HOWARD: Unfortunately, we were on NBC and NBC was at that time in the doldrums. Remember the genius who was at CBS and ABC and finally NBC, Grant Tinker? He came in and I think he wanted to design his own kind of shows and that's what he did. We lasted two seasons. That was about it. I think we deserved better.

JASON: You've done a lot of serious shows, but you've also done comedy. I remember a show that you did with Ida Lupino called *Mr. Adams and Eve*.

HOWARD: We got two seasons out of that one. I thought we ought to have done better than that, but that's the way it goes. We were not perceived as *I Love Lucy*, which we had no intention of trying to do. Some people think we were a little ahead of our time.

JASON: You had some good people on that one too, people like Larry Dobkin and Alan Reed.

HOWARD: Larry used to play the crazy director, the head of the studio, kind of a combination of Harry Cohn and Louie Mayer. Dan Tobin was my friend and Hayden Rourke was our agent. Remember him from *I Dream of Genie*? We had a lot of fun doing it. I can't complain about not being given my head because we made all the decisions about what kind of show we wanted it to be.

JASON: Were you included in any way in Four Star Playhouse?

HOWARD: No, I wasn't, but Ida was. The four stars were David Niven, Charles Boyer, Dick Powell and Ida.

JASON: And originally Joel McCrea and Roz Russell were part of the group.

HOWARD: No kidding?—maybe so.

JASON: I'm sure your favorite role must have been Sam Spade.

HOWARD: It would have to be. It was a lot of fun doing it and I like to do comedy. A lot of people thought of it as comedy.

JASON: It was kind of an early day Mike Hammer approach.

HOWARD: Yeah, we were pretty loose for that time. I'm surprised a lot of the dialogue holds up as well as it does. We had a lot of fun doing it. Well. What the hell, it was one of my favorite things I got to do.

JASON:	It has stood the test of time. A lot of radio has. There are some things that are very dated, but for the most part I think radio has held up quite well.
HOWARD:	Right. We always thought we had it going pretty good. We had no make up or lights to worry about.
JASON:	John Dehner said something to me that I had never considered. He said that radio was a great medium because you could be riding across the plains and you never got dusty.
HOWARD:	That's a good line. I'd like to have that line myself.
JASON:	Now you do.
HOWARD:	Yeah. I've got it now.
JASON:	What would be your favorite movie role? I always liked *Naked City*.
HOWARD:	I don't know that that was my favorite role. The first two movies I made were *Brute Force* and *Naked City*. In *All My Sons* I did a minor character. I think one of my favorite roles that I ever played in a feature picture was one I did with Bob Altman, *The Wedding*, where I played a sort of alcoholic doctor.
JASON:	Dr. Jules Meacham is the character you're referring to. During the wedding reception he was called on to attend someone who seemed to be very ill. Not being in the best of shape himself, the good doctor discovered that the patient was not ill, he was dead, not the best thing at a wedding. It may not sound like it, but it was a very humorous scene. Would you say that there were any recent television appearances you particularly enjoyed?

HOWARD: I enjoyed doing a thing on *Knotts Landing*. I played a very wealthy guy who was a power freak. I've been doing a lot of power freaks lately. The older you get the more you fit those parts.

JASON: That kind of goes with the prime time soaps. Everybody's a power freak.

HOWARD: Everybody's a power freak. Yeah, that's the way it's been going.

JASON: You've had a long career in every form of the media. Tell me what you're up to these days.

HOWARD: Oh, let me see. I play a lot of tennis and I read a lot and I just finished a picture that I kind of like called *No Way Out* with Gene Hackman and a young guy named Kevin Costner and a young lady named Sean Young. I play a kind of powerful southern senator. That's the last picture I've done. I do guest shots on television here and there. I do some voice-overs for commercials. We just moved to Santa Barbara, my wife Judy and I. We love our house. It's a whole new life we've got going here.

JASON: It sounds like you're enjoying life. That's always good to hear.

HOWARD: I have to say that I really do enjoy life. I intend to keep on doing that as long as I'm able. If you live this long you damn well better enjoy it.

****

As I said at the beginning of this segment, Howard Duff really was the man he portrayed on *The Adventures of Sam Spade*. You might have noticed the tough guy image coming through loud and clear in some of the answers he gave. In reality, this interview turned out to be one of the most enjoyable that I ever conducted with anyone, show business or otherwise.

We talked at some length about the blacklisting era. Many folks believe that that was at least the partial cause of Howard's long marriage to Ida Lupino breaking up after thirty-three years. It was just one more of the consequences of those terrible times. They remained good friends. They were both good people.

Howard died in Santa Barbara at the age of seventy-six in 1990, much too young.

ACT VII:
SCENE THREE
THE SAINT

Yes, he did play *The Saint* on radio and yes, he also played many obsessively evil characters in movies, but, as is the case for so many, in fact all of my guests, that was only the tip of the iceberg. I saved him for last because he was the most deeply complex person I ever spoke with from the business of shows of one sort or another. That includes all three volumes of this series. He was actually three diverse and interesting people, but due to the nature of these books I chose to limit most of my questions to his performing career.

When I exchanged words with him on July 27, 1986, Vincent Price did all I could hope for to accommodate me.

****

JASON: Before we go into your background as a performer I want to clear the air about your personality. What we see and hear on the media is definitely not the real Vincent Price; in fact, it couldn't be farther from the truth.

VINCENT: I'd say pretty much so. I don't beat dogs and I try not to scare the kids. I'm afraid that's only very much an acting job.

JASON: I know you've done a great deal of humanitarian work and I also know that you are an aficionado and patron of the art world, paintings and sculpture and you're somewhat of a fanatic when it comes to Pre-Columbian art.

VINCENT: I love it, that and African art are my favorites.

JASON: Is it true that your first entry into the fine arts came at a very young age when you purchased an authentic Rembrandt drawing?

VINCENT: I was still a school boy at that time. I was earning a little money selling magazines and junk. I went to a local art dealer, the only one in town at that time, and I saw that drawing. Right away I knew I had to have it. The price was $37.50, which was a stretch for me. You must consider that this was in the '30s and at that time $37.50 was much more than it is now. I talked the dealer into working with me. He could see how much I was wrapped up in that drawing. He let me give him a down payment of five dollars with a promise that I would pay off the debt in six months. Little by little I brought the balance down, but it was a full year before it was paid off. By the way, I still have it and I treasure the memories it brings to me when I look at it.

JASON: Jumping forward to the present, your house is now a gallery that rivals many museums. You even have a totem pole in your yard.

VINCENT: Not just any totem pole. Most of them look to me like carved telephone poles, but mine is a masterpiece. It was carved by the Haida Indians from the Queen Charlotte Islands in British Columbia. It stands all of twenty-five feet tall and consists of just three marvelous figures. At the bottom is a bear-like creature. On his head is a man holding a huge fish and at the top is a great bird. We got it when they were having a sale of artifacts at John Barrymore's house after he died. The colors are still warm and beautiful. We figured it to be from about the 1870s.

ACT VII: SCENE THREE: THE SAINT

JASON: I believe it's also true that you are a gourmet chef. You can go up against the best of them.

VINCENT: Yes, I've always been interested in cooking. I'm from the Middle West. My mother gathered recipes from all over the world to, I think, escape the Middle West. So we ate in our house in St. Louis on a worldwide basis. She taught my brother and sisters and I how to cook.

JASON: I suppose we should get to the Vincent we all learned to love and fear. In your early pictures you were anything but a heavy. You played such roles as Sir Walter Raleigh in *The Private Lives of Elizabeth and Essex*. You played Joseph Smith in *Brigham Young*, a prelate in *Keys to the Kingdom* and several other roles in that vein. Then it changed around. When did you play your first really evil character?

VINCENT: Well, on radio I played *The Saint* for many years and I played many other things, some of the *Suspense* shows and things like that. Simon Templar was not the nicest person, but I suppose the first really evil part I had was in a play on Broadway called *Angel Street*.

JASON: Your acting career began on the London stage if I'm not mistaken.

VINCENT: I started in theatre in London and then I came to New York. I've done theatre all my life, not always necessarily in New York. I've played in Madison many times at the University there. All actors usually like the theatres best of all.

JASON: You were such an accomplished actor on the stage and in movies. What brought you to doing radio?

VINCENT: When I was in my first play on Broadway with Helen Hayes, *Victoria Regina*, I had a lot of time on my hands and I thought, I'm not going to do anything else for about three years because this play will probably run that long, so I decided to do as many radio shows as I could. It was a difficult time for an actor to get radio shows if he wasn't in a long running soap opera. I did parts anonymously in soap operas. I'd do maybe five or six a day just to learn the business. I've always thought that radio was one of the great ways to learn to act because you have to do everything with your voice. It stood me in good stead. To this day I love radio. I rarely turn down a chance to be on radio.

JASON: What makes it the best is that you can project different images to different listeners. Everyone gets their own idea of who you are.

VINCENT: Absolutely. I think radio has always had a wonderful mixture of comedy and drama and even documentaries. It's a wonderful medium.

JASON: But you said your only regular series was in the role of Simon Templar on *The Saint*.

VINCENT: I think I did that for about four years.

JASON: The show that I remember best was one that was not a regular one for you, but you were on it many times. I'm referring to the aforementioned *Suspense*. Since you were on so many *Suspense* shows you had a chance to work with several fine directors, Bill Robson, Bill Spier, Anton Leader, and Bruno Zirato. Did you have any preference?

VINCENT: I loved Bill Robson. I got to know him very well, Bill Spier too. Radio directors were tremendously

JASON:	It was all live in those days.
VINCENT:	Yes indeed, live. I did one series with Tallulah Bankhead. We had to do it before we did the plays we were in. She was in one play and I was in another. Then we'd have to come back to redo the radio show for the west coast. It was a long day's work.
JASON:	Of all the *Suspense* shows that you did there was one that you did several times and you also did it on *Escape*. It got so familiar that people started referring to it as the story with the rats. You were more a victim than a bad guy on that one.
VINCENT:	Oh yes, he was a victim. I wasn't always the bad guy on those shows. That one was called *Three Skeleton Key*. It was really one of the most exciting shows ever done on radio. It was written by a friend of mine named James Poe. He was sort of angling to get on radio. He was a very famous screen writer, but he wanted to get into writing for radio. He came up with this one which, as you said, I did many times. I think it's really a great classic radio story. The sound effects were superb.
JASON:	I can still hear the rats gnawing on the light house. I have several different copies of that program.
VINCENT:	They used strawberry boxes.

creative people. They had a wide variety of hints to give the actor. They were marvelous. It all had to be done sort of instantaneously because you only had maybe one read through. They were terribly talented and they gave us everything we needed to go on.

JASON: Ida Lupino was also terrific in stories that could stand your hair on end. Do you remember one you did with her called *Fugue in C Minor*? You were extremely evil on that one.

VINCENT: Yes, I do indeed. Ida was a wonderful actress. Radio wasn't really her medium as much as television and, before that, movies, which were great pictures. She was really wonderful, but when she did come over to radio she was one of the few movie actresses who could deliver on radio. Many of them didn't know how to read.

JASON: You must have worked with Agnes Moorehead. She was on *Suspense* quite a lot too.

VINCENT: Yes, I worked a lot with Aggie. I was in the *Mercury Theatre* with Orson Welles, but before Agnes joined it. She really joined it at the very end. I was in it from the very beginning. Then she joined the *Mercury Theatre on the Air*. I was on it in many shows with Agnes and did one movie with her. Actually I did a couple of movies with her, but the one was called *The Bat*.

JASON: Since I brought up directors I think we should mention a couple of others whom I'm sure you know. Do you remember working with Norman Corwin and Norman MacDonnell?

VINCENT: Norman Corwin was one of the real genius geniuses on radio, a brilliant man, and MacDonnell too. I worked with so many of them. One of them who was an actor and a very brilliant comedian was Hans Conried. He was also an excellent director.

JASON: Norman MacDonnell was the head man on *Gunsmoke*, but one of the shows you worked with him was

	Escape. I remember a particularly chilling story called *Bloodbath*, set in the jungles of South America.
VINCENT:	That was a very exciting show too. I did a lot of movies and a lot of different things that were in South America. I don't know why. I think it was in the period when it was romanticized much more than it is now that we're tearing it all down as usual, destroying it.
JASON:	It reminded me a little of *Leiningen vs. the Ants*, another classic. You played some real fright figures as time went on. In 1946 or there about there was *The Lodger* on *Hollywood Star Time*, the story of Jack, the Ripper.
VINCENT:	That was extraordinary because Laird Cregar, who created that role in the movies, really should have done it. I was thrilled to do it because I think it's a wonderful part. I later did plays by that same author.
JASON:	Going back a little further to about 1941, you showed up repeatedly on *Philip Morris Playhouse*. That was with Bill Spier.
VINCENT:	That was also with Tallulah Bankhead. She had this very definite voice, definite delivery. She really couldn't change from time to time and what we were doing was sort of classic short stories, dramatized for radio. It always sounded like Tallulah Bankhead, but it always had a marvelous, glamorous quality. She was a unique woman of the theatre.
JASON:	There were a number of shows you were involved with over the years as a guest or the host. Two of them were anthologies and at least one of them had a surprising date on the calendar. I'm referring to

Family Theatre from the 40s and 50s and the most recent one from 1979, *The Sears Radio Theatre*.

VINCENT: I really had hoped that was going to be a comeback and be a permanent thing because all of us who had worked on radio believed we were the only country in the world where, when television came in, it killed radio. In England it's still as popular as it was in its heyday. I did a series for the BBC called *The Price of Fear* which are now being played on Public Broadcasting here. Radio in England is still much more listened to than television is watched.

JASON: The taxing policies have something to do with it. They have to pay a stiff tax to have an operating television in their homes. That also applies to radio, but it's much less. I had to abide by similar rules when I lived in Holland for several years.

VINCENT: Yes, that's true, but they also do awfully good radio. They have top writers and top directors and actors. I looked through the casts of some of the *Price of Fear* things that I did and there were extraordinary people on them, great, great stars of the English theatre who were interested in radio and also in earning a little extra money.

JASON: I know that some of the older comedy shows are currently re-running in England. I believe they've revived *The Goon Show* recently. That was a favorite of some of the Royals, Princess Margaret in particular. Those were great shows, very funny, but a little outré.

VINCENT: Right on both counts.

JASON: If you were to consider just radio, do you have a favorite role?

ACT VII: SCENE THREE: THE SAINT

VINCENT: I loved doing *The Saint*. I had never done a series that went on and on until then. I never really made up my mind whether I loved them because I loved the character or just because I loved radio and the marvelous people who did it. We were almost like a stock company. I worked with the same people every week.

JASON: I think it's time to interject a portion of one of those *Saint* shows. This is a portion of an episode called "Author of Murder." Simon is rudely awakened by an unknown visitor with murder on his mind.

****

VISITOR: Templar! Mr. Templar!

SIMON: I'm asleep.

VISITOR: Mr. Templar!!

SIMON: Noisy dream.

VISITOR: You're not dreaming. You're not dreaming.

SIMON: That's what you say. I'm alone in my bedroom. I'm in my bed—

VISITOR: You're not alone. I'm here.

SIMON: Go away.

VISITOR: I'm sorry. I didn't climb into your bedroom merely to go away.

SIMON: What do you expect, a twenty-one gun salute?

VISITOR: I expect your attention. You can't see me, can you?

Simon: No, I'd be even happier if I couldn't hear you.

Visitor: I can see you, however. You're situated against the window behind you.

Simon: That's cunning of me.

Visitor: It helps me to aim the gun I'm pointing at you.

Simon: I'm so glad, I'd hate to have your aim suffer. What do I do now, get up and put the lights on?

Visitor: Don't do anything of the kind.

Simon: No? Why? Are you shy?

Visitor: Yes, let's say I'm shy.

Simon: That's why you insist on holding this conversation with me in the dark, a conversation that wouldn't be, obviously, about the weather? What would it be about?

Visitor: Well, I'm a writer.

Simon: A writer—and shy—nonsense.

Visitor: I need some advice.

Simon: The only advice I can give to all writers is—don't.

Visitor: I'm writing a book—about murder. I'm calling it The Story of a Perfect Crime.

Simon: Sounds interesting.

Visitor: Thank you. What I came here for is to have you tell me if the murder I'm dealing with is really a perfect crime.

SIMON: Go on.

VISITOR: The man to be murdered in my book suffers from heart disease. He's a completely unpleasant character, a financier and an unsavory one, a man who deserves to die.

SIMON: Yes and he suffers from heart disease.

VISITOR: For his condition he takes daily, capsules containing medicine, capsules on which his life depends. Now the murderer, in my book that is, decides to poison the financier.

SIMON: That's not cricket.

VISITOR: No, it's murder, murder that will be poisoning without poison.

SIMON: I'm waiting breathlessly for the next chapter.

VISITOR: The murderer steals one of the capsules, pours the medicine out, replaces the medicine with powdered sugar and returns the capsule to the financier's pill box. In due course, the financier reaches the capsule, takes it and his weak heart, lacking the medicine he needs, fails. And there you have poisoning without poison.

SIMON: Hmmm, very intriguing.

VISITOR: I think so. The poisoner can't be traced through the poison he purchased because he didn't purchase any. The murdered man is assumed to have died a natural death. Well, is it the perfect crime?

SIMON:	I can't see any flaws in it.
VISITOR:	If you can't I don't see why the critics will.
SIMON:	Don't you mean the police?
VISITOR:	Why should the police be interested in a book I'm writing?
SIMON:	Why should the critics be interested in the murder you're committing?
VISITOR:	You're not serious?
SIMON:	You are.
VISITOR:	I rather think I must leave now.

****

JASON:	In the next scene a sleazy financier is found dead in his bed from an apparent heart attack. You can guess where it went from there. Let's switch gears and talk about one of my favorite shows on PBS, *Mystery*.
VINCENT:	I do those in Boston for WGBH. They are British shows, some from BBC and some from Thames. They're all different London companies that made the shows. They're purchased in London for *Mystery* which is an American show.
JASON:	So it's just the intros and outros that are done here.
VINCENT:	Yes, I do all of them from Boston.
JASON:	Those are always good shows.

VINCENT: Yes, they're wonderful. The English know how to do it.

JASON: You've done a lot of TV commercials of late. It seems like they nearly always make the most of your image from horror movies. I'm thinking about a couple of examples, one where your wife used her Master Card to get you a fly zapper and also a Cousins spot where you used a very devious method to cut the sandwich, right out of your 1961 movie version of Edgar Allen Poe's classic story, *The Pit and the Pendulum*.

VINCENT: Some of them they do very well. I think it's always fun to make fun of yourself.

JASON: You recently did an animated film that was a take-off on the Sherlock Holmes legend. You did the voice of another villain. The title is *The Great Mouse Detective*.

VINCENT: It's a huge hit. I'm just delighted about it because, all my life I've wanted to do a Disney movie. I think it's in the tradition of the Disney animated films and will kind of live forever. It's a wonderful character I played, Professor Ratagan.

JASON: He's the heavy, isn't he? I haven't seen it yet.

VINCENT: Oh boy—is he ever. He's a rat, really a rat.

JASON: You've worked in over seventy feature films. Would you care to pick a couple you liked the best?

VINCENT: I sort of put them into two different categories. I've done so many different kinds of themes. I think *Laura* for instance was probably as fine a film as was ever made. It's not pretentious. It was perfectly

| | made. I think also that *Dragonwyck* was a very fine movie. Both of those were with Gene Tierney. I think *Song of Bernadette* with Jennifer Jones was a wonderful picture. Then there was *The Baron of Arizona* which I loved doing and which is now having a big revival. And of some of the spooky ones, I would think *Theatre of Blood* is my favorite. |

JASON: What about *The Abominable Dr. Phibes*?

VINCENT: They were absolutely wonderful.

JASON: When you say they you're referring to both *The Abominable Dr. Phibes* and *Dr. Phibes Rises Again*.

VINCENT: That is correct.

JASON: Aside from radio, television, stage and movies, there's another facet to your career. You do a lot of lectures about the business and how to get into it.

VINCENT: I really want to stress the fact that I have always been a lecturer, all my life. In the theatre I feel it's very important to get out and talk to young people who want to follow that path. I always try to say how much I believe in radio as a method of training. Many colleges have very fine radio departments and they're beginning to have good television departments. The radio departments have turned out some very fine young actors. I do think it's a marvelous medium in which to learn the theatre.

JASON: I think it's interesting that you should say that because when I talked with a man from a very different part of the business, Mel Blanc, he spoke of how many times he goes out and lectures at the colleges about his background and not only that, but why he does what he does.

ACT VII: SCENE THREE: THE SAINT

VINCENT: He's an extraordinary man, a great friend. I'm devoted to him and his work.

****

If you want to know more about Vincent Price's dedication to the art world I suggest that you read his early autobiography published in 1959 called *I Like What I Know: A Visual Autobiography*. It is all about his tremendous collection of art from around the world and how he got to obtain nearly every piece.

On a more personal note, I would like to add that when I did most of these interviews I received in return an autographed picture of my interviewee. Mr. Price did them one better. Shortly after our conversation, I received in the mail a fine gold edged copy of *A Treasury of Great Recipes*, a cook book he put together with his then wife, Mary of complete recipes from some of the finest restaurants world-wide. As we said earlier, cooking was one of his avocations.

Vincent Price died in 1993. He left an indelible mark on all of us.

Afterword/Epilogue Criminals & Crime Stoppers

Now it is time to close out Volume Three. I cannot do that without fulfilling my promise to further investigate radio's many ventures into the world of crime and punishment. In no way will I attempt to bring up all of the shows that delved into that particular form of broadcasting. It would take another full volume or two to accomplish anything close to that end. Instead, I will talk of just a few of them, each with a different approach to the overall subject.

One source material for these shows was books. So far we talked about S. S. Van Dine's Philo Vance, Dashiell Hammett's Sam Spade and Leslie Charteris' Saint. There were others based on literature. One of them came directly from the work of Gilbert Keith Chesterton. What makes that one interesting, at least to me, is that it was the early forerunner of a much later successful television series. The radio series was a short lived one season summer replacement called *The Adventures of Father Brown*. It was about a diminutive, humble parish priest who could intentionally look dumb while solving some difficult dilemmas. The television show that it put me in mind of was Tom Bosley's portrayal of Father Dowling on *Father Dowling Mysteries*. This is just my own personal interpretation. Father Dowling was in modern times while Father Brown was a character of the nineteenth century, but there were definite similarities.

Next on the list of detectives who came right out of fiction are a married couple who dramatized the works of Frances and Richard Lockridge. Their alter egos were two people who were not really detectives at all. He was a publisher and she was a house wife, but they had a nasty habit of stumbling onto a corpse each and every week. They were just average people who solved run of the mill murders on each episode. The show was *Mr. And Mrs. North* starring Joseph Curtain and Alice Frost as Jerry and Pam North. Pam was usually the one who came up with the solution to each case.

Yet another show with literary background was originally from the pen of Earl Derr Biggers, although as is the case of all of these examples, he did not write the radio version. The leading character was an oriental sleuth named *Charlie Chan,* played by Ed Begley. Charlie had so many children that he could not ever remember their names so he simply referred to them as Number One Son, etc. He used all sorts of strange theories to come up with his conclusions, but somehow, they always worked.

The last descendent of the printed page was someone who was usually on the wrong side of the international law system. He was primarily a jewel thief who would never be involved in murder or anything else quite so heinous. He was always on the run, usually in Europe, but he was never caught throughout the two year run of the show. The story line came from Graham Greene. Orson Welles played the main character. The series was called *The Lives of Harry Lime* or alternately, *The Third Man.*

Taking a different approach to the subject we come upon three entries from Jack Webb's repertoire. Everyone remembers his droll impersonation of Joe Friday on *Dragnet,* both on radio and television. He never let anything excite him very much. All he ever wanted was "The facts Maam." Not as many folks recall what was in my mind his best entry into the world of crime and capture. The broadcasts owe a good deal of their credit to the incredible writing of Richard Breen who could twist a phrase with the best of them. You had to listen closely because if you did not you would miss yet another amazing line. *Pat Novak, for Hire* was its name. Pat was a Private Eye who started each show with a quip like, "Yeah, My name is Pat Novak. I rent boats and tell a few lies if the price is right." His location was the seedy underbelly of the San Francisco waterfront. For pure listening enjoyment, *Pat Novak* was hard to top. The third Jack Webb venue was a little different from the other two, but in some ways similar. It was called *Pete Kelly's Blues.* He was a down and out cornet player working in a gin mill in Kansas City. He was always on the run, just like Harry Lime, but for different reasons. In every episode he would find a way to run afoul with some member of the KC crime family and he spent the rest of it worming his way out of trouble. If you like jazz this was an excellent show to listen to.

On the feminine side we had another PI who was gorgeous, but could be hard as nails when the situation called for it. The shows always began with her answering her phone in her San Francisco penthouse with her phone number, YUkon 2-8209. She was played by Natalie Park (Masters). The title was *Candy Matson*.

We cannot forget the newspaper gumshoes. There were several of them. One was *Big Town* starring Edward G. Robinson as Steve Wilson, managing editor of the *Illustrated Press*. He was a constant crusader for justice. A different approach was *Casey, Crime Photographer*. He was played, at different times, by Matt Crowley, Jim Backus and finally, Staats Cotsworth. He would go to a crime scene, snap a picture and then go on to solve the case.

We also had the lawyers from both sides of the law. *Mr. District Attorney* was after the felons, but *Roger Kilgore, Public Defender* was forever protecting the ones he thought to be innocent of any wrong doing.

Finally there was an entry from the comic pages, *Dick Tracy*. The drawings in the funnies were executed by Chester Gould, but once more, he did not write the show. Dick was portrayed by many actors; among them was the ever present Matt Crowley.

That was just a small sampling of what was available. Some of my examples were short lived shows while others ran for many years.

THANKS FOR LISTENING!

BIBLIOGRAPHY

Allen, Steve. *Hi Ho Steverino: My Adventures in the Wonderful Wacky World of Television.* New York: Barricade Books, 1992.

Arden, Eve. *Three Phases of Eve.* New York: St. Martin's Press, 1985.

Backus, Jim and Henny Backus. *Forgive our Digressions: An Autobiography.* New York: St. Martin's Press, 1988.

Backus, Jim. *Rocks on the Roof.* New York: G. P. Putnam, 1958.

Dunning, John. *On the Air: The Encyclopedia of Old-Time Radio.* New York: Oxford University Press, 1998.

Idelson, Bill. *Story of Vic and Sade, The.* Albany, Georgia: BearManor Media, 2007.

Ives, Burl. *Wayfaring Stranger: An Autobiography.* New York: Whittlesey House, 1948.

Leonard, Sheldon. *And the Show Goes On: Broadway and Hollywood Adventures.* New York: Limelight Editions, 1984.

Price, Vincent. *I Like What I Know: A Visual Autobiography,* Garden City, New York: Doubleday and Company, Inc., 1959.

INDEX

14 August, 345
26 by Corwin, 162
60 Minutes, 16
101 Dalmatians, 219p, 265

A

Abbott & Costello, 41
Abbott & Costello Meet the Invisible Man, 94
Abbott, George, 120, 168
Abominable Dr. Phibes, The, 388
Adams, Ansel, 50
Adams, Nick, 112
Adventures by Morse, 287
Adventures in a Vast Wasteland, 190
Adventures of Father Brown, 391
Adventures of Frank Merriwel, 7
Adventures of Maisie, 81
Adventures of Sam Spade, 53, 126-127, 230p, 355, 357-365, 370, 372, 391
Adventures of Superman, 229p
Afflick, Mary, 14
After the Thin Man, 294
Ainley, Joe, 322
Albad, the Oaf, 170
Aldrich Family, The, 22, 41
Alexander's Ragtime Band, 156

All My Sons, 371
All You've Got is Time, 42
Allen, Gracie, 31
Allen, Irwin, 190
Allen, Steve, 173-192, 214p, 215p
Allen, Woody, 354
Allison, June, 110, 125
Allman, Elvia, 301
Altman, Robert, 371
Amazing Mr. Malone, The, 54
Ameche, Don, 19, 86, 246, 252, 260, 261-262
Ameche, Jim, 19, 86
American Album of Familiar Music, 37
Amos and Andy, 83, 128, 153, 154
Amundsen, Robert, 328
Anatomy of a Murder, 319
And the Show Goes On, 94
Anderson, Eddie, 82
Androcles and the Lion, 116
Andy Griffith Show, The, 91, 255, 368
Angel Street, 377
Anna and the King, 255
Anthony, Susan B., 179
Antoinette, Marie, 179

Anybody Can Play, 56
Aplon, Boris, 23
Apple Annie, 92
Arden, Eve, 203p, 224p, 225p, 265, 307, 320
Armed Forces Radio, 47, 125, 126, 357
Arnaz. Desi, 319
Arnheim, Gus, 137
Arnold Grimm's Daughter, 259
Arnold, Eddie, 76
Arnold, Edward, 265
Astaire, Fred, 154, 188
Auerbach, Artie, 82, 145
Aunt Mary, 265
Auntie Mame, 309, 326
Author of Murder, 383
Author, Author, 351

B

Baby Snooks, 125
Bacall, Lauren, 93
Bach, Segunner, 12
Bachelor Father, 337
Back Where I Come From, 162
Backus Strikes Back, 101, 114-115
Backus, Henny, 95-118, 206p
Backus, Jim, 95-118, 206p, 207p
Baer, Parley, 76, 239, 327
Baker, Carol, 164
Ball, Lucille, 75, 77, 127, 151, 291, 297, 310, 321, 328, 338, 369
Ballard, Kay, 319
Bankhead, Tallulah, 379, 381
"Barbara Allen", 159
Barber, Red, 36, 42
Barbera, Joe, 301
Barefoot in the Park, 309
Barnes, Paul, 23

Baron of Arizona, 388
Barret, Robert, 121
Barrymore, John, 376
Barty, Billy, 320
Baruch, André, 33-48, 198p, 199p
Basie, Count, 189
Bat, The, 380
Batman, 367
"Battle of the Century", 286
Beck, Jackson, 5, 6, 228p, 229p, 265, 341-354
Bellamy, Ralph, 272
Benaderet, Bea, 76, 291, 325, 330
Bendix, William (Bill), 335-336
Benedetti, Florio, 22-23
Benny Goodman Story, The, 183
Benny, Jack, 26, 31, 81, 82, 83, 106, 125, 140, 141, 152, 192, 247, 297, 298
Berg, Gertrude, 299
Bergen, Edgar, 26, 60
Berle, Milton, 176
Berlin, Irving, 180, 189
Bernstein, Leonard, 309
Best of the Week, 323
Bester, Don, 140
Betty & Bob, 259
Beverly Hillbillies, 338
Bianchi, Carlo, 20
Bickford, Charles, 164
Big Country, 163
Big Eddie, 86-87
Big Town, 76, 127, 393
Bill Idelson's Writing Class, 256
Black, Frank, 140
Blair, Jules, 322
Blanc, Mel, 6, 81, 82, 105, 142, 301, 327, 388

Blaufuss, Walter, 254
Block, Martin, 174
Blondie, 223p, 293-299
Bloodbath, 381
Blyth, Anne, 225p
Blum, Myrt, 142
Bob Crosby Old Gold Show, 323, 337
Bobbie Benson and the B-bar-B Riders, 6, 33-34
Bogart, Humphrey, 93, 166, 294, 360
Booth, Shirley, 310
Bop Fables, 182
Bosley, Tom, 391
Box 13, 264
Boyer, Charles, 370
Boyle, Peter, 94
Boys from Syracuse, The, 167-168
Bradley, Curley, 14-15
Bradley, General Omar, 61
Brady Bunch, The, 125
Brando, Marlon, 93
Breakfast Club, 324
Breen, Richard, 51-52, 392
Brice, Fannie, 125
Brickhouse, Jack, 23
Brigham Young, 377
Brinks Job, The, 93
Broadway, 120
Broadway Is My Beat, 83
Brooklyn Dodgers, 36-37
Brookshire, Norman, 41
Brother Orchid, 11
Brother Rat, 11
Brothers, The, 77
Brown, John, 87, 336
Brown, Les, 42

Browning, Elizabeth Barrett, 179
Brownstone Theatre, 347-348
Brute Force, 371
Bryan, Arthur Q., 301, 327
Brynner, Yul, 255
Burns & Allen Show, The, 76, 127
Burns, George, 47, 130, 141
Burr, Raymond, 53
Burroughs, Edgar Rice, 70
"Bury Your Dead, Arizona", 286
Bushkin, Joe, 138
Butler, Daws, 301
Butterfield, Billy, 138
Butterfield, Herb, 326

C

Caesar, Sid, 55, 113
Caine Mutiny Court Martial, 326
Camel Caravan, 348
Candy Matson, 393
Cannon, John, 24
Canova, Judy, 81, 82, 130, 291, 308
Capra, Frank, 92-93
Captain Midnight, 5, 15, 23, 26-28, 197p
Caravan of Courage: An Ewok Adventure, 170
Carol, Sue, 264
Carpenter, Ken, 31
Carson, Jack, 323
Casey, Crime Photographer, 350, 393
Cat on a Hot Tin Roof, 165, 168
Catherine, the Great, 179
Cats Don't Dance, 272
Cavanaugh, Eddie, 25
Cavanaugh, Fannie, 25
Cavanaugh, Hobart, 120
CBS Mystery Theatre, 351

Chadwick, Kamilla, 274
Challenge of the Yukon, 7
Chandler, Jeff, 314-315, 318
Charlie Chan, 392
Charteris, Leslie, 339, 391
Chase, Chevy, 320
Chekhov, Anton, 356
Chesterton, Gilbert Keith, 391
Chevillat, Dick, 153
Chez Show, The, 16
Christmas Carol, A, 72
Cinderella, 272
Cinnamon Bear, The, 70-72
Cisco Kid, The, 6, 346
Clarke, Ian, 77
Cleopatra, 179
Club Matinee, 324
Coast to Coast on a Bus, 34
Cobb, Buff, 16
Cohn, Harry, 296, 370
Cole, Buddy, 138
Coleman, Ronald, 72
Collins, Jazbo, 182
Collins, Ted, 40
Collins, Tom, 287
Columbia Presents Corwin, 170
Columbia Workshop, 170
Command Performance, 125
Concentration, 57
Connors, Chuck, 213p
Conrad, William (Bill), 64, 125, 326
Conried, Hans, 54, 82, 105, 129, 130, 363, 380
Coons, Johnny, 248-249
Cooper, Wyllis, 265, 267
Corwin, Norman, 3, 162-163, 170, 256, 345, 380

Cosby, Bill, 89, 90, 369
Cosby Show, The, 369
Costner, Kevin, 372
Cotsworth, Staats, 350, 393
Counterattack, 342
Coward, Noel, 356
Crawford, Joan, 367
Cregar, Laird, 381
Crenna, Richard, 311, 318, 326, 333
Crosby, Bing, 183
Crosby, Norm, 80
Crowley, Matt, 350-351, 393
Crusinberry, Jane, 268-270
Cugat, Xavier, 137
Culp, Robert, 89
Curtain, Joseph, 392

D

Dagmar, 15
Dallas, 64, 141, 170, 268, 369
Damon Runyon Theatre, 87
Dana, Bill, 183
Dangerous Assignment, 287-288
Danny Thomas Show, The, 83, 87, 91, 92, 129, 255, 337
Dante, 368
Darnell, Linda, 156
Davis, Edith, 247
Davis, Joan, 337
Davis, Nancy, 247
Day, Dennis, 81, 142-145
Day, Doris, 177-178
Dead End Kids, 34
Dean, James, 111-112, 164-166
Dear John, 359
Death Valley Days, 342
Dehner, John, 326, 355, 371
DeMarcos, The, 137
Dennis The Menace, 77

Dick Tracy, 393
Dick Van Dyke Show, The, 89, 217p, 255, 256
Diletskii, Nikolai, 190
Disney, Walt, 59, 60, 265, 272, 387
"Dizzy Fingers", 34
Dobkin, Larry, 370
Don Winslow of the Navy, 271
Donaldson, Dan, 42
Donlevy, Brian, 267-268
Doran, Ann, 112
Douglas, Kirk, 128, 326
Dowd, Bob, 360
Dr. Phibes Rises Again, 388
Dragnet, 52, 83, 84, 130, 131, 392
Dragonwyck, 388
Drake, Betsy, 91
Duff, Howard, 230p, 231p, 355-374
Duffy's Tavern, 34, 81
Dumont, Margaret, 64
Duncan, David Douglas, 50
Dynasty, 268, 369

E

Earn Your Vacation, 175
East of Eden, 164-165
Ebsen, Buddy, 308
Eddie Cantor Show, The, 32, 81
Edwards, Jane, 108
Edwards, Ralph, 41
Einstein, Harry, 80
Ellen, Minetta, 279
Ellington, Jackie, 89
Elliott, Bob, 283
Ellis, Georgia, 53
Erickson, Louise, 331
Escape, 379, 381
Ethel & Albert, 352

F

Falcon Crest, 268, 369
Falk, Peter, 95, 113
Fall of the City, 344
Family Skeleton, 288
Family Theatre, 382
"Farmer in the Dell, The", 147
Father Dowling Mysteries, 391
Father was a Fullback, 111
Fatherhood, 91
Fatool, Nick, 138
Fawcett, Farah, 158
Faye, Alice, 81, 211p
Feinstein, Michael, 188
Felony Squad, 366
Fenneman, George, 49-64, 200p, 201p
Ferrer, Jose, 114
Fibber McGee & Molly, 31, 72-74, 321-323, 333-334
Fields, W. C., 332
Fine, Mort, 84
Fio Rito, Ted, 137
Firestone, Eddie, 239
First Nighter, 258, 261-261, 322, 324, 348
Fisher, Carrie, 320
Fitzgerald, Barry, 288
Flash Gordon, 7, 68, 69
Fly, The, 234p
Flying Time, 265, 266
Flynn, Bernadine, 216p, 239-240, 246-247
Flynn, Charles, 19
Flynn, Fahey, 23-24
"Foggy, Foggy Dew", 160
Fogle, George, 260
Fonda, Henry, 129

Forsyte Saga, 276
Fox, Bernard, 217p
Fountain, Pete, 155
Freeman, Paula, 53
Friedkin, David, 84
Frost, Alice, 392
Fugue in C-Minor, 380
Funny, Funny Films, 50
Furness, Betty, 351

G

Gabor, Eva, 76
Gallop, Frank, 41
Galsworthy, John, 276
Gangbusters, 106
Garbo, Greta, 322
Gardner, Ed, 81
Garner, Earl, 185
Garner, James (Jim), 155
Gasoline Alley, 238
Gaylord, Slim, 182
Gaynor, Mitzi, 303
Gershwin, George, 188
Gerson, Betty Lou, 218p, 219p, 257-272
Get Smart, 256
G. I. Joe, 352
Gibby, 256
Gilligan's Island, 103, 107, 125
Gilman, Don, 276, 277
Ginsberg, Ralph, 25
Girl of the Night, 294
Glass Menagerie, The, 258
Gleason, Jackie, 335
Gluskin, Lud, 54
Gobel, George, 15
Godfrey, Arthur, 160
Goff, Norris, 124
Golden Days, 51

Golden Gate Quartet, 162
Golden Girls, 369
Golden Years, 101, 114
Goldwyn, Sam, 93
Gomer Pyle: USMC, 94, 255
Good News, 293, 294
Goodwin, Bill, 31, 84, 105, 337
Goon Show, The, 382
Gordon, Don, 15
Gordon, Gale, 7, 67-78, 82, 85, 151, 153, 202p, 203p, 314, 320, 326, 328, 333, 350
Gould, Chester, 393
Goulding, Ray, 283
Granby's Green Acres, 76
Grand Hotel, 262
Grant, Cary, 84
"Gravy Waltz", 181
Grease, 319
Great Gildersleeve, The, 73, 302, 323-327, 330, 332, 334-335
Great Man, The, 114
Great Mouse Detective, 387
Greb, Art, 270
Green Hornet, The, 6, 16
Greene, Graham, 392
Griffin, Merv, 100
Griffith, Andy, 91, 368
Ground is our Table, The, 178
Guedel, John, 62
Guiding Light, 258, 263, 270
Guinness Book of World Records, 185
Gunsmoke, 64, 130, 380
Guthrie, Woody, 162
Guys and Dolls, 92-93
Gwenn, Edmund, 110, 112-113

H

Hackett, Buddy, 187

Index

H

Hackman, Gene, 372
Hacop, Frank, 38
Haig, Albert, 170
Haines, Larry, 344
Hall, Monte, 56
Hallop, Billy, 34
Hallop, Florence, 34
Halstead, Henry, 136
Hamilton, Clayton, 348
Hammett, Dashiell, 339, 360-361, 391
Hanna, Bill, 301
Hannah, Dan, 120
Happy Days, 256
Harold Teen, 238
Harrington, Pat, 11
Harris, Phil, 81, 82, 135-156, 159, 182, 210p, 211p, 297, 321, 323, 332
Hart, Lorenz, 168
Hartzell, Clarence, 247
Harvest of Shame, 179
Hauser, Dwight, 53
Hausner, Jerry, 119-132, 208p, 209p, 300, 326
Havoc, Joan, 348, 363
Hayes, Helen, 299, 304, 378
Haymes, Dick, 53
Haynes, Larry, 129
Hellman, Lillian, 360
Hello Dolly, 309
Hello Frisco, Hello, 156
Hepburn, Katherine, 322
Herlihy, Ed, 331
Herman, Woody, 42
Heston, Charlton, 164
Hewitt, Alan, 357
Hewlett, Ted, 351

Hey, Nonny, Nonny, 303
Hi Ho, Steverino, 192
High and the Mighty, The, 155
Hill, George Washington, 46
Hintz, Ralph, 190
His Honor, the Barber, 288
Hog Breeder's Journal, 240
Hollis, Tim, 123
Hollywood Star Time, 381
Honest Harold, 331
Hop Harrigan, 5
Hopalong Cassidy, 6
Hope, Bob, 81, 120, 128, 178, 308
Hopkins, Pauline, 270
Hopper, Dennis, 112
Horn and Hardart Children's Hour, 7
Horse with the Flying Tail, The, 60
House of Myths, 276
How to be Funny, 176
Hubley, John, 129
Huddleston, Dick, 123
Hudson, Rock, 167
Hummert, Anne, 37-38, 259-260, 270
Hummert, Frank, 37-38, 259-260, 270
Huston, John, 258, 360
Hymn Singer, The, 161

I

I Dream of Genie, 370
I Fly Anything, 53
I Like What I Know, 389
I Love a Mystery, 53, 274-275, 283, 286-287, 289-290
I Love Adventure, 287, 289
I Love Lucy, 127, 227p, 291, 338
"I Love You Today", 180
I Married Joan, 106

I Spy, 84, 89, 92
I've Got a Secret, 181
Idelson, Bill, 216p, 217p, 237-256
"Impossible", 181
In Old Chicago, 156
Indiana Jones, 284
Inherit the Wind, 326
It Happened One Night, 110
It's a Mad, Mad, Mad, Mad World, 112
It's a Wonderful Life, 92, 205p
Ives, Burl, 157-171, 212p, 213p

J

Jack Armstrong, the All-American Boy, 15, 17-19, 196p, 246, 262
Jackpot, 128
Jackson, Michael, 189
James, Harry, 41
James, Jason, 360
Jarvis, Al, 174
Jennay, Jack, 138
Jetsons, The, 108, 293, 295, 301
Joey Bishop Show The, 337
John, Elton, 190
Johnny Fletcher, 84
Johnny Mercer Show, 189, 328
Johnny Modero, 83
Jones, Jennifer, 388
Jones, Margo, 170
Jordan, Jim, 328-329
Jordan, Marian, 329
Jubilee, 125
Judy and the Rockers, 301
Judy Canova Show, The, 81, 82, 130, 291, 308
Jungle Jim, 351
Just Plain Bill, 38

K

Kahn, Bill, 268

Kate Smith Show, The, 37, 40-41
Kaufman, George, 58
Kay Kyser Show, 337
Kazan, Elia, 164-165
Keeler, Ruby, 303
Kelk, Jackie, 22
Kelly, Patsy, 303
Kern, Jerome, 174
Keyes, Evelyn, 303
Keys to the Kingdom, 377
KGO, 51, 275
Killer at the Wheel, 274
King Leonardo, 353
King, Wayne, 141
Klein, Manny, 138
KMX, 177
Knott's Landing, 372
Knotts, Don, 176
Kohl, Jeff, 64
Korean Orphan's Choir, 169
Koufax, Sandy, 100
Kramer, Mandel, 344
KSFO, 51
Kubrick, Christiane, 209p
Kubrick, Stanley, 128

L

Ladd, Alan, 264, 268
Lake, Arthur, 109, 223p, 298, 299, 300
Lamar, Nappy, 138
Lampell, Millard, 162
Landsberg, Larry, 59
Lansbury, Angela, 299
Lassie, 94
Lauck, Chester, 124
Laura, 387
Lauria, Louis, 218p
Lavish of Sin, A, 275

Lawrence, Jerome, 126, 304, 309, 326
Leader, Anton, 378
Ledoux, Leone, 300
Lee, Robert E., 126, 304, 309, 326
Leemans, Tuffy, 17-18
LeGrand, Dick, 333-334
Leiningen vs the Ants, 381
Lemmon, Jack, 110, 121
Leonard, Sheldon, 79-94, 204p, 205p
Let's Pretend, 7
Levine, Benny, 191
Lewis, Cathy, 130, 325, 363
Lewis, Elliott, 83, 125, 126, 145, 147, 326, 350, 357
Lewis, Forrest, 15
Lewis, Jerry Lee, 190
Lewis, Tom, 125
Life of Riley, 335
Lights Out, 267
Lincoln, Abe, 162, 258
Lineup, The, 83
Little Lulu, 353
Little Orphan Annie, 6, 193p, 238
Lives of Harry Lime, The, 392
Lockridge, Frances, 391
Lockridge, Richard, 391
Lodger, The, 381
Lofner, Carol, 136, 137
Lofner-Harris Band, 136
Log of R-17, 162
Lomax, Alex, 162
Lombardo, Guy, 41
London, Julie, 114
Lone Ranger, The, 6, 322
Lonely Women, 260
Lonesome Train, 162

Loretta Young Show, 128
Lost Horizon, 110
Louise, Tina, 107
Love in the Rough, 294
Love, American Style, 255
Lovejoy, Frank, 54, 126, 344
Loy, Myrna, 294
Luddy, Barbara, 260, 261, 322
Lum and Abner, 122-124
Lupino, Ida, 231p, 367, 369, 373, 380
Lux Radio Theatre, 127
Lynch, Peg, 352

M

*M*A*S*H*, 256
Ma Perkins, 29, 245, 260
MacDonnell, Norman, 380
MacGregor, Jock, 347
Mack, Gil, 351
Mack, Nila, 7, 163
MacKenzie, Gisele, 131
MacMurray, Fred, 111
Mail Call, 125
Make Believe Ballroom, 174
Make Room for Daddy, 92
Maltese Falcon, The, 360
Man Behind the Gun, 343-344
Manhattan Transfer, 40
Mankiewicz, Joe, 93
Mantz, Paul, 266
Marcellino, Muzzy, 137
March of Time, 80, 349, 351
March, Hal, 54, 326, 363
Marie, Rose, 256
Marie, the Little French Princess, 38
Marks, Sherman, 23, 28
Martin, Mary, 305
Marx, Groucho, 57, 64, 201p

Marx, Harpo, 57
Massey, Raymond, 164-165
Mature, Victor, 116
Mayer, Louis B., 370
Mayer, Wally, 126
McCambridge, Mercedes, 285, 288-289
McCarthy, Clem, 42
McCormick, Myron, 344
McCrea, Joel, 370
McDonald, Eddie, 126
McIntire, John, 362
McMillan, Gloria, 319
McNeill, Don, 324
McNulty, Marianna Dorothy, 294
Meadows, Jane, 173, 179, 215p
Meet Me at Parky's, 80
Meeting of the Minds, 179
Mel's Fix-it Shop, 105
Melody Cruise, 154
Mercer, Johnny, 189
Mercury Theatre, 380
Mercury Theatre on the Air, 380
Meredith, Burgess, 344, 345, 367
Meredith, June, 261
Merkel, Una, 325
Merman, Ethel, 305
Messick, Don, 301
Miami Vice, 346-347
Mickey Mouse Club, The, 59, 60
Midstream, 259, 270
Mildred Pierce, 225p, 309
Miller, Eddie, 138
Mineo, Sal, 111, 112
Miner, Jan, 351
Miracle on 34th Street, 110
Miracle Worker, The, 170
"Misty", 185

Mitchell, Shirley, 226p, 227p, 321-338
Moh, Chuck, 136
Molina, Carlos, 138
Montefuscos, The, 258
Moore, Gary, 324
Moore, Sam, 325
Moore, Tom, 28
Moorehead, Agnes, 301, 380
More Bop Fables, 182
Morgan, Brewster, 345
Morgan, Frank, 303
Morgan, Gus, 294
Morgan, Henry, 9, 181
Morgan, Jane, 265, 311
Morrison, Brett, 41
Morrison, Patsy, 104
Morse, Carlton E., 220p, 273-290
Mosher, Bob, 153-154
Mothers in Law, 319
Mr. & Mrs. North, 392
Mr. Adams & Eve, 369
Mr. and Mrs. Blandings, 85
Mr. and Mrs. Music, 46
Mr. District Attorney, 393
Mr. Magoo, 106-107
Mr. President, 265
Murder, She Wrote, 299
Murphy, Eddie, 187
Murrow, Edward R., 178-179
My Favorite Husband, 291, 310
My Friend Irma, 130
Myrt & Marge, 305
Mystery, 386

N

Naked City, 371
NBC Mystery Serial, 276
Nelson, Frank, 81, 105, 125, 145, 302

New Adventures of Gilligan, The, 108
Newhart, Bob, 258
Newman, Paul, 165-166
Newton-John, Olivia, 319
Night Court, 34
Nightingale, Earl, 24
Nightingale, Florence, 179
Niven, David, 370
No Way Out, 372
No, No, Nanette, 303
"Nola", 34
Nolan, Jeanette, 363
Nolan, Lloyd, 127, 359-360
Nordine, Ken, 23
North, Sheree, 86
Nye, Louis, 176

O

O'Conner, Ralph, 11
O'Hara, Maureen, 110-111
O'Leary, Pat, 10
O'Malley, Walter, 36-37
Oboler, Arch, 267
Odd Couple, The, 256
Of Mice and Men, 125
Off Limits, 128
"Oh, You Beautiful Doll", 254
Olsen, George, 140
On a Note of Triumph, 345
On Campus, 50
One Fella's Family, 283
One for the Plot, 77
One Man's Family, 221p, 238, 269, 275, 277, 279, 282-289, 288-289, 305
Osmond, Donnie, 58
Osmond, Marie, 58
Oswald, Glen, 136

Our Miss Brooks, 72, 77, 203p, 265, 310-319

P

Painted Dreams, 261
Paley, Bill, 16
Palmer, Eric, 128
Palmer, John, 128
Parish, Tony, 9-30
Parker, Dorothy, 58
Parks, Bert, 58
Pat Novak, for Hire, 51-52, 83, 392
Paterson, Walter, 284
Pathé News, 42-43
Paths of Glory, 128-129, 209p
Patrick, Lee, 121
Payne, Virginia, 29, 260
PBS *Mystery!*, 232p
Peary, Hal, 302, 325, 330, 334
Peck, Gregory, 164, 213p
Perlman, S. J., 58
Perritori, Tony, 12, 26
Personal Album, 125
Pete Kelly's Blues, 52, 392
Petticoat Junction, 337
Phantom Pilot, The, 357
Phil Harris-Alice Faye Show, The, 81, 211p
Phillips, Barney, 130
Phillips, Irna, 238, 258, 261, 270
Philo Vance, 391, 347
Pierce, James, 70
Pink Elephant, The, 177
Pious, Minerva, 336
Pit and the Pendulum, The, 387
Pitchford, Donnie, 123
Please Don't Eat the Daisies, 337
Pocket Full of Miracles, A, 92
Poe, Edgar Allen, 387

Poe, James, 379
Poor Little Rich Girl, 157
Popeye, the Sailor, 6, 228p, 353
Porter, Cole, 180, 188
Powell, Dick, 368, 370
Powell, William, 294
Preminger, Otto, 367
Prentiss, Ed, 28-29
Presley, Elvis, 190
"Pretend You Don't See Her", 181
Price of Fear, 382
Price, Vincent, 232p, 233p, 234p, 375-390
Private Lives of Elizabeth and Essex, 377
Producers, The, 113
Pryor, Richard, 187
Punky Brewster, 256

Q

Quedens, Eunice, 308-309
Quinn, Bill, 344
Quinn, Don, 73, 325, 329
Quinn, William J., 276

R

Radio Days, 354
Radio Free Europe, 128
Raffetto, Michael, 278, 279, 284, 287
Raft, George, 11
Randall, Tony, 289
Ray, Nick, 112
Real McCoys, The, 337
Rebel Without a Cause, 111, 112, 114
Red Channels, 171, 336, 361, 362
Reed, Alan, 370
Reid, Elliott, 363
Reiner, Carl, 89, 255
Reis, Irving, 345

Remley, Frank, 136, 138, 145, 147-150, 321
Renfrew of the Mounted, 7
Requiem for a Heavyweight, 114
Rhymer, Paul, 239, 248, 256
Rich, Irene, 359
Ritter, Thelma, 110
Rivera, Chita, 306
Road of Life, 259, 263, 270
Robb, Mary Lee, 331
Roberts, Ken, 41, 331
Robinson, Earl, 162
Robinson, Edward G., 76, 127, 393
Robson, Bill, 343, 345, 361, 378
Rocks on the Roof, 97, 101, 115
Rockwell, Bob, 315
Rocky & His Friends, 353
Rodgers, Richard, 168
Roger Kilgore, Public Defender, 393
Rogers, Ginger, 154
Romance of Helen Trent, 260
Rooney, Mickey, 112-113
Roosevelt, Eleanor, 162
Roosevelt, Franklin D., 12, 162
Ross, David, 41
Ross, Earl, 328, 334
Ross, Steve, 188
Rourke, Hayden, 370
Royal, John, 121
Rubin, Aaron, 89
Rubin, Benny, 82
Rudy Vallée Show, 323
Runyon, Damon, 86, 87, 92, 191
Russell, Rosalind, 370

S

Sad Sack, 103-104, 130
Said, Faud, 90
Saint, The, 233p, 375, 377, 378, 383

Sanderson, Junior, 38
Sandrich, Mark, 154
Sanger, Margaret, 179
Schubert, Jake, 293, 308
Scott, Zachary, 225p
Screen Guild Theatre, 127, 359
Scully, Vin, 36
Sears Radio Theatre, 326, 382
Second Husband, 38
Secret of Mystery Lake, 59
Seymour, Anne, 268
Shadow of Fu Manchu, 72
Shadow, The, 41, 80
Shakespeare, William, 356
Shark, Ivan, 28
Shaw, Artie, 41, 42, 138
Shawn, Dick, 113, 128
Shearing, George, 185
Sherman, Alan, 56
Sherman, Ransom, 322, 323, 324
Shirley, Will, 24
Show of Shows, 55
Showboat, 168
Silver Chalice, 166
Silver Theatre, 127
Simmons, Jean, 169
Simon and Simon, 84
Simon, Neil, 309
Sinatra, Frank, 93, 174, 189
Sing Out, Sweet Land, 168
Singer, Ray, 153
Singing Story Lady, 7
Singleton, Doris, 104
Singleton, Penny, 76, 105, 109, 222p, 223p, 293-306
Skelton, Red, 291, 323
Sky King, 5, 16, 23, 24, 53
Smile Time, 175

Smith, Leonard, 319
Smythe, J. Anthony, 279
Song of Bernadette, 388
Song of Love, 308
Sophie, 180
Sothern, Ann, 81
"South Rampart Street Parade", 181
Space Patrol, 7
Sam Spade, The Adventures of, 53, 126-127, 230p, 355, 357-365, 370, 372, 391
"Speak to Me of Love", 330, 331
Spiegel, S. P. (Sam Spiegel), 360
Spier, William, 126, 127, 360, 363, 378, 381
Spiral Road, The, 167
Stafford, Hanley, 72, 125, 301
Stafford, Jo, 328
Stander, Artie, 89
Stang, Arnold, 353
"Stardust", 174
State Fair, 156
Stern, Billy, 112
Steve Allen Show, The (radio), 174
Steve Allen Show, The (TV), 175
Stewart, Chuck, 89
Stewart, Jimmy, 92, 128, 319, 359
Stone, Ezra, 41, 168
Stonewall Scott, 348
Stories of the Black Chamber, 70
"Story of Esther, The", 163
Story of Mary Marlin, The, 268
Story of Vic and Sade, The, 256
Straeter, Ted, 40
Stuff the Lady's Hatbox, 275
Sunday Evening Serutan News, 51
Superman, 6, 229p, 346
Superman, Adventures of, 229p

Surprise Package, 56
Suspense, 105, 126, 377-380
Sweeney & March Show, The, 54
Sweeney, Bob, 54
Swing Your Lady, 294

T

Take the Money and Run, 354
Talking Picture Time, 261
Tallman, Bob, 360
Tarkington, Booth, 120
Tarzan, 70
Tatum, Art, 185
Taylor, Elizabeth, 165
Tell it to Groucho, 56
Temple of Vampires, 285, 286
Temple, Shirley, 125
Terry & the Pirates, 6, 21-22, 23, 194p
Tetley, Walter, 150, 322, 333
That Good News, 294
"That's What I Like About the South", 139, 140
The Saint, 233p, 375, 377, 378, 383
The Shadow, 41, 80
Theatre of Blood, 388
"Theme from Picnic", 181
Third Man, The, 392
This is Harris, 154
Thorson, Russell, 289
Those Websters, 239, 258
Three Skeleton Key, 379
Tierney, Jean, 388
Tinker, Grant, 369
To Have and Have Not, 93
Tobin, Dan, 370
Today Show, The, 182
Today's Children, 29, 260-261

Todd, Michael, 165
Tom Mix and the Ralston Straight Shooters, 5, 13, 14, 195p
Tonight Show, The, 175, 176, 182, 191
Too Many Cooks, 54
Tracy, Spencer, 120
Travolta, John, 319
Treasury of Great Recipes, A, 389
Tremayne, Les, 260, 322, 337
Truex, Ernest, 121
Tucker, Les, 181
Tucker, Sophie, 180
Turner, Roscoe, 265, 266
Tuttle, Lurene, 126, 325, 331, 362
Tweedles, 120
Twenty Years Ago and a Day, 351
Twilight Zone, 255

U

Under the Rainbow, 320
Underwood, Cecil, 325, 328
United States Steel Hour, 37

V

Van Cleave, Nathan, 344
Van Cleave, Patricia, 299
Van Dine, S. S., 339
Van Harvey, Art, 216p, 239
Van Rieper, Karen, 68
Vance, Vivian, 227p
Vaughn, Beryl, 23
Vic and Sade, 216p, 237-255
Victoria Regina, 378
Vigran, Herb, 104, 130, 327
Von Zell, Harry, 41
Vonn, Veola, 291
Wade, Laureen, 121, 122
Wain, Bea, 39, 45
Wake Me When It's Over, 128

Wake, The, 177
Waldo, Janet, 108, 126, 301, 325
Wallace, Mike, 9, 16, 23, 154
Wallace, Mina, 154, 155
Wallace, Tom, 262
War According to Anna, The, 274
Ware, Harlan, 278
Waring, Fred, 40
Warner, Gertrude, 348
Warno, Mark, 41
Waterman, Willard, 86, 239, 260, 302, 330-332
Watkins, Pierce, 121
Wayfarer's Notebook, 169
Wayfaring Stranger, 169
Wayne, John, 155
WBBM, 13, 20, 24
WBOW, 161
Webb, Jack, 51, 52, 83, 130, 392
Wester, Carl, 263
Wedding, The, 371
Weeks, Anson, 137
Weems, Ted, 140
Weiss, Seymour, 141
Weist, Dwight, 42
Wells, Dawn, 107
Welles, Orson, 41, 80, 380, 392
WENR, 28
West, Brooks, 311, 319
Weston, Paul, 328
WGCU, 34
WGN, 25, 28, 238, 260, 358
What Are You Doing After the Orgy?, 101
Whedon, John, 325
Wheeler Dealers, The, 155
Where Did Everybody Go?, 101
White, Alice, 299
White, Bob, 260
White, Josh, 162
WIBJ, 11
Wicker, Ireene, 7, 261
Wiener, Lee, 50
Wilcox, Harlow, 31, 329
Williams, Andy, 54, 191
Williams, Tennessee, 258
Williams, William B., 174
Wilson, Don, 31, 142
Wilson, Marie, 130
WIND, 12
Wizard of Oz, The, 320
WMAQ, 28, 358
WNUP, 28
Woman in Hiding, 231p
Woman in My House, 238, 289, 323
Woman in White, 259, 263, 270, 322
Wonder, Stevie, 189
Wonderful Town, 309
Wood, Natalie, 110, 111, 112
Woods, Leslie, 351
Woollcott, Alexander, 58
WOR, 351
WPBR, 46
Wright, Steven, 187
Wrightsman, Stanley, 138
WTAM, 122
WTOP, 12
WTR, 11
Wyler, William, 164
Wynn, Ed, 114
Wynn, Keenan, 101, 114

X

Y

Yagatti, Paul, 183
Yank Swing Sessions, 125
Yarborough, Barton, 278, 284, 287

You Bet Your Life, 51, 56, 60, 64, 175, 201p
Young Love, 126, 325
Young, Alan, 101, 102
Young, Loretta, 125
Young, Sean, 372

Youngman, Henny, 41
Your Hit Parade, 37, 39, 41, 45, 46

Z

Zanuck, Darryl, 135, 136
Ziegfeld Follies, 308, 309
Zirato, Bruno, 378

www.ingramcontent.com/pod-product-compliance
Lightning Source LLC
Chambersburg PA
CBHW050832230426
43667CB00012B/1963